THE DISASTROUS LOVE AFFAIR
OF MOON AND MARS

THE DISASTROUS LOVE AFFAIR OF MOON AND MARS

CELESTIAL SEX,
EARTHLY DESTRUCTION
AND DRAMATIC SUBLIMATION
IN HOMER'S ODYSSEY

By
ALFRED DE GRAZIA

metron

ISBN: 978-1-60377-098-9
© Metron Publications, February 2019
All Rights Reserved

To Immanuel Velikovsky (1895-1979)

Iron sharpens iron, and one man sharpens another.
Proverbs, IV, 27.17

TABLE OF CONTENTS

FOREWORD   10

INTRODUCTION   12

Part One:
SACRED SCANDAL & DISASTER

1. An Athena Production   18
2. The Song of Love   22
3. The Love-Affair as the Mask of Tragedy   30
4. Catastrophe and sublimation   37
5. Holy Dreamtime   42

Part Two:
GODS, PLANETS, MADNESS

6. The Rape of Helen   55
7. Crazy Heroes of Dark Times   64
8. The Two Faces of Love   88
9. The Ruined Face of a Classic Beauty   117
10. He Who Shines by Day   126
    Appendix to 10:
    Logic of Identifying Relations   144
11. The Blasted Career of the Mighty Swordsman   148
12. The Laughing Gods   161
13. How the Gods Fly   173

Part Three:
THERAPY FOR GROUP FEAR

14. The Uses of Language   190
15. The Birth and Death of Memory   208
16. The Transfiguration of Trauma   223
17. Settled Sky and Unsettled Mind   235

Appendix: Characters of the Book   247

FOREWORD

In this book, I extract a dreamy bedroom comedy from Homer's *Odyssey,* analyze it as a dramatic form of myth, detect that it might have a real astronomical origin, seek this origin in world-wide disasters, and assert that an unconscious parallel occurs between astronomical events and artistic production.

The narrative is well suited to readers of venturesome tastes, who may have a passing acquaintanceship with the history of the theater and ancient Greece, with psychoanalysis, with mythology and the ideas of catastrophism and astronomy.

The work was written and offered for publication over a decade ago. Well-founded criticism from several British experts on mythology, particularly Peter James, Malcolm Lowery, Brian Moore and Martin Sieff, led me to withhold the manuscript, despite the encouragement coming from other quarters to publish it. I have indeed held it, to near the end of the Quantavolution Series, and release it now, benefited, I believe, by the amendments that my friends induced.

Thanks on this occasion go also to professor William Mullen of St. John's College, whose advice extended from Greek poetic meter to the full ancient oecumene; to Eugene Vanderpool of Athens, Greece, who was consistently sympathetic; to Dr. Elizabeth Chesley-Baity, who discussed with me the archaeo-astronomical anthropology of dances, fire-rites, ballgames, and sword ceremonies; to the late Dr. Zvi Rix of

Israel, whose enchanting letters on problems of mythology kept the book and its author warm over the years of its hibernation; to George English for his editorial advice and Jungian interpretations; to my colleague, Professor Cyrus Gordon, for his appreciations of the values in my approach; to the late Professor Livio C. Stecchini, whose absence from the scene of ancient history and science is sorely felt; and to Dr. Jay Lefer who responded keenly to the questions here raised in the field of psychiatry. Finally, I would acknowledge the inspiration afforded by my friend, the late Immanuel Velikovsky, who designated the Greek gods as sky-bodies threatening the Earth.

INTRODUCTION

The theory to be expressed here is hardly believable. We discern behind a famous Homeric scenario about the misconduct of the gods the shadow of a second scenario of astronomical catastrophe. By pursuing the connection relentlessly, many reasons are uncovered to suspect that the human drama is unconsciously imitating what the human eye witnessed as a prior catastrophe in the skies. Chant and catastrophe, dance and disaster seem to be historically linked.

Can a dance and poem be a piece of astronomical history, tightly, not vaguely, related? If they are, then an idea that many psychologists have considered: that humans have a tendency to suppress the memory of terrible events, but also are somehow compelled by unconscious psychic forces to reenact the events - this idea is supported by our theory.

It appears that the reenactment may take place through religious rites, through wars, through literature, through individual and group behavior of many kinds. Here it is through the sublimated medium of poetry and dance. I think that such a process is occurring in the story of the Love Affair of Venus and Mars. If my readers will agree, then we shall begin to shape a consensus on a matter of great importance to several fields of science and the humanities.

The literature referred to is a brief lyric of a hundred lines, sung in

Book VIII of the *Odyssey*. It tells how the bright-crowned goddess Aphrodite loved Ares, god of battle, and how they met repeatedly to make love "in the home of fire," until they were entrapped in a marvelous net made by her outraged consort, the god Hephaestus, and released only when Ares pledged to reform his conduct.

The lyric tells of a much longer opera ballet sung and directed by the sightless bard, Demodocus, who, some say, is Homer's self-image. The recital plays to a fascinated audience at the palace of Alcinous and to his guest, Odysseus, or Ulysses, hero of the War against Troy. The frank sexuality is Homer's, no matter how often it has been translated vaguely. The story is the archetype of the adulterous love triangle, as neat a plot and piece as anyone has ever composed, and a model for a thousand imitations. But it may also be the masking of a catastrophe visited upon the Greeks from the skies.

I studied the lines and read some translations of them. I rendered them in something like the original epic hexameter, and shall present them below (Chapter 2) in that form. Still, examining the words was but the beginning of an investigation that carried me on Odyssean wanderings into various fields of knowledge.

I asked myself what spirit breathed into Homer and saw that it was the goddess Pallas Athena. Athena moved the Homeric Age. She led the Greeks in the *Iliad* and guided Odysseus through his many adventures of the *Odyssey*. I found her everywhere. She dominated the skies as a phenomenon, and human strife on Earth.

I concerned myself with the context of the song and discovered that it was a Holy Dreamtime song, not a sacrilegious burlesque. It was presented as an opera-ballet, meant to take place among the gods in heaven. The same art form exists today among the aborigines of Australia.

I asked myself how such holy songs could arise, and found an answer in the modern theory of catastrophism. Precedents and parallels from many countries and cultures justify searching for catastrophism behind the lines of the love song of Demodocus. Greek culture was badly damaged by natural disasters of the eight and seventh centuries before this era, and Homer's poetry (which I place later than is usual) shows both the effects of the disasters and the ways in which the Greeks recovered from them.

The song of the love affair of Aphrodite and Ares is to be stripped of its facade. It is to be considered as a song about planetary gods doing violence to the world. I assign this Aphrodite of Homer to the Moon, with reservations that I believe are fully explained herein, rather than to the planet Venus. Ares stands for planet Mars without doubt. Hephaestus or Vulcan, though male, surprisingly stands for the planet Venus in this episode. Sea-god Poseidon represents the worried Earth, and persuades Hephaestus to release Aphrodite and Ares from the invisible net by which he has trapped them. Poseidon stands bond for Ares. All this suggests the unspeakable horror of natural disasters brought by these planetary gods upon Earth and humanity.

That Aphrodite was always a great goddess of the Moon is maintained, again with reservations, for she may also have had her name assigned to other sky-bodies, especially planet Venus which the Greeks and Romans, following the Orientals, came to call Aphrodite. We tell of how the Moon-Aphrodite received in Homeric times the wanton, irresponsible, and imperturbable character by which later ages came to know her. Aphrodite is tied to Helen of Troy, and Helen to the Hellenes or Greeks. The Trojan wars evolve psychically into campaigns to recapture the Moon from planet Mars (Ares) by the followers of planet Venus (Athena).

The stories of the Trojan wars thus use the historical and mundane battles to play out on Earth the drama of the skies. The skies of the Homeric age must be recent: 776 to 687 B. C. - or so I calculate, taking up Velikovsky's chronology. Although natural disasters had befallen the numerous settlements of Troy (possibly Hisarlik) throughout its history, a final major destruction by natural forces may well have occurred during Homer's boyhood. It was an awesome tragedy to him and others, which could not be recalled without pain, fear, and distortion.

It is to be expected that the life of survivors of worldwide natural catastrophes would be fearful and turbulent. Hence I argue that the social psychology of the Homeric Greeks is framed in a concept of mania and madness, rather than in the conventional view of a primitive people gradually achieving a higher culture.

Further, as on Earth so in heaven, there must be signs of the cosmic disasters of the age. I examine the Moon, as the astronauts have seen and sampled it for evidences of recent disaster, and shall recite indications that it did experience torrid bouts in the near past involving immense electro-gravitational stresses.

I do the same with the planet Mars, from the evidence of the latest explorations. Mars has been the victim, it appears, of recent abysmal ruptures and explosions; I explain how these might have been caused by near encounters with Earth, Moon and Venus. Planet Venus is played by Hephaestus in the love Affair. He is a stand-in for Athena, director of the show, who is more frequently identified with the planet Venus than he. Venus is exceedingly hot, and marred beneath her dense atmosphere by shallow surface craters of great diameter.

The other gods of the Love Affair introduce to the first modern bedroom comedy its humor, which can be explained in Freudian theory as yet another cover-up of the disaster. In reality they too are heavenly bodies. The role of the Sun, Helios, is shown to be secondary to that of the planetary gods and responsive to their behavior, as it is pictured in the earliest development of theology everywhere.

If the characters of the Love Affair are to be placed in heaven, their motions too must be given meaning. The best explanation lately offered has the Sun and planets forming an electric system, subordinate to and part of the galactic electrical system. They act as charged bodies separated from an oppositely charged space plasma by space-charge sheaths, the rupture of which destroys a balance and creates havoc through discharges among the bodies. These efforts seem to be discernible in the special motions of the characters of the Love Affair.

We present physical and historical evidence in general agreement with the love song sung by Demodocus. How the human mind manages to react to such events in a way to preserve its own balance, and to give forth its most beautiful literary expressions, needs to be learned. An examination of the language of the Love Affair, and of Homer generally, brings forth a theory of myth: to succeed in telling the truth about an unspeakable event, a myth must fail to convey the truth. This fateful contradictory task is achieved successfully through the Love Affair.

Homer was probably an editor and publisher of such great myths. He labored to write down in a fresh and convenient alphabet what he thought should be sung. He was a bringer of peace between gods and men, and the symbolizer of a unified Greek culture.

Memory, I offer, is of traumatic origin. Human memory begins in horror and the need to forget. To remember is to forget; to forget is to remember. From the beginnings of true human nature until now, no one has been exempted from the rules of amnesia, not even the philosophers whose sublimation of the terrors of becoming a creature of memory have seemed to carry them very far from particular events.

Myth and dreams coincide, operating according to similar laws. The conscious and unconscious parts of the mind exchange with each other what is required for a sense of control to exist so life can go on. Still the balance is scarcely a happy one. Human nature is imprinted by a deeply buried, unresting, and generalized great fear. The fear is reflected today and in the earliest human institutions of religion, politics, sex, schools, commerce, and war.

I concluded in the end that the hundred lines of the Love Affair dramatize subconsciously the history of a catastrophic encounter of the planets at or near 687 B. C. Further, the mythical and literary transformations of the event mark a high point in the development of the European mind and its culture.

I ask the reader - no matter that he may disbelieve me - to pursue his disbelief through the pages to follow, and acquire, at the least, a reasoned disbelief. To the reader who is familiar with my ideas, I offer assurances that the revelations contained in this introduction do not exhaust the surprises that he will encounter, one after another, as he moves through these pages upon his personal *Odyssey*.

PART ONE

SACRED SCANDAL & DISASTER

CHAPTER ONE

AN ATHENA PRODUCTION

The Love Affair, as I shall call it, is a story of how the arrogant god of war, Ares, made love to the Golden Goddess Aphrodite in the bed she was supposed to share with her husband, Hephaestus, the lame blacksmith god. Hearing of their adultery from Helios, the sun-god, Hephaestus fashioned an invisible net that trapped the pair in bed. Returning from a pretended trip, he called upon the gods to witness their guilt and would release them only on the promise of the sea-god, Poseidon, to stand bail for the disreputable Ares.

Perhaps this was the first bedroom farce of literature. Its producer, in a manner of speaking, was the Goddess Pallas Athena, patron of the arts and crafts, daughter and favorite of Zeus, father of the gods. She was born some centuries before 1500 B. C. [1] and was originally envisioned in the planet Venus.

Athena was not only the producer of the 'Love Affair' but also of the

---

[1] William Mullen, "A Reading of the Pyramid Texts," III *Pensée* No 1 (1973), 10; pp. 13-4.

Iliad and the *Odyssey,* as I shall seek to show: so she was not a novice in the field of dramaturgy. Her versatility was proverbial. She probably inspired the magnificent setting of Phaeacia and directed the scene closely. She sang it in the guise of the god-inspired Demodocus. Like Shakespeare she acted in her own plays: as herself, she planned the occasion for the story, and in the person of Odysseus, was the honored member of its audience. "I am Pallas Athene, Daughter of Zeus, who always stands by your side and guards you through all your adventures," she reminds Odysseus at one point.

Odysseus's name means "troublemaker" or better "the inveterate troublemaker." Writes George Dimock, "In the Odyssey *odyssasthai* means essentially 'to cause pain (odynë) and to be willing to do so.'" [2] In her unruffled and sanguine way, often behind the scenes, Athena is the world's greatest troublemaker, as we shall soon learn.

Though she is a mistress of disguises, Athena permitted a picture of her natural human form to develop over the centuries. E. V. Rieu, who has provided one of the many translations of the *Odyssey* that are available, writes that "we may think of her as a tall and beautiful woman, with brilliant eyes, clad in the white robe, with the *aegis,* a goatskin cloack, across her breast, a crested helmet on her head, and a long spear in her hand."[3] Sometimes an owl and a snake accompany her. However, we would warn that Athena's appearance is as varied as her characterizations, and her names are so many that some are still to be unearthed.

"Most vivid and alive of Homer's gods," writes Rieu, "she dominates the *Odyssey.* And this is true even though there are moments when we are at a loss to say whether the poet means us to imagine her actual presence or to understand only that his characters are exercising the motherwit which she personifies."

The whole story of the *Odyssey* itself can be retold briefly here. The saga begins with an assembly of the Gods. Athena catches her father Zeus reminiscing on the just killing of an evil man, and, taking advantage of the absence of Poseidon, reminds him that the worthy Odysseus has still not reached home, although it is the tenth year after the destruction

---

[2] George E. Dimock, Jr., "The Name of Odysseus," in George Steiner and Robert Fagles, eds., *Homer: A Collection of Critical Essays,* New York: Prentice Hall, 1962, p. 106.

[3] *The Odyssey,* Penguin edition, introduction.

of Troy; for seven years he has been detained by the nymph Calypso on an island. And for three years before then, he had wandered: he had sacked a town, landed among the lotus-eaters who relished an amnesia-promoting vegetable, and had been captured by a giant man-eating Cyclops whom he blinded in order to escape.

This proved to be unfortunate. The Cyclops was a son of Poseidon, whose enmity now marked Odysseus for unending disasters.

The wanderers landed on the floating island of Aeolia where they were treated royaly. Upon departing, Odysseus was given a bag of rushing winds that was not to be opened, and granted a fair breeze for home. But his crew, acting in the typically greedy and impetuous manner that was to destroy them all ultimately, opened the pouch in envy of its supposedly precious contents. The fierce winds escaped; the way was lost. A landing among savage Laestrygonians brought a slaughter of many of the company. Fleeing, they found the island of the witch, Circe. After some difficulties (she changed a number of the men into pigs for a time), they conciliated her and spent a luxurious year at her palace.

Upon his departure, Circe gave Odysseus means of discovering his own fate and reviewing the history of many a departed soul through a visit to Hades and a talk with the seer Teiresias. Pausing at Circe's island afterwards, Odysseus received further instructions that would carry him past the seductive Sirens, and through the narrow straits between Scylla, a grasping monster, and Charybdis, a swallower of ships.

However, he is overruled by his men when he begs them to sail past the Island of the Sun. They land, and are kept ashore by storms until out of supplies. While Odysseus sleeps, the crew seize and eat the fat cattle of Helios. The Sun protests to Zeus (Jupiter) who destroys their ship and lets Odysseus drift alone for nine days until washed up on the shore of Ogygia, the island of Calypso. Seven years pass.

Then it is that, following upon Athena's plea, the order of Zeus moves him on and he was sailing well until Poseidon, returning from a visit among the Ethiopians, spied him and dashed his little boat to pieces. The nymph Ino helped him to stay afloat and Poseidon turned away, satisfied. Athena smoothed the winds and seas so that he might survive, and arranged for him to fall into the hands of the Phaeacians.

Now it is to the Phaeacian episode that I shall attend closely, but a few words more will bring the story to an end. Odysseus is transported from Phaeacia, with many gifts, and laid upon Ithaca, asleep. Athena appears to him and advises him: his wife, Penelope, still withholds her choice of a betrothed, though it is demanded of her by her many suitors, who meanwhile feast at the expense of the palace. His son, Telemachus, also faithful, is young and indecisive. Odysseus is to go first in disguise among his people, then to prepare his weapons, then, with the help of his son and two loyal slaves, to challenge and slaughter the suitors. So he does, and wins back his possessions and his wife. A final battle with the surviving opposition ensues but Athena calls Odysseus off, for he is supported but warned by Zeus. "So spoke Athene, and he obeyed, and was glad at heart. Then for all time to come a solemn covenant betwixt the twain was made by Pallas Athene, daughter of Zeus, who bears the aegis, in the likeness of Mentor both in form and in voice."[4] Thus ends the *Odyssey*.

---

[4] A. T. Murray, translator, *Homer: The Odyssey*, 2 vols. (New-York: Putnam's Sons, 1919), II, 443. Mentor was the lifetime guardian and advisor of Odysseus. He had been left behind when Odysseus sailed for Troy. (All line references to the Greek text will be to the Murray translation.)

CHAPTER TWO

THE SONG OF LOVE

Here then is this song of love. It is presented fifth-hand: my literal verse is based upon a number of translations of what is ultimately a tenth century A. D. manuscript in Greek (the earliest extant - as written down in the seventh-century B. C. and reedited in the next century) of Homer's *Odyssey,* which reports what was sung by a blind harpist, Demodocus, in a time and place that have been debatable questions for over two thousand years.

Alcinous the King announced the event:

Now, all and one of you dancers, Phaeacia's finest!
form in your corps de ballet so our stranger and guest can tell all his
friends upon going back home, we're surpassing all manner of mankind;
We are the paramount sailors on sea, and in running a foot race,
singing of songs, and in dancing. So someone around us here go,
go without loitering, bring to us here for Demodocus's

*use, that precious harp that so clearly resounds; it's the lyre
carefully standing, it's somewhere, I know, within one of our great halls."
Sacred commands of Alcinous! Quickly arose a herald,
seeking to find and to fetch him the resonant harp from its palace place.
Rising as well were a chosen nine men who were Lords Ceremonial,
publically called, whenever the people foregathered and needed an ordering.
These cleared out space for the dancing to come; they measured a broad ring.*

*Meanwhile the herald returned; he carried the clear-intoned lyre.
Taking the lyre in hand, Demodocus moved in the midst of the young boys
standing there, all of them skilled in the dance though they blossomed with fair youth.
Down stamped their feet on the floor made for beauteous magical dances.
Spellbound Odysseus marvelled as dancing feet twinkled in mid-air!*

THE SONG LITERALLY RENDERED IN ENGLISH VERSE

Whereupon the song of the Love Affair begins.

*Striking his masterly chords in the prelude to singing his sweet song,
Demodocus charmingly told of Ares' love affair and Aphrodite,
Golden of Crown. In secret they lay in the home of Hephaestus.
Ares came carrying all manner of gifts to dishonor the Lord's bed.*

*Straightaway then went with the news, of course, Helios, who'd spotted them loving.
Shocked and dismayed was Hephaestus to hear of the painful story.
Deep down below to the depth of his forge he proceeded; there,
placing a thunderbolt stone on the block of the anvil, he struck, and
struck off unbreakable fetters that no one could hope to dissolve, for
fixing the lovers in bondage, right where they loved, was his fierce aim.
Then having fashioned his snare, imbued with a wrath against Ares,
up to his chamber he went, by his bedstead of love, and all over,
everywhere, round the four posts of the bed he moved, spreading the ligaments,
dropping a number of them from above, from the beams to the floor, too,*

fine as the web of a spider, so fine that the Blessed Immortals,
looking for them could not see them, such excellent craft was he capable of.

Soon as the bonds had been stretched over all of the lovers' trysting couch,
Hephaestus pretended to move on the way to his well-founded Lemnos,
dearly loved island. Wherewith the unwavering gaze of the Golden-bridled Ares
fixed without fail on Hephaestus, Most Famed among Artisans, going
off. And Ares straight made his way to the house of the Famous Hephaestus,
eager for love of Cytherean Aphrodite of the Bright Crown.
She had in fact come before him just now from her father, mighty Son
of Kronos, and rested herself to await his arrival. Ares
entered directly the house, reached for her hands, and spoke calling her name:
"Dearest one, come to bed now with me; let us together lie.
Hephaestus is no longer here or about and I do think he's gone.
Lemnos must have him; he's gone to his Sintians who speak like barbarians."
He spoke like that, and she was quite thrilled to lie in his lean arms.
Going to bed, they laid themselves together. But upon them
showered the bonds engineered by versatile Hephaestus, tight drawn. Try as
they might, they couldn't remove their limbs or even move them.
Then they did realize no way could be found to escape the close bonds.

Nearing them now, having turned himself back before reaching his Lemnos,
came close the Famous, the Strong-armed, the God with Disabled Legs.
Helios had watched as before and again had delivered the story.
So, to his mansion once more he returned, his heart so heavy.
Standing astride of the door he was seized by a wild anger.
Terrible cries went up; all of the Gods heard his shouting:
"Zeus, my father and all of you Blessed Gods who are Eternal, come down!
See for yourselves here a laughable matter, unyielding fact.
Aphrodite, the daughter of Zeus, has ever shunned my lameness, but
loved Annihilator Ares who is handsome and straight-footed,
born to stumble that I am! Yet no one to blame save my parents.
Better had they not begotten me. Here you can see how this pair
climbed into my bed and twine around each other so lovingly.
I am torn apart by the sight. But believe me, their desire will vanish.

However in love, their lust is gone, and an end to their fornication.
Nevertheless, the trap and the net will not let them go free.
Gifts that I gave for the right to the bride, with her eyes of a spaniel,
first must be paid back to me by her father; fair though his daughter,
she is a wanton and reckless." So spoke Hephaestus,
seeing the Gods had now met at the house by its brazen bright threshold.

Poseidon came, the Mover of Earth, and Hermes the Helper, too.
Lord and Director of Far-removed Works, Apollo: he came.
(Goddesses were absent, they remained home, away from the shameful scene.)
Standing around the door, then, were the Gods, the Givers of Good Things.
Laughter arose from the Blessed Gods, inextinguishably gleeful
they were at the sight of Hephaestus' shrewd craft and cunning,
saying amongst themselves, glancing at each other, "Bad deeds
prosper poorly. The slow one can catch the most swift. See how
Hephaestus, though slow he may be, has caught up with Ares,
fastest of Gods who command high Olympus. Lame although he be,
yet he has caught him by skill, so Ares must pay the just fine
owed by one in adultery." To each other they spoke in this manner.

Apollo, Lord and the son of Great Zeus, said aside to God Hermes,
"Hermes, the son of Great Zeus, and our Messenger, Giver of Good Things:
would you be willing, on oath, to wed with the Golden Aphrodite,
even though trapped by strong bonds?" The Messenger God,
Slayer of Argus, retorted: "Would that this happened to myself!
Yes, O Master Apollo, Unfailing Marksman. If unbreakable
bindings of three times the number would fasten me down, yes,
and all of the goddesses were to be looking upon the two of us.
Would that it happened that I should be sleeping with Golden Aphrodite!"
Speeches like this caused new laughter to rise from the Heavenly Deities.

Poseidon laughed not at all; he besought on the contrary Hephaestus,
Supreme-of-all-Craftsmen, to let go of Ares, speaking in winged words:
"Loose him, I promise, when ordered by you, to compel him to pay you
all that is right, and I swear this before all these Gods, the Immortals."

Famous and Strong-armed Hephaestus replied: "Do not ask this.
Think! Poseidon, Earth-Surrounder. Bail for a reprobate!
How can I place you in bondage among the immortal gods,
granted that Ares will avoid both the debt and the bail and depart."
Still the Shaker-of-Earth was insistent; Poseidon declared,
"Surely if Ares shall flee from his debt I shall pay you Hephaestus."
Then the Famous, the Strong-armed Hephaestus conceded in answer:
"I am not right to deny you, nor would such an action be proper."
Suddenly, so saying, the Mighty Hephaestus unfastened the bindings.
Straightaway, freed from their powerful bonds, the lovers sprang upwards.
Ares proceeded to Thrace, but Aphrodite, Lover of Laughter,
went on to Cyprus, to Paphos, her domain with her fragrant-smoke alter.
There she was bathed by the Graces, who salved her with oils of immortals,
ointment refulgent on Gods who are Deathless. And they clothed her body.
Such was the beauty of raiment, the vision astonished the eyes.

HAPPY ENDING

The opera is over, its audience charmed and relaxed:

This was the song that the famous bard sang and Odysseus rejoiced;
glad in his heart was the guest while he listened; glad, too, the Phaeacians,
men of the long oars, famed for their sea-going vessels.
Forthwith Alcinous bade Halius and Laodamas to dance by themselves.
No one could match them. They grasped in their hands a beautiful purple
ball that Polybus the Wise One had fashioned for them and their dancing.
One would lean backwards and toss it up high towards the shadowy clouds. His
brother would leap off the ground in the air, and skillfully catch it,
even not touching the ground with his feet until holding it firmly.
Showing their skill at casting the ball straight up high was a prelude;
Now they began a new dance on the bounteous earth, flinging the same ball
to and fro, to and fro, as other youths stood in the wings, beating time.
Great was the din that arose! Odysseus then turned to Alcinous, saying:
"Lord and Renowned among mankind, you boasted of your dancers;

best you had said that they be, and true are your words in our full sight. Looking upon them, amazement takes hold of me here."

Alcinous is gladdened by this praise. He impetuously ordains that all manner of rich gifts be heaped up for the guest to carry along home when he leaves Scheria.

THE PHAEACIAN UTOPIA

The "Love Affair" stands as a complete story in itself. More exactly, it is a summary of a long dramatic presentation which will never be heard or seen. And this long story is of course part of only one episode of the Phaeacian Adventure.

Phaeacia itself is a marvelous creation of Homer-Athena. If the "Love Affair" as a literary genre can be called the first bedroom farce, Phaeacia may be called the first Utopia, to be succeeded by hundreds of utopias in the millennia to come. It has aspects of More's *Utopia,* of Campanella's *City of the Sun,* of Defoe's *Robinson Crusoe,* of Hilton's *Shangrila,* of Skinner's *Walden II,* and of many another.

Phaeacia means in Greek the "Shining Land". It is a new community, now in its second generation. Its people were once settled in Hypereia, probably far to the East, when they were oppressed by savage giant neighbors, "a quarrelsome people who took advantage of their greater strength to plague them", says Homer.

Their first king, Nausithous, father of the present king, the divine Alcinous, "made them migrate and settled them in Scheria [probably a mythical name, like Phaeacia and Hypereia], far from the busy haunts of men."

"There he laid out the walls of a new city, built them houses, put up temples to the gods, and allotted the land for cultivation." They have an abundance of food and water, and of niceties of civilization. "We run fast and we are first-rate seamen. But the things in which we take a perennial delight are the feast, the lyre, the dance, clean linen in plenty, a hot bath, and our beds." The wash is done in "the noble river with its never-failing pools, in which there was enough clear water always bubbling up and swirling by to clean the dirtiest clothes." [1]

The beautiful princess, Nausicaa, is impelled by Athena to go with attendants to the river banks to wash clothes and play games, activities suggestive of the rites of Spring to at least one authority, Emile Mireaux.[2] There she inevitably encounters Odysseus, begrimed from his many days adrift but refreshed from sleep. Her ball falls near the thicket where he lay, she meets him and he wins her trust. She in turn reassures her playmates.

> Stop, my maids. Where are you flying to at the sight of a man? Don't tell me you take him for an enemy, for there is no man on earth, nor ever will be, who would dare set hostile feet on Phaeacian soil. The gods are too fond of us for that. Remote in this sea-beaten home of ours, we are the outposts of mankind and come in contact with no other people."[3]

A town square, marketing-place and meeting place, well-paved, adjoins the Temple of Poseidon, chief of the gods favoring the city, for he fathered king Nausithous. Poseidon is not always pleased with his Phaeacians, because they are sometimes too hospitable to travelers who have offended him, and it was fore-told by King Nausithous that Poseidon would be jealous enough one day to petrify a vessel of theirs and swing about the mountains behind them into a ring that would foreclose the sea.

Meanwhile they lived well and gave their energies to the building and sailing of fleet ships. They held commerce, too, in contempt. Neither grim warriors nor merchants, yet they enjoyed all the good things of life.

The King's name of Alcinous (Alkynoos) is significant. The central star of the Pleiades, the gate to Paradise and to the world of spirits, is Alkyone. Alkyonic Lake is the waters of death leading of Paradise. There has since time immemorial been a worldwide knowledge, among tribes and great civilizations, about the Pleiades, early November celebrations

---

[1] A. T. Murray, translator, *Homer: The Odyssey*, VI.

[2] *Daily Life in the Time of Homer*, trans. by Iris Sells from the 1954 French edition (New York: MacMillan and Company, 1959), . 102. Vol I, chap. X.

[3] A. T. Murray, translator, *Homer: The Odyssey*, VI..

occur centering upon them.[4]

The palace of Alcinous, too, is shining and grand, "for a kind of radiance, like that of the sun or moon, lit up the high-roofed halls of the great king." The palace enjoys a large household of retainers and its gardens extend into a bush-enclosed orchard.

Homer is as respectful of women as anyone in this age of brutal male chauvinism. Queen Arete, mother of Nausicaa, "sits at the hearth in the light of the fire, spinning the purple yarn, a wonder to behold, leaning against a pillar and her hand maids sit behind her,"[5] but she is a powerful factor in setting policy for the realm. If you secure her favor, Nausicaa tells Odysseus, you may hope to regain home and friends. "On mother's wishes much depends."[6]

The places of public assembly can hold "many thousands": all of the nobles, their families and the population. The king is beloved, but ruler by consensus. Social and political functions are performed by men chosen, perhaps elected, from the aristocracy. For example, when the performance of "Love Affair" was announced, a committee of nine official stewards took matters in hand. "They were public servants who supervised all the details on such occasions."

The Phaeacians are a well-organized community. They have a public opinion. There are conventional moral standards: gossip, respect, a time for marriage, a place for everyone and for strangers: these seem all the more utopian as they seem real.

A peaceful people, we are induced to believe, a people beloved by and respecting the gods, a people who lived serenely under an ultimate belief that their special god, Poseidon, would take away their sea, their precious sea-faring way of life.

In the end, we are told, these beautiful people, hospitable, who had sublimated all terrors to the arts and crafts, were punished as Poseidon had promised: for their kindness to Odysseus, their returning ship was frozen to stone and a range of mountains was about to encircle them.

---

[4] R. G. Halliburton, 25 "Nature" (Dec. 1, 1881) 100-1; E. B. Tylor 25 *Nature* (Dec. 15, 1881) 150-1; R. G. H., 25 Nature (Feb. 2, 1882) 317-8.

[5] A. T. Murray, translator, *Homer: The Odyssey,* I, 229.

[6] Robert Fitzgerald, *Homer: The Odyssey* (New York: Doubleday, 1961).

CHAPTER THREE

THE LOVE AFFAIR
AS THE MASK OF TRAGEDY

The song is sung. The play is over. Now the question is, "What does it represent?" It represents, I think, and I must take the rest of this book to explain myself, a shocked spell amidst conditions of horrifying natural disaster. The Greeks experienced it, suppressed its memories, remembered it subconsciously, and converted it ultimately into the symbolic form of a comedy.

The Greeks assumed the Love Affair took place in the sky nor could it have any other location. The gods move swiftly from place to place, the Sun is one of the actors, some of the brilliant imagery such as of "the brazen bright threshold" suggests the heavens, the gods involved are all sky-gods, and the decor and associated games are celestial. Hyginus is not alone in speaking of the play as going on in the sky; speaking of Venus exciting Mars, he writes that "since she inflamed him violently with love, she called the star Pyroeis, indicating this fact."[1]

---

[1] *Poetica Astronomica,* II 42. The root "pyr" denotes "fire."

The Love Affair As The Mask Of Tragedy

Hyginus' *Poetica Astronomica* also says that: When Vulcan married Venus he watched so Mars could only follow but never catch her.

This indicates the nature of the "love-affair" as a planetary engagement and hints at prior close encounters of Vulcan with Aphrodite and then a relationship such that Vulcan would always be closer to Aphrodite than Mars could be.

Effective planetary encounters must be accompanied by grave disasters.

Probably the primordial elements of The Love Affair were composed of the incoherent, intense feelings of people in a frenzy of despair and fright.[2] Words of today cannot express their feelings. The biblical prophets convey some impressions of the state of mind in the throes of disaster. The mind of today, developed in the imagery of nuclear bomb devastation, can perhaps understand something of their feelings. Accounts of historically experienced natural disasters such as Vesuvius, Krakatoa, the Pestigo (Wisconsin) forest fire, and the great Lisbon earthquake lend analogous material.

What had really happened had probably caused repeated surges of disjoined symbols and thoughts. The poetry must have sprung originally from a chaos of sounds, sights and human babel and ejaculations, uttered by many tongues, over hours and days of time. A "normal" adult would probably have been reduced to bodies of expression such as follows:

> "The worst is happening... just as feared!... all sacrifices failed... here it is... annihilator... oracles... monster-body... war... death sun... red dogs, blood... Aphrodite... sex... moon... darkness... thunder... trumpets... golden... Ares... Zeus... sword... stretched fireballs... moon rape... heat... god, god... who... suffocation... stinks... stand still... run... hide... don't move... a giant in the sky calling... he was away... his flares are out... moon is his... we give it... pray take it... all this can't happen... we did not mean it... abah, awah, abah... we are dying... glowers... shakes... where is he going... where has she gone... din... deafness... the sky and land are afire... Poseidon stop it... shake them off... take everything... let us be... uh."

And so on. But the horror once past paved the way for music and literature. The state of mind of the audience of Demodocus can be reconstructed into a more coherent story in which the matching of a new plot with the original real story is nicely achieved. The original memories

---

[2] Alfred de Grazia, "The Palaetiology of Fear and Memory," (Lethbridge, Canada: University of Lethbridge, 1976), Part I.

and anxieties are blended and smoothed over by the new story so that they erupt under control. History cannot be forgotten, but it can be made tolerable. The Song of Love is telling something that only the collective unconscious can understand, and which the unconscious rarely permits to be verbalized. I shall try, nevertheless, to force to emerge some of the unexpressed and unconscious feelings of the people of Phaeacia as the Love Affair is sung and played. To do so I may resort to a rhetorical device.

AN ANCIENT PRIEST EXPLAINS

If an old priest of Delphi were to be instructing acolytes about events of the song, we imagine that lecture-notes upon his discourse would read as follows:

> "We know these gods for what they are, uncontrollable and primeval; we cannot say what we think of them; we must not even say who they are or where we first met them; we must not say what they did to us or in any way accuse them; we must not even remember too much lest we feel agony and panic. The rhythms and the chords keep our feeling under control, reinforcing the screen of words alone. The story, as Demodocus signs it, is familiar. Yet it contrives to excite and appease us. We shall feel better afterwards. That is because otherwise we might be compelled to confront the true story, which is rather like what follows, although we cannot be sure that it is more than a terribly realistic dream."

THE HIDDEN STORY

Ares and Aphrodite are the planet Mars and the Moon. The Planet Mars is ruddy and far away now, but was then close to the Moon who was bathed in her golden aura. Hephaestus is the planet Venus. He is not married to Aphrodite. He approached her on various occasions in times past, and ourselves too, our Earth, and was terribly destructive. And the Moon was disturbed and drawn to him and then was drawn back, and so we gave her in marriage, or rather Zeus gave her in marriage, for how else could they be legitimately coupled save by the ruler of the skies and of humanity, who has for three thousands years dominated us.

Mars and Moon are not in love, nor do they make true love. They are destroying each other and us. Mars' huge body which once seemed like a flaming sword interjects itself between Moon and Earth. And the whole primal violence of

The Love Affair As The Mask Of Tragedy

extreme sexual activity occurs on a world scale. The bed of Earth shakes, the skies glare brilliantly, electricity is all-pervasive, the Moon disappears and reappears. A massive rape is occurring. Hephaestus is far away. It is night but for the brilliance of the scene, secret night when sex flourishes and Aphrodite, the Dark One, makes love. Perhaps if he would return, he would divert the assailant Mars and spare us from total destruction. We would ourselves imitate this orgy, if we were engaging in an alternate mood of anxiety-therapy, or we would propitiate by sacrificing ourselves or what belongs to us or whatever and whomever we can lay our hands on.

We know what "gifts of Ares" are. They are meteors. They are the steeds of Mars. They have struck us and are showered upon Moon. When our King Nausithous led us out of Hypereia, it was because of the stone-giants which Mars and his horde had hurled upon our land.

The secret will be exposed. Helios the Sun is rising. He never takes part. He cannot rescue us. But he will attract the attention of the Planet Hephaestus and perhaps an intervention will occur.

It does. Planet Hephaestus looms large, in blazing anger, his immense arms and stunted legs making him look like a comet. Then he disappears. He does not approach the lovers closely. He goes to the other side of Earth. We wonder whether he will reappear. The destruction upon Earth is terrible. Mars is twice the size of the Moon. We are struck repeatedly by his "gifts"- gases, stones, quakes. The waters are disturbed. The tides are high, the volcanos are erupting. Will the other gods do nothing? Now the Moon and Mars are behind us, leaving us rocking and quaking. But Hephaestus is once more in sight. He is as large as Mars, brilliant, and trailing electric sparks even against the gray sky. But if his legs drag, not so his arms. His huge arms flap as they hammer out the sparks. The whole sky around him is brazen. He drops flashing clouds over our heads and from the corner posts or pillars of the sky.

But again he departs and again come Mars and Moon. She had returned separately to the region of Jupiter and comes back once again to meet Mars who has come flying along parallel to us. Moon attracts Mars once more. Great electric sparks envelop them. They are perturbed. They pause and move, pause and move. Now Moon appears in an unusual phase or position, now she disappears behind Mars and he moves ahead showing another part of her. Mars is closely following the Moon, which is to say that he is moving swiftly parallel to the Earth.

But Hephaestus now approaches, even larger than he was a few hours ago (who can measure such agonizing time?) A thunderous noise fills the heavens, like the enraged shouts of the cuckolded husband. It is something to cause ugly laughter; it is a tangible, an enormous, a highly visible fact, this entanglement of the two.

We shall now witness the catastrophe, as we Greeks call the end of an age and also that part of a drama which brings the culmination of a plot.

"The Gods of the Sky must come!," says the thunderous noise. The scene must attract them, for it is their milieu. It is the end of the age, the end of the world.

They will be our salvation or our doom. Hephaestus is lying. He knows he is not the son of Zeus but was cast down by Jupiter and took his strange misshapen form (compared with the other Olympians) from the accident. The bed of Hephaestus is by the Moon, not as it is today, even though he is often far away and invisible in the northern sky.

But Mars has climbed upon this bed and is trapped in the invisible electrical-gravitational net. The sex bout has ended with the bodies suddenly largely stilled. Our Earth also pauses.

Hephaestus hovers in the sky, glowering, raging, exchanging bolts with Mars. Mars tries to emerge from the bed of the Moon. Hephaestus demands his brideprice back from Jupiter. They are the same "gifts" as Mars, which Hephaestus had showered upon Moon in olden time, when the marriage was first consumated and we have not recovered from that marriage of the gods yet.

Jupiter stays away. He is retiring more and more. He has claimed to set up the order of the skies, such as it is. He is scarcely responsible, it seems to us, for he should return to strike Mars with thunderbolts and drive him away. Instead of the conflict being adjudicated, it will have to be compromised.

Other gods gather. Actually they do not. But memories of them do because of the terror of our experience. New terrors pile upon the old and explode them. Here we see Hermes and Apollo, the lucky and the wise. What can we except from them? Hermes is the helper. We say he is so, because we hope he will help and because once long ago he had been near us when we were going through a similar crisis; he fled to safety and we followed; so we say he led us.

But now he is tormenting us. Prompted by Apollo, he tells the grim truth as a sexual joke; he is an old lover of Moon too, and great is the ruin they brought upon each other and ourselves but great also is the attraction these gods of the sky have for one another. They laugh at the tragedies of others because they suffered the same themselves and no one consoled them. The goddesses stayed away, "out of shame", we sing. The goddesses are not ashamed; it is male conceit. Their names are taken by the male gods whenever they please. Artemis "is" Apollo. Hera "was" Poseidon and "is" now Jupiter. And Athena? Well, Athena "is" Hephaestus, the only planetary female, so she is here in fact and deed.

Hephaestus-Venus will stay married to the Moon. We know how it will end. The only question is whether Mars should pay anything. Apollo remains aloof and laughing. But for Earth and Sea it is no laughing matter. Poseidon stands for Earth when Mother Earth is absent, as well as for the all-encircling seas and waters. He is The Earth-Shaker! He repeatedly beseeches the Planet Venus on our behalf to uncouple Mars and Moon. Earth is already paying its price and willing to pay more if only the disasters will cease.

The tension is terrible to bear. Fortunately, Venus-Hephaestus is about to move away. The disaster cannot continue. He therefore accepts the offer of the Earth-Shaker who may be growing tired of his own exertions. More will be paid by Earth to the Planet that shines in daytime. This bodes ill. More songs, more dances, prayers, sacrifices, suffering will be required in the future, from Venus as well as from Mars.

So the two bodies are loosed and spring up and away. Thank the Gods! The break happened fast. As Venus withdrew, Mars speeded away in a new orbit to the Northwest, propelled by the planets Earth and Venus, and the Moon, violently abused, flew Southwest where all smoke and fires were quickly quenched and she emerged soon, appearing as round and golden as she did before but she now carries new pocks and scars. The character of the Moon is unchanged. The Gods are uncontrollable; we must not offend them; we must not pretend to be like them; but we cannot help but sing and dance about them. It is one of the few things we can do to prevent our utter destruction in the future and suppress our intolerable memories of the past.

And the old priest would conclude with a warning to the acolytes: "Someday you will understand this, but what I have told you must always remain a secret from everybody."

The song, the music, and the dancing are ended. The transition to the ordinary frame of mind occurs. The sons of the good King Alcinous perform a dance to lighten the minds and hearts of the audience. They cast a beautiful purple ball far into the air, leaping to catch it. It seems to reach the shadowy clouds. They seem to touch the sky, to be as light as air. This heavenly sphere has no counterparts on earth. Perhaps it is a stretched and round-stitched bladder or skin filled with feathers, fashioned by a master hand, or a round-shaped gourd ball. It makes contact with the celestial spheres - Sun, Moon, Planets. They keep them up and leap after them; all is done quickly; it is a *trompe l'oeil*, a dazzling coda.

AUTHOR'S CODA

If the preceding replay of Demodocus' song as a representation of the unconscious contains both a new "real" parallel plot and a certain "madness," one need not be repelled or even surprised. Literature was not invented by humankind out of boredom with spending long nights in caves. It emerged as a method of controlling psychological distress.

Both the "real" story and the "madness" will come in for more lengthy discussion. One asks here simply for a beginning of understanding. As the plot breaks down under analysis, it should evidence some well-known psychoses of which the mind is capable under stress. In its suffering and terror the mind engages in many forms of delusional thought. An important effect is the belief that the skies and the earth are alive with beings who resemble oneself and are similarly motivated. This anthropomorphism helps the transfiguration of the uncontrollable and huge forces into the images of sex, social power, and property that the mind is accustomed to dealing with.

Ambivalence to the gods erupts quickly, once the gods are born out of nature. Hate is just as quickly suppressed and turned upon oneself, for fear that one will be terribly punished if it becomes known to the gods. A persecution complex occurs instantly; one cannot evade the mighty punishers. Symptoms of schizophrenia are abundant: attempts at shutting out the real world; attempts at reconstructing quickly a new world of one's own in which events are controlled only by the mind.

Forgetting and distortion proceed quickly. As soon as possible, means will be invented to screen off both the real story and its effects on the psyche. Literature, songs, and games will be invented. Wars will be waged, for one must handle the urge to punish oneself by moving out wildly and attacking others. Temples and palaces for the provision of security and order must be erected; these will celebrate, in a different screening language, of course, the events of those days; they will see to it that the right food is eaten and digested and the proper mating and reproduction will occur.

CHAPTER FOUR

CATASTROPHE & SUBLIMATION

One may dare to suppose that the Love Affair stands for a tragedy of humanity if there is borne in mind a larger theory, already considerably developed, even if not yet widely employed. The larger theory, the modern scientific theory of ancient catastrophes - quantavolution - functions as a kind of general engineering scheme to guide the reconstruction of the song of Demodocus. It is both chronological - telling *what* happened *when* - and analytic - telling *how* it happened. As a consequence of work done in quantavolution, many ancient and recent discoveries have come together, attracted as if by a magnet.

THE GENERAL THEORY OF CATASTROPHE

I state here the several components of the general theory of ancient catastrophes and quantavolution, shaping it to present needs to a degree, and illustrating it to the minimal extent required for its comprehension. Ample documentation and qualifications are to be found in the

"Quantavolution Series" [1] and other works - of a controversial nature, to be sure.

1. *Grave catastrophes have befallen the planet Earth.* The evidence of geology, oceanography, meteorology, paleomagnetism, and archeology are continuously bringing forward new evidence, and rediscovering old evidence, that in times past the Earth suffered repeated devastation by quakes, floods, fires and winds whose dimensions are fantastically beyond any historical experience of the last 2700 years. The surface of the Earth has been twisted and turned, sunk and raised, scoured and ploughed on a continental scale. The orbit of the Earth, the rotation of the Earth, and the axial inclination of the Earth to the plane of the ecliptic have changed suddenly, with frightful consequences.

2. *The catastrophes have been initiated in great part by changes in the solar system.* Planets have changed their orbits and other motions, nearly collided, acquired or discarded satellites, become heated and cooled, accumulated and discharged electricity, and, on some of these occasions, involved the Earth in their titanic activities. One planet, Venus, may even have been newly created out of Jupiter. The number of meteors that have struck Earth is large but responsible for only a portion of the catastrophic damage, since atmospheric, electrical, tidal and seismic disturbances can occur with or without body impact.

3. *Some catastrophes have had large effects upon mankind.* They have been allocated to past periods during which hominids and humans lived, whether these are traced back thousands or millions of years. The last ice age has been moved up to a point where *homo sapiens* is readily recognizable, and has been given by many geologists a huge, abrupt beginning and/or conclusion. All agree that, on occasion, as far back as the fossil record may carry and up to the dawn of history, many species were quickly and concurrently wiped out or reduced to a few survivors.

4. *Some catastrophes have occurred at times within the capacity of humanity to transmit their memories to successive generations.* All peoples have myths of chaos and creation, and of the destruction of civilizations and their recreation, in a set of cycles. As one moves from earlier to later catastrophes the linkages between oral (and transcribed) myths and factual reportage, recognizably modern in form, increase. Additional

---

[1] The reader is referred to the volumes of my *Quantavolution Series* (Metron Publications, Princeton, N. J., 1981-4), especially *Chaos and Creation* and its bibliography.

corroboration comes from the developing science of myth-analysis, contributed to by classicists, anthropologists, philologists, psychologists, and archaeologists. In addition, archeology has disclosed periods of total and simultaneous devastation of existing civilizations in areas stretching from the Atlantic Ocean to China, and from Mexico to Peru.

5. Wherever symbolic and linguistic evidence is available, and usually also where only oral traditions are preserved, *the catastrophes suffered on Earth and by humanity were attributed to changes in the celestial system*, and particularly to Ouranos (the Sky), the planets Saturn, Jupiter, Apollo (now transmuted beyond ready identification), Mercury, Venus, and Mars. The latest catastrophes are associated with the erratic and destructive behavior of Mars in the years 776 to 687 B. C., ending that is, 2662 years ago. These precise years, which Velikovsky initially proposed, cover the scenarios of this book, and in my view are generally acceptable.

6. Putting aside the sudden destruction of many civilizations in the course of thousands of years and granting that the sheer survival of these species was all-important, retroactively considered, and furthermore leaving to my book *Homo Schizo I* the question whether a highly significant mutation took place among proto-humans in a cerebral or endocrine form that contemporary paleophysiology can barely recognize, *the greatest effect upon humanity of the catastrophes was their contribution to the making of the human mind and human nature.*

The *exceedingly heavy experience of disaster* from all forms of elemental turbulence, with its associated disruption and dissolution of human communities, caused widespread amnesia. As much as they could and as quickly as possible, surviving humans suppressed the memories of those times.

But the fear and the anxiety produced now by one and then by another catastrophe could not be forgotten and surged repeatedly to the surface of consciousness. *The massive collective anxiety was displaced onto many different subjects, altered the ways in which these subjects were viewed and treated, until finally our modern human nature emerged,* replete with a variety of sublimations, that is, the continuous and partly controlled discharge of the never-to-be forgotten experiences and fears of disaster.[2]

---

[2] These matters are discussed at length in *Homo Schizo I* and *II*.

THE DISPLACEMENT OF AFFECTS

The sublimations of catastrophic anxiety diffused into three major areas: expressive communication; passive controls; and active controls.

In the area of expressive communication, the primitive language was expanded and grew more abstract and conceptual to describe the behavior being observed in the skies. The astral events were associated with prior experiences of the closest analogous types, especially sex and conflict, and humanized. The terrific visible sky-forces were understood then to be human-like but superhuman to the nth power. (" The Lord made the mountains skip like rams," recited the Hebrew psalmist.) All manner of recounting the events was called for; no matter which mode, it was bound to be loaded with anxious affect.

The different modes were sorted out, the most heavily charged from the less, the most denotative from the more connotative. Different formulas were worked out for handling the modes of expression; those that were the most direct or challenging to the superpowers had to be the most carefully licensed and regulated. Little by little, songs, ballads and fables were developed that could be granted more freedom of expression. So began the history of literature, both liturgical and profane.

Passive controls include the incorporation of catastrophic anxiety into prescribed conduct, whether personal or social. The governance of behavior by taboos, fixation of archetypes and stereotypes, and the performance of rituals alone and in crowds received so much impetus from the catastrophes and their aftermaths that they practically may be said to have sprung from them. If a word had to be chosen to represent the motivation for all of these passive controls, it might be an obsession, which may be defined as the inability to move one's conscious attention from the centerpiece of one's anxiety without enchaining the attention.

The greatest taboo of all is to forget the circumstances of disaster. One freezes like death, like the possum, like the soldier against a brilliant flare, like the humans who were turned into statues by the Greek gods, like the Judaic sect whose members immobilize at the first moment of the Sabbath, in the position of the moment, until the Sabbath passes. A great proliferation of ideas and customs can come from this attitude but they will all be deductively connected to the primeval chaos and creation. "Good" education comes to be making the young both as fearful and as habituated as oneself. People think, "If I do something new, it, the thing, nature, god, will do something new" and therefore it isn't worthwhile; it is taboo in fact, to try to do so.[3]

The third great area affected by catastrophe governs human efforts at active control of other people and the environment. Here is included the sharp growth of the power motive (and corresponding ability) in individuals that start up the centralized kingdoms (and which prospers from the passive control behavior just noted). The urge to wage destructive warfare is enhanced, but also the proliferation of invention: all in imitation of the celestial forces who hammered, shouted, put on dazzling displays of light, showered down many types of materials and objects, and changed many species of animals and plants. "For the Spartans," wrote Lucian, "Lycurgus drew from the sky his ordering of their whole polity."[4]

The Love Affair is an example of the first area of sublimation, the expressive communication, and of one kind of myth, the holy dreamtime song. But, as has become already apparent, the words alone are an inadequate description of the event. It dwells upon what was the last or nearly the last of the great catastrophes. Every major element of the general theory of ancient catastrophe put forward above is represented in the song, its latent meaning, and its physical and social contexts. At the same time, every element of the general theory of catastrophe had happened before in earlier disasters, as in the case of the repeated incursions of Venus upon the Earth's orbit, which occurred between 1500 B. C. and the time of our story and which have been described in detail by Velikovsky, by the "Quantavolution Series," and in related works. And it all happened again and again before 1500 B. C., which is a vast and difficult history only now being told.

---

[3] Cf., e. g., Eliade, *Myth and Reality*, pp. 6-7 et passim.

[4] From "Astrology," p. 367, Vol. V of *Works* (Loeb ed., Harvard University Press, 1936).

CHAPTER FIVE

HOLY DREAMTIME

Before the Love Affair had been played and sung, Odysseus was reduced to tears by Demodocus' singing of the Trojan War. And, later on, hours after the Love Affair has been played, Odysseus offers a gift to Demodocus and addresses him:

> Demodocus I proclaim you the most distinguished of all mortals. Either the Muse, daughter of Zeus, instructed you, or Apollo you directly. For you chant the fate of the Achaeans absolutely according to its proper ordering: What they did and had done to them and what distress they suffered - as if, in some way, you had been present yourself or had heard it from someone who was there.[1]

One may wonder whether, although Odysseus does not recognize it, the Love Affair, too, is sung "absolutely according to its proper ordering," and as if Demodocus "had been present" himself "or had heard it from someone who was there."

Strange it is that Odysseus, when the song is ended, has been transported and is joyfully at ease. One would imagine that the story of

---

[1] A. T. Murray, translator, *Homer: The Odyssey,* VIII, ls. 487-91.

an adulterous love triangle might have reminded him of his own plight - long away from his palace and beset by rumors of his wife's unfaithfulness. One might believe that the song was in bad taste, or that afterwards he might gnash his teeth and rend his garments. Not at all. Homer and he obviously did not feel any such connection between the performance and his plight.

When the singer, Demodocus, "struck the chords in prelude," his audience was already entranced. He himself is blind; Homer, whose image he may reflect, is also called "the Blind." He is Homer's "good minstrel, whom the Muse loves above all other men, and gave him both good and evil; of his sight she deprived him, but gave him the gift of sweet song."[2]

There is a hint here that ancient bards were sometimes blinded, as smiths were ritually lamed, and young singers castrated, to heighten their symbolic role and competence. No god might then envy the bard, especially not Apollo, and his blindness is an assurance that he will not see what is divinely forbidden to see. Athena, too, was known to play tricks with human sight.[3] Furthermore, his audience will not be discomfited at being viewed in their musing mood by a sensibly alert musician. And, of course, a blind man may develop epic powers of memory. An alternative, less radical, would be to sing with eyes closed, or blindfolded.

The audience is settled around as an organized community, king and queen, nobles, council of state, the citizens and retainers, and the Hero, Odysseus. The dancers continue their movements, acting out the scenes of the sacred play. Those who have competed in sports rest, their aggressiveness dissipated, their minds relaxed to receive now a flow of aesthetic communication.

The singer carries the melody; it is sung in long, measured lines. His lyre was originally a gift of Mercury and Apollo, and is a beautiful instrument; its strings are attuned to the heavenly bodies, as Pythagoras will demonstrate mathematically a century hence. Although the earliest lyres held three strings, the age of seven-stringed lyres may have already arrived. The rhythms are supplied by the ballet who stress the

---

[2] VIII, I. 62-4; V. I, 263 in Murray, *op. cit.*

[3] Graves, I, 23: I, p. 87.

movements of the opera.

The production is a drama, not a ballad or folk song. Its plot is conventionally complete, perhaps the earliest of the dramatic plots of what is to become the literary history of Classical Greece, therefore a great invention, with a pair of protagonists, an antagonist, the development of a line of conduct, its interruption, a climax, a resolution, a disposition of participants and values. All happens in a time span close to what Aristotle discovered, centuries later, to be the ideal unity of dramatic time.

One notes particularly, in the jargon of literary analysis employed from the time of the early Greek tragedians, the "catastrophe." The word means "the climax," "the point of *denouement*," in general, the word means "the turning-down point," and also "the end of a period of time." Yet it was historical experience that lent itself to the definition of plot, not plot of history. It was first an unconscious invention, then a conscious one, that ordained the classical climax of drama. The archetypical plot is that when the end of an age arrives, the gods foregather, and societies turn abruptly downward, after which the cycle begins once more. The Love Affair is a relic of the end of the Mycenean Age of Greece.

THE SCANDALOUS LITTLE PIECE

What has been made of the Love Affair? It is at least a song, for it was chanted to the chords of a lyre, to the accompaniment of rhythmic dancing. Perhaps, first off, I should stress that its 'songness' has been variously imparted. In the version by the famous Alexander Pope, one would sense a different spirit. The bard, Demodokos,

The loves of Mars and Cytherea[4] *sings;*
How the stern god, enamour'd with her charms,
Clasp'd the gay panting goddess in his arms,
By bribes seduced.

---

[4]Cytherea is one of the epithets given Aphrodite. Cytherea was the holy island which the newly born goddess touched while floating towards her destination of Cyprus.

And as Hephaestus traps the lovers, Pope's Homer sings:

Stern Vulcan homeward treads the starry way:
Arrived, he sees, he grieves, with rage he burns:
Full horribly he roars, his voice all heaven returns.
"O Jove, (he cried) O all ye powers above,
See the lewd dalliance of the queen of love!
Me, the awkward me, she scorns; and yields her charms
To that fair lecher, the strong god of arms.

Translation of the *Odyssey* are numerous. One that interested me to the point of inquiry was by Thomas Hobbes (1588-1679,) prepared when he was in his eighties. His long life as natural philosopher and political scientist carried him through the extensive revolutions and religious debates of the times and up to Newton and Whiston. This was the Hobbes whose view of mankind included the famous phrase that in a state of nature man's life was "nasty, brutish, and short." Poetically, I must agree with Pope, who said that Hobbes' version of Homer was "too mean for criticism."[5] But did he treat the Love Affair in some unusual way? Not at all - though it contains a touch of unwarranted political expertness:

And the judges rise
In number nine, who had elected been
By public-vote, of games to hold assize,
And order took for large room in the middle, And
made it to be planed well and even.[6]

But, as a I shall explain, even if beautifully rendered, the lines of Homer must read as the pale representation of their original pronouncement and context.

Experts upon Homer have generally denied serious consideration to his song about a love affair. It seems to be what Alexander Pope makes it out to be, burlesque entertainment for a visiting sailor. One seems to

---

[5] *The English Works,* Vol. X (London: ed. 1677; John Bohn, 1844, W. Molesworth, editor), p. iv.

[6] *Ibid,* p. 376.

hear the typical commentator: "A bit scandalous, but then you know how lightly the Greeks took their gods and goddesses!"

One translator, Professor Murray, indicates conscientiously that "the whole passage was on moral grounds rejected by some ancient critics."[7] Walter Otto tells us that "even in antiquity many readers, Plato among them, found this story offensive, and in modern times it is generally regarded as a frivolous burlesque."[8] Professor Finely, an expert upon the society and economy of Homeric Greece, speaks of "the little pieces, like the myth of the adultery between Ares and Aphrodite"[9] that infiltrate the *Odyssey*. George Sarton, the encyclopedic historian of science regards the whole of the *Odyssey*, indeed, as a story of peace, a gentle romance.[10] Such observations can only reflect the nostalgia for one's school-days: the blood and guts spilled in the *Odyssey*, and the terrors entailed, would put to shame the authors of a typical evening of violence and horror on American commercial television. T. B. L. Webster mentions the possibility that "the light-hearted treatment of the gods in some Egyptian stories may have influenced Demodokos' lay of Ares and Aphrodite in the eight book of *Odyssey*."[11] E. V. Rieu, introducing his translation of the *Odyssey*, says that "in the famous Lay of Demodocus" Homer provides "a treatment that we can only regard as humorous." This merely betrays, he claims, "a very tolerant understanding of their motives and frailties," not an absence of respect for the power and beauty of the gods.[12]

But, then, the distinguished Robert Graves, premature women's liberationist that he is, says: "though masquerading as an epic, the *Odyssey* is the first Greek novel; and therefore wholly irresponsible where myths are concerned." Graves tends to agree with Samuel Butler, author of the utopia, *Erewhon,* who, in another book, *Authoress of the Odyssey*, ascribed the work to a young and talented Sicilian noblewoman of the district of

---

[7] A. T. Murray, translator, *Homer: The Odyssey,* p. 276.

[8] *The Homeric Gods,* trans. by Moses Hadas (London: Thames and Hudson, 1954).

[9] M. I. Finley, *The World of Odysseus* (Middlesex, England: Penguin Books, 1954, 1967, 1972), p. 40.

[10] *A History of Science: Ancient Science through the Golden Age of Greece,* 1958 (New York: John Wiley and Sons, 1964), p. 135.

[11] *From Mycenae to Homer* (New York: W. W. Norton, 1958, 1964), p. 88.

[12] Page 5.

Eryx.[13]

Experts can be piled "Ossa upon Pelion" without reaching heaven. Otto's elaborate concern over reason and respect reminds one of a prude explaining why his sister is loitering on a Piraeus street corner. "The story is naturally not a moralizing sermon, but that does not make it frivolous. Its tone of lofty humor removes it from both moralizing and frivolity." Ares is a bloody savage, disliked by everyone. "All interest centers upon the discreditable role played by Ares... And Aphrodite? If we consider the story carefully we suddenly realize that she receives no attention whatsoever." His final gaff regarding Poseidon is monumental: "Poseidon is so touched by Ares' situation that, unable to laugh, he prevails upon Hephaestus to release his hapless victim and is so kindly as to provide a guarantee for him."[14] This comment would perhaps have made the surly Poseidon laugh for once.

BURLESQUE OR RELIGION?

One cannot be satisfied with these explanations: a little piece, a casual ballad, a joke at the expense of the gods, or a pardonable escapade. Suppose the passage is reread, beginning with the paragraph before the song commences.

"Sacred commands of Alcinous." Do godlike kings incite simple public pornography?

"Quickly arose a lithe herald, seeking to find and to fetch him the resonant harp from its palace place." Are treasured instruments of music employed casually?

"Rising as well were a chosen nine, men who were Lords Ceremonial, publicly called, whenever the people foregathered and needed an ordering." These are nobles. They are nine, the magic number of days in the week may then have existed or once existed in a 36-day or 27-day

---

[13] *The Greek Myths,* 2 vols. (New York: Braziller, 1957). Cf. v. II, pp. 376,365.

[14] A. T. Murray, translator, *Homer: The Odyssey,* p. 245.

month.¹⁵ They are chosen representatives of the community, a council of ministers of public order. Are these august personages activated for the sake of a ditty?

"They cleared out space for the dancing to come; they measured a broad ring." Is a large dancing ring being readied without apprehension and excitement?

Demodocus "moved in the midst of the young boys." He is the star performer, blind, revered, also godlike (of these qualities we read in other passages). "All of them skilled in the dance though they blossomed with fair youth." This is not to be improvised. The performers know their places. They have all achieved high competence.

"Down stamped their feet on the floor." The rhythms begin, even before the lyre sounds. "Spellbound Odysseus marveled as dancing feet twinkled in mid-air!" The little song is introduced, it is clear, as a full court opera. The preliminaries portend a significant event. Odysseus, and the rest of the audience, have become transformed by the rhythm, flashing movements, and apprehension into an unusual state of mind, a new mood.

The mood is not vulgar or profane. It is not lecherous. Something more profound is to occur. The audience has experienced it all before; their contagion affects Odysseus. The incident, from its very beginnings, portends an affair of state, not a moment of minstrelling, a story of significance rather than cocktail hour music. It is to be even rather sacred, I think.

Perhaps reassurance is needed. Is this behavior, this kind of performance, unanalyzed in science? Not at all. It is universal and has been generalized. Mircea Eliade, a distinguished religious ethnologist, would lend his support:

> All dances were originally sacred;...they had an extrahuman model... The model may have been revealed by a divinity (for example the pyrrhic, the martial dance created by Athena) or by a hero (cf. Theseus' dance in the Labyrinth). The dance may be executed to acquire food, to honor the dead, or to assure good order in the cosmos. It may take place upon the occasion of initiations, of magico-religious ceremonies, of marriages, and so on... What is of interest to us is its

---

¹⁵ Immannuel Velikovsky, *Worlds in Collision*, hereafter cited simply as *W in C*, (New York: Doubleday and Co., Inc., 1950), pp. 343-4.

presumed extrahuman origin (for every dance was created *in illo tempore,* in the mythical period, by an ancestor, a totemic animal, a god, or a hero.) Choreographic rhythms have their model outside of the profane life of man; whether they reproduce the movements of the totemic or emblematic animal, or the motions of the stars; whether they themselves constitute rituals (labyrinthine steps, leaps, gestures) performed with ceremonial instruments - a dance always imitates an archetypal gesture or commemorates a mythical moment. In a word, it is a repetition, and consequently a reactualization, of *illud tempus,* 'those days. '"[16]

The Love Affair appears then as a sacred song, not bawdy lyric; or at least its context is unmistakably holy, putting aside its plot and words. One cannot be sure of either its full context or words, of course, because Demodocus tells of another, apparently long operatic ballet that we are not privileged to watch and hear.

THE PIOUS DRAMATIST

The Phaeacian audience is *in illo tempore.* It is in Holy Dream-time, a state of being in the past and in the present, where a great event is happening and still away from it in the here and now, in the presence of those who were involved in the action. One cannot watch the Phaeacians as R. M. Berndt did the aboriginal Australian Wonguri in a similar format and mood,[17] or as other anthropologists have observed primitive tribal performances; one must imagine them with the aid of all the evidence that can be brought to bear upon the scene. If one is successful, it will be owing to another scholar, in this case Giovanni Patroni, whose total immersion in ancient Mediterranean sources has permitted him elaborately to reconstruct the format of the song of Demodocus. He says:

> The most important observations that the singing of Demodocus merits (and has too long awaited) concern the generic type of the song, its aim and function in Homeric and pre-Homeric society, the probable frequency and importance of recitations analogous to that we see held in the agora of Scheria by Demodocus with the aid of a corps de ballet or a chorus that will interpret the

---

[16] *The Myth of the Eternal Return,* originally in French, 1949(Princeton, N. J.: Princeton University Press, 1954, 1965), pp. 28-9. As a well worked out case, see R. M. Berndt, "A 'Wonguri-Manzikai Song Cycle of the Moon-Bone," XIX Oceania (September, 1948, 16-50)

[17] *Ibid.,* and see my note on this song in *The Burning of Troy.*

> narrative of the singer (but we do not mean exclusively) through the medium of movements and dance figures.
>
> This is not epic poetry. Nor is it a song, nor a fragment of a song, nor an episode of an Achaean saga... Neither, for that matter, notwithstanding that its subject concerns exclusively the gods, a sacred hymn. If it is the last, it reflects the higher personal, profound and polemical religiousity of Homer; in this sense it should be entitled: 'The triumph of Mediterranean religion over the foolish and sacrilegious heresy of Olympia. '"[18]

By this, Patroni means that Homer adores the ancient Great Goddess, detests the single-minded destructive god Ares, and upholds the peaceful sovereignty of the female principle that antedated the barbarous incursions of the Achaeans into Minoan and Mycenaean civilization.

In effect, says Patroni, the Song is not sacred poetry because one could not come out openly and formally to the greater glory of Aphrodite, even though the Song carried her through a tedious trial at the hands of a repulsive husband and a mindless warrior lover.

So Patroni classifies the cantata of Demodocus as "opera theatre," midway between our ballet and melodrama with dance, a musical satire perhaps.

But, in fact, Patroni goes beyond his own real interpretations, so prejudiced for the archaic Mediterranean religion is he (and alike to Robert Graves in this regard). We must insist that he stay with his own judgement - it is sacred poetry even if influenced by the personal religion of Homer. It is sacred enough, as he points out immediately, to prompt extraordinary preparations, measure the magic circle, place the venerated poet in the center that is to be occupied many years later by an altar of Dionysus, use the sacred instrument of religious and funereal singing of the Minoans, and employ the incredible acrobatic dancing of the bull-leapers of Tyrins and Knossos. The song, he knows, is the abbreviation of a long performance, and takes place in the halls of the prince.

Indeed, such is the enthusiasm of Patroni for what he believes must have occurred in the opera-theater of the Love Affair that he uncovers ultimately the vast majority of criteria that for anthropologists and psychologists denote the Holy Dreamtime. And he forgets that he has for a moment faltered and said that the hierarchs could not allow a religious character to be granted the triumph of Aphrodite.

---

[18] *Commenti Mediterranei all'Odissea di Omero* (Milano: Marzorati, 1950), p. 249

He gives, actually, a full set of stage directions for the production of the Disastrous Love Affair of Mars and Moon. Dancers leap high into the sky. The Sun mandates a messenger to Hephaestus (for the sun, reasons Patroni, cannot move from its course). Direct quotations are sung by actors, the rest by Demodocus. The climax brings together all of the actors to determine the resolution of the plot, and the finale must be beautiful and ecstatic; Ares is summarily dismissed, but Golden Aphrodite, unabashed, flies to her island where she is perfumed, beautified, and made virginal altogether.

> The goddess - impersonated by an actor - hid herself momentarily in the base of the tower that had been put at the disposition of the spectacle, while the music and ballet entertained the audience; and, from another exit that gave upon the sea (at Scheria the agora was next to the arsenal: it was the same in all the maritime cities; elsewhere the sea was simulated by pulling a boat with a pulley) she embarked on a boat kept in readiness and reappeared from the other side, landing and reentering the arena with all of her cortege, quickly then joined by the entire corps de ballet which, having given further proof of its unmatchable competence, composed itself for the final scene. And what could be the meaning of the scene if not: *The Triumph of Aphrodite*?

The answer to his rhetorical question would disappoint him. It could be, it was, the Triumph of Athena the Producer and Director of the opera. Zeus said to Hera in the *Iliad* when Hera proposed to fight Ares: "Go to it then, and set against him the spoiler Athene, who beyond all others is the one to visit harsh pains upon him."[19]

The chorus of this Mycenaean drama moved directly into the classical Greek chorus, says Patroni (p. 250). Here is one more indication of the interface between Mycenean and Greek, rather than a five hundred year chasm of barbarism. The circle we see in Scheria, too, persisted in the theatre at Epidaurus.

Patroni's informed visions of the dramaturgy of Homer are captivating. The production of the Love Affair in Scheria was complete and elaborate, as much so as the Dreamtime production of the Moon and the Dugong that I mentioned above, though relative to the culture of the indigenous Australians. Patroni's assertions, that Homer was heir to the Minoan and Mycenaean theatre, and that he was a fully experienced choreographer and dramatist, are acceptable too.

The anthropological and mythological evidence should induce

---

[19] Richard Lattimore, *The Iliad of Homer* (Chicago: Univ. of Chicago Press, 1962), p. 148.

Patroni to acknowledge his own immense cultural panorama and to grant that the "marveling" and "spellbound" Odysseus, along with the Phaeacian audience, was in the state of Holy Dreamtime, midway between the pomp and circumstance of the religious "mass" and the nearly secular games that preceded the spectacle.

Here Emile Mireaux has hit the target briefly and sharply:

> Choral lyric poetry naturally remained closer to its religious origins. It was really the poetry of the sacred songs, with their accompaniment of music and dancing... (It included the *hyporcheme* which involved mime dancing.) The mischievous story recited by Demodocus... may be simply a *hyporcheme*... All these Collective displays were designed to 'inspire' the community and lead to the exorcizing of the 'demons' of envy, discord and civil strife.[20]

The Olympic Games themselves, agglomerates of athletics and poetry, had been instituted in the year -776, and no one doubts their religious and cultural aims. Then and at the time of the Love Affair, the Greeks, of many ethnic subcultures with local versions of the gods, and with all manner of archaic and foreign vestiges, were pulling themselves together. The divine Homer was striving to lead them.

---

[20] *Daily Life in the Time of Homer,* trans. by Iris Sells from the 1954 French edition (New York: MacMillan and Company, 1959), p. 102.

PART TWO:

GODS, PLANETS, MADNESS

CHAPTER SIX

THE RAPE OF HELEN

It began during the furious quarrel between Odysseus and Achilles at the rich feast of the gods, sings Demodocus, "for it was at this very moment that calamity began to unroll upon both Trojans and Danaans by the plans of the Great Zeus."[1]

The *Iliad* is sung as the wrath of Achilles on one level - the Poet says so - but is of a type with the battles of the sky gods recited in Scandinavian, Finnish, Hindu, Mexican, Babylonian, and other epics. The Greek gods of the Trojan Wars engage in plain soldiering, hurling rocks and spears, shooting arrows, and driving chariots. They make onslaughts from heaven; they launch disasters upon Earth: plagues, fires, hurricanes, earthquakes, floods, hail of stones and arrows, famines, fogs, and darknesses in the day.

The gods negotiate amongst themselves and with humans. They engage in fighting, trickery, argument, and bribery amongst themselves. They build morale and conduct psychological warfare; they provide

---

[1] *Od.* VIII, 81-2.

military intelligence but also distort information for the good of their favorites. They counsel the warriors on tactics. They enforce rules of warfare that they sometimes themselves violate. They manufacture weapons. They promote and reverse events, battles, and decisions of leaders.

Whole sections of the *Iliad* are devoted to the warring of the gods. On the Achaean side there range Athena, Hera, Poseidon, Hephaestus. On the Trojan side, the line-up includes Ares, Aphrodite, and Apollo. The victory is with the Achaeans and their gods, although the Homeric element ends with Achilles' killing of Hector, the burial of Hector, and a mere pause in the struggle; however, all known versions of the rest of the story, occupying the tenth year, agree that the Achaeans "won the war" and razed Troy. Whether or not Troy was actually destroyed by the Achaeans cannot be told from the ruins of the city. Troy VI and VIIa are the best candidates for the historical city; Schliemann's Troy (now referred to as Troy IIg) is not regarded anymore as a possibility; I have written of this case in the Book, *The Burning of Troy*. Troy IIg was destroyed by an atmospheric conflagration; Troy VI by an earthquake; Troy VIIa by an atmospheric conflagration. These, to Homer and his audiences, would be the gods in battle, the effects of "a divine-kindled fire of stones" *(Iliad)* and other superhuman operations. The "Fall of a City" is a legendary symbol in various cultures for a disaster, that is, the disruption and end of a celestial order. It is likely that the Fall of Troy was such a catastrophe, in which human agency played less of a role than the divine.

THE INDESTRUCTIBLE LADY HELEN

Some of the Trojan story is reported in the *Odyssey,* by Demodocus no less, and by Odysseus from Hades. There and elsewhere the post-war adventures of the Achaean heroes are recounted and it would appear that for the most part they received very little for their pains except more suffering, mishaps, treachery, and misadventure.

But let us examine, with Finley's words, the case of

> Helen, who is a very peculiar figure. Helen, daughter of Zeus and Leda, was Aphrodite's favorite, and thanks to the gifts of the goddess she succeeded in embroiling Greeks and Trojans in a gigantic struggle that cost both sides dearly.

> Helen was no innocent victim in all this, no unwilling captive of Paris-Alexander, but an adulteress in the most complete sense. For Paris there was no atonement ... But Helen received no punishment, and scarcely any reproach. She ended her days back in Sparta, administering magical drugs obtained in Egypt, interpreting omens, and participating in the life of the palace much like Arete [queen of the Phaeacians and a strange, powerful figure] and not like a proper Greek woman.[2]

The "enigmatic" and "complicated" image of Helen, that Finely alludes to, has a simple solution. Helen of Troy stands for the Moon. She represents the goddess Aphrodite. Paris-Alexander, Prince of Troy, represents the god Mars-Ares. The Moon that had been "embraced" over centuries by Hephaestus (Athena-planet Venus) in his encounters with the Earth is taken away from him; Athena-Hephaestus and their allies must repossess it. Helen is the Moon Goddess and the world is the male version of Helen, father of the family of all Greeks. Etymologists have also indicated a connection between "Selene" and "Helios," the latter deriving from the same Indo-European root as *sun* and *solis*.[3] Thus she symbolizes in the battle of the gods the coming of the Hellenes into their revived nationhood in conjunction with the triumph of the Athena faction of the family of Zeus.

Let us read in Graves briefly:

> The Ionians and Aeolians, the first two waves of patriarchal Hellenes to invade Greece, were persuaded by the Hellads already there to worship the Triple-goddess and change their social customs accordingly, becoming Greeks (*graikoi* 'worshippers of the Grey Goddess, or Crone'). Later, the Achaeans and Dorians succeeded in establishing patriarchal rule and patrilinear inheritance, and therefore described Achaeus and Dorus as first-generation sons of a common ancestor, Hellen - a masculine form of the Moon-goddess Helle or Helen... Aeolus and Ion were then relegated to the second generation, and called sons of the thievish Xuthus, this being a way of denouncing the Aeolian and Ionian devotion to the orgiastic Moon-goddess Aphrodite - whose sacred bird was the *xuthos*, or sparrow, and whose priestesses cared nothing for the patriarchal view that women were the property of their father and husbands.[4]

Hans Jones, author of *The Gnostic Religion*, may also be quoted. For he has traced a very old belief in the connection between Moon and Helen:

---

[2] *The World of Odysseus*, p. 150.

[3] So I am informed by the linguist, Malcolm Lowery, who adds, "conversion of original s - to h - is also exampled by *hex-six* and *hepta* (septem, seven).

[4] Graves, Robert. *The Greek Myths*, Vol. I., p. 161.

> Some Greek mythological speculation seems to have associated the Homeric Helen with the moon, whether prompted by the similarity of Helene and Selene, or by her fate (abduction and recovery) interpreted as a nature myth, or by Homer's once comparing her appearance to that of Artemis. One story had it that the egg which Leda found dropped from the moon; and the late Homer commentator Eustathius (twelfth century A. D.) mentions that there are some who say that Helen fell down to earth from the moon, and that she was taken back up when the will of Zeus was accomplished. When and by whom this was said, Eustathius does not state; neither does he say (or imply) that in this form of the myth Helen served as a symbol of the *anima*...[5]

The plot of the *Iliad*, then, would become the plot of the Love Affair, where the central action concerns the recapture of Aphrodite from Ares by Hephaestus (Athena). The theory would explain many problems (and no doubt will create some). The question raised endlessly by students, "How could people of little discipline fight so murderously and for so long over a mere woman in an age when women were nearly ordinary chattels?" is answered. Beautiful Helen, eternally unravishable and unconquerable, was Moon-Aphrodite. Aphrodite was also a Great Goddess, and retained qualities of a Great Mother Goddess; so the psychic prize was not only the Moon and the beautiful women, but also the Mother of Greece.

The connection between the two wars - one of men, the other of gods - is often explained as a form of hyperbole and egocentrism: it "heightens the glamour of the human warriors." This kind of explanation would no longer be necessary. The two wars are inextricably and originally linked now; they *must* be told together because they happened together. As for the city of Troy and the Trojans, it is as much a mythical place as the Shinning Land of Phaeacia. The Trojans are the Moon-capturing followers of Ares.

As has been argued increasingly for two decades, the Trojans may have been Greeks who were set up by Homer to provide a counterforce to the Achaeans. Perhaps no saga in all mythology treats the enemy so objectively, even with positive sympathy. An epic singer usually delights his audience by heaping sins and defeats upon the enemy. Even Achilles may have to assume a new character, that of Athena-Hephaestus, triumphant, but falling finally through a wound of the foot from the

---

[5] (Boston, Beacon Press, 1958) Fn. 9, p. 109.

arrow of Paris-Ares-Apollo-Aphrodite.

If this were generally so, and it is not to be demonstrated here, then at least the Love Affair portion of the *Odyssey* may be fixed as concurrent with the Battle of the Gods in the *Iliad*. It has been affirmed that the Love Affair is a late piece of the *Odyssey*. We would not contest this placement at all. We are thinking of the middle 7th century for the composition of the *Iliad,* and of the culture and the skies being both of the preceding two generations.

Yet one more theory needs to be put forward respecting the *Odyssey*, before agreeing that the work may well be composed of older materials and have its own hidden plot. Compare the strong affection that Athena holds for Odysseus in the *Iliad*. He has her traits. See him again in the *Odyssey*. Again he has her traits... From beginning to end, the work of the *Odyssey* is the divine work of Athena. She was not only the producer of the Love Affair, and of the *Iliad,* but also of the *Odyssey* as a whole, and as she was the principal actor in the first two, so she is once more the principal actor. For the *Odyssey* is, in its latent plot, the story of the wandering planet Venus between 1500 B. C. and her final settling in her present orbit, personified in her human mirror-image, Odysseus. She it is who saves him at the beginning from the enraged Sea-Earth god, Poseidon, and places him safely in command of his royal sphere in the end. If the Love Affair is a Holy Dreamtime cycle, and the *Iliad* is sacred History, then the *Odyssey* is to be categorized as Sacred Saga.

For all of this we praise Homer and his kind. He chose for the *leitmotif* of his works the natural history of seven centuries. He rationalized the sky-gods for the Greeks and transfigured unbearable truth into tolerable myth. His myths coordinated the basic activities of sexuality, subsistence, respect, power, technology, and wealth into a consistent cultural pattern and created the archaic Greek character. He restored to the Greeks an ethnic identity consistent with the changed nature of the Gods and heaven.

THE AGE OF MARS

"When the gods fought" was a stock phrase among the ancient Greeks. Or they referred to "the strife of the Gods," meaning something that was not simply confined to passages of the *Iliad* but was a historical event. According to Velikovsky, the period 776 B. C. to 687 B. C. experienced at least four catastrophes at fifteen-year intervals that were felt throughout the world. There were probably six terror-filled episodes.

This disastrous agenda began with an earlier event, which he dealt with in the first part of his work called *Worlds in Collision* and in his *Ages in Chaos*. The former amassed evidence that the planet that we know as Venus appeared before our ancestors as a comet and nearly destroyed life on Earth around 1500 B. C. Thereafter the eccentric orbit of the planet threatened the Earth at intervals of fifty-two years. The comet was worshipped as a god, Pallas Athena, in the Greek world. Sometimes before 776 B. C. and perhaps close to that year, Venus, in a diminishing elliptical orbit, encountered Mars. Thereafter, and until both planets were impelled to take roughly their present safe orbits, now one and now both approached Earth and Moon with consequent devastation to the participating bodies.

Awe-inspiring celestial phenomena accompanied the founding of the Greek Olympic Games in -776. Hercules is supposed to have organized the games, ushering in what later came to be a quadrennial all-Greek spectacle of religion, athletics, and poetry. The Greek Mythikon calendar ends in -776. The Historikon calendar begins. But Stecchini says that it may have actually begun, or soon was redone, in -748/7[6] And this would conform to those who say that Hercules did not enter upon the games until they had been operative on eight prior occasions.

In the west, the town of Rome was founded in -748 or -747. Some say -753. It was a period of commotion. Fabius Pictor's ancient adoption of the date -747 seems most likely to have been accepted for an event which probably did not take a single day but had best, for patriotic reasons, to accompany some climactic events.

The founding of Rome was in the name of Romulus who was sponsored by Mars. Romulus was the direct descendant of Aeneas, hence of Aphrodite, mother-protector of Aeneas. Aeneas founded towns in her names on his long journey to Italy. Barely had the Trojans become latinized when Rome was founded. Once more, the revised chronology connects well with an ancient tradition.

In the time of Romulus the week and month were reckoned long, and

---

[6] "Astronomical Theory and Historical Data," in Alfred de Grazia, ed., *The Velikovsky Affair* (New York: University Books, 1965), pp. 158-9.

the early calendar began with the month of Mars and proceeded in four nine-day weeks for ten months, a total of 360 days. Romulus himself disappeared on the occasion of a natural tumult during which, says Ovid, the earth shuddered, clouds obscured the heavens, and the sky was riven by flames; "The people fled and the king soared upon his father's steeds to the stars."[7] (His "father" was Mars.) No people on earth came to be dominated more by Mars and imbued with the spirit of ruthless, single-minded warfare personified by Ares-Mars.

In a study of the validity of carbon-dating in ancient times, H. E. Suess has come upon "a most conspicuous and so far unparalleled irregularity in the *C14 as a function of time. There was a "rapid C14 increase at the beginning of the 8th century B. C. and the sharp maximum between 780 and 770 B. C... It is also the time of a general climate change that took place on the North American continent... The climatic change was not a temporary one; it marked the beginning of a completely new climate epoch."[8] So severe a change introduces the probability of extraterrestrial encounters, for reasons that I have advanced and supported in *The Lately Tortured Earth*.

In Egypt it was the time of the Libyan and Ethiopian dynasties. These were foreigners, whose domination over the greatest of empires has not been satisfactorily explained, except as a consequence of natural disasters. In Italy, Vesuvius exploded with a fury not to be approached until the milder eruption that buried Pompeii and Herculaneum. In Judah, heavenly commotion excited the populace and brought destruction in the times of Uzziah (783-742), Ahaz (735-717), and Hezekiah (717-687); the kingdom of Israel was dissolved and its people dispersed at this time. The Assyrians were under six different kings, the last of whom, Sennacherib, saw his army blasted to death before the city of Jerusalem in a single night of the year -687. It was the period of a Babylonian-Chaldean empire; of Laomedon and Priam of Troy; of the destruction of the now Greek-speaking Cretans at Knossos; of the

---

[7] My source is a discussion with Stecchini. On nine-day divisions of the months, see in *Worlds in collision*, II, viii citing Sicke (1892), Kaegi (1891), Kugler(1907), Naville (1875), Roscher(1903, 1904); and Ovid; for the ten-month year, he sites Schiefner (1857), Male (1846), Nilssen (1920), and Frazer (1931) together with Plutarch, Eutropius and Procopius.

[8] "The Three Causes of the Secular C14 Fluctuations. Their Amplitudes and Time Constants," *Radiocarbon Variations and Absolute Chronology* (Proceedings. 12th Nobel Symposium at Uppsala Univ. 1969), ed. Ingrid V. Olsson (Almquist and Wiksell, Stockholm, 1970), p. 602, quoted in *Pensée*, Fall 1972, p. 41.

destruction of Mycenae; and, at the end of the period, there came Homer and Hesiod. They are the oldest known Greek writers, and the first whose writing have appeared in the classical Greek script and alphabet. The adoption of a new calendar by the Assyrians in -747, the beginning of the "Age of Nabonassar," suggests that heavy disturbances occurred in the first and second encounters; probably the Earth's orbit, rotation, and axis all underwent changes.

Thales, one of the great "seven sages," calculated the Greek calendar, perhaps shortly after Homer and possibly around -600. But, as Velikovsky points out, Thales *re-calculated* the seasons and year after the period of turmoil and changed celestial periodicities. For, "all around the globe the years following -687 saw activity directed towards reforming the calendar."[9] Velikovsky asserts, too, that the day shortened in -717 and lengthened in -687. These would indicate orbital changes, axial tilts, changes in rotational speed, or a combination thereof.

Accordingly, in the Greek-speaking and Middle East areas, crushing damage to late Mycenaean and early Hellenic civilization occurred in the period -776 to -687. One or more of the type of encounters pictured in the Love Affair took place, with Moon and Mars largely barren of atmosphere, and susceptible to nearly complete destruction on the faces that they turn to Earth.

Velikovsky dates the last disaster as centering upon 23 March -687. It is noteworthy that the Romans celebrated the festivals of both Minerva (Athena) and Mars about the same time. The Exodus has also been assigned this day by Velikovsky, over seven centuries earlier. Probably this is more than a coincidence, and the double celebration is evidence of both bodies participating in an encounter about 23 March -687. That the same date would also correspond roughly with the spring fertility rites in which the Moon would have long played the major role would stress, too, the occasion.

This Seventh Century date would put the story that Homer writes down and Demodocus sings in the period of heavy Greek colonization of the Western Mediterranean. The physical destruction of the pre-existing civilization, the movements of people, the loss of their written language, the capture of initiative on the part of the uncouth survivors, the loss of memory (that is, loss of will to report the disaster), the revival

---

[9] *Worlds in Collision,* p. 358.

of poetic forms, the mastering of the forms and then the Homeric collection and integration of them in writing would have to take place in no more than a hundred years. Only a radical reformulation of the nature of Homeric studies would permit this. But one must pursue this approach, for, in the words of Lucian, "It is the conjunction of Venus and Mars that creates the poetry of Homer."

CHAPTER SEVEN

CRAZY HEROES OF DARK TIMES

It was early Springtime[1] in Pylos, a Mycenaean town of the Peloponnesus, facing the western sea. The year was between 776 and 687 B. C. It may even have been March 23, -687. A force of 800 men was posted along 150 kilometers of shoreline. With them were liaison officers from the Palace of King Nestor. The famous old sage of the Achaean warriors himself would have been home from the siege of Troy.

A clay tablet, one of those inscribed "immediately before the destruction which baked them and rendered them durable"[2] begins, "Thus are the watchers guarding the coastal regions."[3] What could they be watching for? Obviously no enemy had been sighted nor could the men be in fighting formation, so thinly dispersed were they. It might be

---

[1] *The Cambridge Ancient History* (1973), Vol II, Part I, p. 611. We recall the suggestion that Odysseus may have awakened to Nausicaa's spring washing rites.

[2] *Ibid.*

[3] *Cf.* Velikovsky, *Worlds in Collision,* (1950), p. 214 *et passim.*

as in Jerusalem around this time, when Isaiah the Prophet was answering the call, "Watchman, what of the night?"[4]

Another tablet may have been the last:

> A single large tablet bears evidence of haste and changes of mind during its writing.
>
> The retention of such an ill-written document in the archive might occasion surprise, unless it was in fact only written in the last day or two before the palace fell. The meaning of some key words is still uncertain, but there is no doubt that it records offerings to a long list of deities. The offerings are in each case a golden vessel, but the principal deities, if male, receive in addition a man, or, if female, a woman. It has been suggested that these human beings were being dedicated to the service of the deities, but the grisly possibility that they were human sacrifices cannot be lightly dismissed. At all events the offering of thirteen gold vessels and ten human beings to a whole pantheon of divinities must mark an important occasion; and what occasion more likely than a general supplication on the receipt of news of an imminent attack?[5]

The "occasion more likely" is catastrophe. Tidal waves were to be watched for, and the setting of the sun behind the flaming horizons. Matters quickly worsened. The news was bad. The gods and goddesses had taken to the skies. "The whole pantheon of divinities" was supplicated, with the richest offerings; gold and human bodies. Not a solitary god of the sea, or a single god of the hearth, or of love, of battle. All of the great sky-gods seem to have been involved.

So Pylos perished. The Palace was destroyed in a "holocaust" which "consumed everything that was inflammable within it, and even melted gold ornaments into lumps and drops of metal." The flames melted brick and stone into "a solid mass... as hard as rock." In one room two large pots were fused "into a molten vitrified layer which ran over the whole floor." Everything that a human invader might desire was reduced to shapelessness. Stone was burned into lime.[6] No human hands and hand-set fires could have wreaked such ruin. Only blasts from the sky - electrical, gaseous or both.

---

[4] Cf. Velikovsky, *Worlds in Collision*, (1950), p. 214 *et passim*.

[5] *The Cambridge Ancient History*, loc. cit., 626.

[6] The above details of this paragraph come from Israel M. Isaacson, 'Carbon 14 dates and Velikovsky's Revision of Ancient History." III *Pensée* no. 3 (1973), 26, p. 29 who is quoting C. W. Blegen and M. Rawson, *The Palace of Nestor at Pylos in Western Messenia* (Princeton: Princeton U. Press, 1966), I, pp. 167, 40, 199, 210, 169, 66.

THE SAGE WHO BRIDGED THE DARK AGES

The name of King Nestor graces both the annals of the siege of Troy in the *Iliad* and the Linear B tablets. Which came first, the burning of Troy, or the disaster at Pylos, or did they occur simultaneously? If Pylos were consumed by fire at the same time as Troy was, than its King Nestor would have been away at the siege of Troy. He would have been, shall we say, fifty-five years old, with plenty of fire left in him. One day, before the gates of Troy, he told a long story, whose irrelevance is only seeming. Professor Denys Page refers to it significantly as "a brilliant piece of late Ionian composition, but it has a continuous pedigree ascending to the Mycenaean era."[7] That is, ascending 400 years or so, by his reckoning; by mine, Nestor was a Mycenean in the Homeric Age of 800 to 650 B. C.

When Nestor was a child, Hercules had descended upon Pylos and a battle of the gods ensued. Hercules and Athena were on one side, while Ares was on the other, and Hercules bested Ares. "Herakles had come in his strength against us and beaten us in the years before, and all the bravest among us had been killed. For we who were sons of lordly Neleus had been twelve, and now I alone was left of these, and all the others had perished."

Little by little the Pylians had recovered until they were able to raid their northern neighbors and revenge themselves somewhat for the ravages of old. The revenge came when Nestor was still young - shall we say fifteen years older? Perhaps he was nineteen, for he had been warned from the fight because of his youth, yet had become its hero. If he was fifty-five in -700, say, he would have been nineteen in -736. The disaster that killed all but a few Pylians would have come around -747.

Working in the other direction, one learns something else about the wise old time-clock. Nestor lived to entertain Telemachus, son of Odysseus, shortly before the latter's homecoming in Ithaca. Therefore, we would add ten years to Nestor and ten years of life also to his palace. It could not have been destroyed when the city of Troy was. Supposing Pylos to have been consumed by an atmospheric disaster, and Troy VIIA by the same (for it was indeed incinerated), it is possible still then that

---

[7] *History and the Homeric Iliad* (Berkeley, Calif.: Univ of California Press, 1959), p. 255.

the end of Troy VI, which was wrecked by earthquake, might have marked the end of the Trojan War and the departure of the Greeks. We recall two stories of the war: Poseidon battered down the famous Achaean defensive wall near the sea after the Achaeans departed; further, the breech in the Trojan Wall was made to admit the Trojan Horse, which may have been the symbol of Horse-Tamer Poseidon, whose tides swept over all barriers like charging steeds.

If such were the case, Pylos and Troy VIIa would go down in -687, along with pitiable Phaeacia. Troy VI would go down eleven years before. And the War of Pylos involving Hercules, Ares and Athena would be set around -747.

We may take this occasion also to tie in the "neighboring giants," who made life impossible for the Phaeacians when they lived in Hypereia. These were probably astral phenomena of monstrous shape who hurled debris upon them from the skies. The Babylonians were chanting in their hymns to Mars-Nergal: "Great giants, with awesome members, run at his right and at his left."[8] This may have been part of the terrible destruction wrought in Asia Minor in -747 in the time of King Uzziah.[9] For King Nausithous led them to Scheria, and he was the father of their present King, Alcinous, who is in the prime of life.

The excavations of Schliemann and Blegen at Hisarlik were valuable as ordinary archaeology; they contributed almost nothing to solve "the Homeric Questions." What we derive from their reports is an important negative: if either Schliemann's Troy or Blegen's Troys were "the real Troy," then Troy was destroyed not by the Achaeans, but by "the gods" - by earthquake and by conflagrations exceeding any possible human agency.[10]

Unfortunately, one cannot at this point be certain of how many celestial encounters in the period -776 to -687 involved simply Mars alone. As we shall see, the years -687 and -747 are candidates for the triple encounters.

If the Battle of the Gods and the Love Affair took place in 698 then, accepting the end of the Trojan War in its tenth year and then years of

---

[8] Velikovsky, *Worlds in Collision*, 281, quoting Bollenbucher, *Gebete and Hymnen an Nergal*, p. 29.

[9] *Worlds in Collision*, p. 213.

[10] T. Blegen, "Troy VI," *Cambridge Ancient History* (1973), p. 685.

wanderings of Ulysses, one would have the destruction of Pylos and Odysseus' killing of the Suitors[11] occurring at the same time, eleven years later, 687 B. C. On both occasions, both Venus and Mars were active in the sky. This is not impossible. Venus was "seeking" a circular orbit. Mars may have been "knocked out of the ring" of its more regular orbit. Professor Earl R. Milton and I discuss this matter in Solaria Binaria. Two encounters with Earth as a participant might have been needed.

This interpretation is preferable to one that would dissolve the Odyssean temporal sequence and have Pylos come crashing down at the same time as Troy, with Nestor in two places at the same time. The scene at Pylos upon which Telemachus, son of Odysseus, happens, when in search of news of his father, is convincing. Nestor tells him that he himself had hastened home from Troy (wise old man that he was) in fear of divine wrath, and that those who tarried suffered greatly. Now we find the King and his whole people on the seashores sacrificing a hundred rich cattle to Poseidon. The skies and Earth have not settled. It may be that a month later, Pylos will be destroyed by "star-fire" or astro-flame. If we check back upon Velikovsky's accounting of concurrent events in the Middle East, we see that Sennacherib's Assyrian Army was blasted in 687 B. C. but also that the army of Esarhaddon, his son, fled in terror of astral phenomena on a successive invasion of Palestine.[12] Here again, the puzzle was whether to unite the two events or treat them successively, and Velikovsky chose the latter course, as do we.

The present state of speculation may be conveyed in tabular form:

---

[11] The interpretation of this event, which we cannot take at face value, must await a later day.

[12] *Worlds in Collision,* pp. 268-9, quoting Sidney Smith's *Babylonian Historical Texts* (1924), p. 5. I refer the reader to *The Lately Tortured Earth* for explanations of the phenomena of extraterrestrially produced incineration and blasts.

Table:
Hypothetical Benchmarks:
Planetary Encounters and Historical Coincidences

Calendar date (B. C.)*	Elapsed time between periods	Nestor's possible age	Personal events	Other events	Sky encounters
776				Olympic Games Founded	Venus/Mars/Earth-Moon
761	15			Hercules Destroys Troy and Wins Olympic Games	Mars/Earth-Moon
747	15	5	Nausithous Moves to Phaeacia; Iliad and Odyssey begin Career as Epic Cycles; Hercules and Heraclids in Peloponnesus (Nestor Sole Survivor)	Pylian War of Gods	Venus/Mars/Earth-Moon
732	15	20	Atreus and Thyestes	Pylians Raid Elians (Nestor a Hero)	Mars/Earth-Moon
717	15		Alkinous Becomes King of Phaeacia		Mars/Earth-Moon
702	15	45	Nestor and Odysseus at Troy	Start of Trojan War	Venus/Mars/Earth-Moon
698		55	Nestor at Troy; Agamemnon Fights Memnon the Ethiopian Prince (Egypt)	Troy VI destroyed by Earthquakes (War of Gods)	Mars/Earth-Moon
687	11	66	Demodocus Sings - Odysseus Returns. Nestor and Telemachus at Pylos. Homer Born.	Troy VIIA Destroyed by Fire; Pylos Falls (Last War of Gods); Phaeacia Falls by Earthquake; Sennacherib's Army Destroyed at Jerusalem	Venus/Mars/Earth-Moon
					Skies clear
670				Greek Alphabet Developed	Calendars Reordered; Earth Trembles
630			Iliad Revised and Transcribed by Homer Odyssey Revised and Transcribed by Homer		Present skies

*The six major intervals are 15 years each, placed largely on the reasoning of

Velikovsky, *Worlds in Collision,* pp 362 ff., that Mars' present orbit is in "favorable opposition" respecting Earth every 15 years. Since Mars had a different orbit before -776 and might have changed its orbit at every encounter between -776 and -687, we must of course ultimately use historical evidence to plot all of the encounters. We must bear in mind, too, that the geological and ecological aftermaths of disaster provoked by celestial behavior can continue for some time. Here, also, we have reasoned that only an 11-year interval separated the last two disaster, that is. Mars was on its way to becoming an outer planet and suffered two encounters close together. Although the problem is not insoluble, it will require a great deal of research to establish empirically the dates of several peak disasters and the rate of subsidence of disturbances in the aftermaths. (*Worlds in Collision,* pp 274-8).

The Pylos story is not ended, however. There is more to it, and it fashions a warning to scholars who have accepted faithfully the theory that a Mycenaean age was ended about 1200 B. C. by barbarian invasions and a "Dark Age" set in that was to be illuminated by the great poets, Homer and Hesiod, finally around 800 B. C. The Love Affair holds a light to the Dark Age and the disposition of the Dark Age provides a key to the Love Affair.

To return to the story, we call upon the research of Isaacson on Pylos. The destruction of Pylos has been compared with the destruction of Gordion, in Asia Minor. The city whose Gordian knot was later cut by Alexander, perished also in a disaster. Pylos was of Mycenaean Greek culture: Gordius was Phrygian. At Pylos were found ceramics that resembled Mycenaean ware that was associated with Egyptian ware and therefore assigned the Egyptian dates because these were the basis of Near Eastern chronology. The Phrygians, however, are honored by their own archeological and historical dating system and Gordius is said to be of the eighth century before Christ.

Charcoal of both burnt-out sites was tested at the same laboratory at the same time to determine its carbon-14 loss. For it is by living that a plant or animal ingests carbon 14; after death the ingestion stops and a decay of this radioactive substance begins. Measuring the loss of Carbon 14 in charcoal samples of the two towns, the investigators discovered what they had expected: the samples of each site could give dates that conventional archeology had already established. But to do so, the investigators performed miracles of purification of the Gordian sample to reduce its age by several hundred years, while they let the samples of Pylos go by polluted and unchallenged because they "proved" what was expected.

Not content with casting the Pylos samples back into the ash-heap, Isaacson advanced three further conclusions from the materials of these two towns far apart, whose dates may now be said to be close together. He discovered that the C14 dates of the olive pollen in a core from the bottom of a lake near Pylos conveyed eighth century readings when the pollen was at its peak. Reasoning that Pylos was tending a maximum of olive trees when the town was flourishing, and that there would be little cultivation in the "Dark Ages" when the population would be sparse, Isaacson logically deduced that the maximum of the short-lived pollen in the eighth century could mean that Pylos was in full flower then as well, although, once destroyed, it remained uninhabited ever after.

He went on to a second point. Analyzing the famed reports of the University of Cincinnati excavations at Pylos, he read in their pages accounts of the mysterious mixing of Mycenaean pottery and geometric pottery in strata where neither could have intruded upon the other. Yet these two types of ceramics were supposed to have been fashioned centuries apart.

Now the basic and perhaps the only unassailable law of geology and archaeology is the law of superposition. Unless proof of accident is brought forward, what is on top is younger than what it rests upon. The Mycenaean and the Geometric Ages then had to be contemporaneous! The "Dark Ages" of 400 to 500 years appeared to have been squeezed out at Pylos.

Pondering this point, one is led almost reluctantly to the third point of Isaacson. Gordion of Phrygia in the 8th century has walls that strikingly resemble the walls of Troy VI, which were devastated by earthquake. Archaeologists who are faithful to their conventions must bargain with an architectural similarity that flatly denies their 400 years' or more gap between Gordius and Troy.

Isaacson's work was following a trail already laid by Velikovsky, who had observed that archaeologists of the 19th century had somehow lost their way. Velikovsky exposed the problem and its probable solution in 1973 by the long-deferred publication of his manuscript on the famous rampant lions gate of Mycenae.[13]

In 1881, W. M. Ramsey had noted that the Gate closely resembled a

---

[13] "The Lion Gate at Mycenae," *Pensée*, III (1973). p. 31. supported in the same issued by Lewis M. Greenberg, "The Lion Gate at Mycenae," p. 26.

Phrygian tomb gate of the 8th century. Flinders Petrie, the renowned pioneer of Egyptian archaeology and history, had established an authoritative chronology of Egypt which could be applied wherever Egyptian artifacts were discovered, or conversely when foreign artifacts were discovered in Egypt. Petrie discounted Ramsay's evidence, because Mycenae had already been "dated" by the association of its artifacts with those of Egypt. Resemblance or not, the Lions of the two cities were moved four hundred years apart.

Petrie's Egyptian chronological imperialism, spreading over the Near East and the Mediterranean islands, compelled scholars to invent a long period of Hellenic culture in which "little happened," barbarism prevailed, the Greeks were illiterate, the arts and sciences were lost - the Dark Ages of Greece, in short, conventionally dated between 1300 or 1200 B. C. and 800 B. C., a span of perhaps 500 years. Not until Velikovsky[14] challenged the Egyptian chronology frontally could any scholar imagine that various baffling puzzles of Phrygia, Mycenaean Greece, and Homeric Greece would have ultimately simple solution; the Gordian Knot was cut. Isaacson's studies of the excavation records at half-a-dozen famous sites, following Velikovsky's hypothesis, have shattered the empirical foundations of the theory of the Dark Ages.[15]

SOCIETY IN SHOCK

Speaking of the aftermath of catastrophe, Plato declares of the survivors; "At first, they would have natural fear ringing in their ears which would prevent their descending from the heights into the plain."[16]

If one were, at this pint, to take up in order the authoritative works of history and archaeology it might be shown that they are in every case affected by a blind spot in regard to the Dark Ages. This method would

---

[14] *Theses for the Reconstruction of Ancient History* (1946); *Ages in Chaos* (1950); "Astronomy and Chronology," III Pensee, No. 2. 38.

[15] I. Issacson, *op. cit.*, and "Applying the Revised Chronology," IV *Pensée* (Fall, 1974), 5. Posthumous studies of Velikovsky are expected in re Dark Ages and Issacson's (Schorr's) studies are being prepared by him for publication.

[16] Plato, *The Laws*, III, p. 57 of the translation of B. Jowett, *Dialogues of Plato,* v. V (London: Oxford Univ. Press, 1871).

be repeating much of Isaacson's work and would expand unduly the present text. It may be better to fashion a new model of the Homeric Age and, by demonstrating its consistency and efficiency, to buttress the theory that the Love Affair portrays an astral and earthly disaster that had recently occurred. Let us call this model, "The Crazed Survivors of Disaster."

It stands in contrast to the conventional "Greek Dark Ages" model. The latter holds that the Mycenaean Age collapsed over the period of a century because of barbarian invasions and that these barbarians in the course of centuries acquired the mentalities and facilities of a civilized people.

The "Crazed Survivors" model is constructed from the theory that a general catastrophe involving great ecological and cultural damage is followed by a shocked society. The shocked society would exhibit a complex of expected behaviors that distinguish it from stable or moderately changing or even revolutionary societies, or more significantly, from a society that is slowly evolving from a "primitive" to a "civilized" culture. In the societies of crazed survivors, personal and mass self-destructiveness and destructiveness of others and of culture increase as terror and guilt interact on a complex and massive scale. Depending upon the extent of the disaster, a totally amnesiac and stupefied society of cultural degenerates may ensue or a more furious cultural coping that may eventuate in a flowering of religious institutions, crafts, and arts.

The Homeric heroes, Odysseus and Achilles among them, typified the bands of survivors of the extensive Mycenaean civilization that was largely destroyed in the catastrophic interventions of the planets Mars and Venus in the Earth-Moon system in the 8th century. The plots of the *Iliad* and *Odyssey,* despite 2700 years of trying to make something else of them, clearly point to the skies as the source of the disruptive and awful events that produced the crazed heroes of the dark times. Western civilization has treasured and imitated the posturings of these mad warriors, hardly ever realizing what they were and how the docile mind of later generations would be affected when this madness was presented to it as normality and for inspiration. We shall proceed now to enumerate and describe briefly a number of psychological and social indications that we are dealing with human beings behaving in the aftermath of catastrophe.

The Homeric Greeks developed a pantheon of skygods and assumed that these gods would continuously manifest themselves by thunderbolts, showers of arrows, tidal waves, earthquakes, meteorites, and so on. They venerated all sky signs and objects from the sky, such as meteoric iron and stones. The earth itself was a living animal and thoroughly animated in its parts.[17] A number of gods and demi-gods contributed to a continual geological and ecological restlessness. Animals, plants, and rocks changed readily into humanoid forms and vice versa. Ovid's *Metamorphoses* elaborates this theme interminably.

By the time of Thucydides, free will and controlled change were accredited to mankind, but the Homeric Greeks were yoked to *moira*, fortune, destiny, lot - the law of chance that determines human fate.[18] Uncontrolled license and little self-discipline were ascribed to (projected upon) the gods. Well-developed priesthoods had dissolved, just as other specialized occupations crumpled into individuals. (Finley calculates that over 100 occupations discernible in the linear B tablets dropped to a mere dozen in Homer.) Nevertheless there were ritual guardians and diviners with prodigious memories, aides to kings but not members of kingly families. Priests, bards, and madmen were possessed by gods.

The priests "were guardians of ritual and of the forms and language of the sacramental songs; preservers of the motions and rhythms for the due observance of ceremonial; interpreters of those signs and often obscure sayings by which the gods manifested their decrees, desires or warnings; and, lastly they were the custodians of the science of precedents in all domains."[19]

The preceding Mycenaean bureaucratic and feudal order had broken down. Finley and other experts have described an *oikos* (household) system as a kind of feudal plantation system that survived the collapse of bureaucratic urban centralism. It is true that the *oikos* system prevails, but it is really a piratical or ship-wreck system in which people gathered around surviving leaders. A great many expatriates, outcasts, outlaws and refugees were to be found among the community. There is a remarkable lack of the stable assignment of social, economic, and political rights to

---

[17] Mireaux, *Daily Life in the time of Homer,* p. 24.

[18] Mireaux, *Ibid.* p. 28.

[19] Mireaux, *Ibid.* p. 79. Cf. p. 14.

the types of people who clustered in these strongholds.

Practically all of the titles of hierarchical officialdom disappeared. The chiefs of households (that it would be a mistake to call "clans")[20] ruled a mixed community as judge and religious-political protector.

The "Argive Kings" and the kings who were supposed to have developed *from* and *after* the Homeric heroic age were actually the same traditional kings whose Greco-Mycenaean kingdoms had come tumbling down in the disasters of the 8th and 7th centuries.[21] The warlords and oligarchies followed. Alcinous of Phaeacia rules like Agammemnon. We quote Denys Page:

> When history dawns on the island of Lesbos in the seventh century B. C., we discover there a mode of government hardly distinguishable from that of Agamemnon at the siege of Troy. The will of the sovereign power, Agamemnon himself, is not absolute: he must first summon a council of elders, and whatever they approve must be declared to an agora, an assembly of all lesser noblemen. In the seventh century B. C., at Lesbos the political constitution is exactly the same; and it happens that the sovereign power is still in the direct line of descent from the family of Agamemnon.[22]

This startling claim is followed by one even more sweeping: "In this place certainly, and in other places presumably, the royal family survived throughout the dark ages from beginning to end." We cannot grant either the Lesbos presumption or the general presumption. It is rare in the annals of history to find a genuine 400-year old dynasty, and hard to imagine one that would have suffered 400 to 500 years of the so-called Dark Ages. If the family of Agamemnon of Troy still ruled Lesbos in the seventh century, it is simply because the Trojan War took place less than a century beforehand.

Indeed, Agamemnon himself had probably an upstart pedigree like most of the Homeric heroes. The heroes spoke of home frequently but there is a lack of definition of their homes, Nestor's account being exceptional in the *Iliad* and those of the *Odyssey* being largely mythical and savage. The heroes boasted in the names of their parents, some of their grandfathers, and usually stopped at this point; some lapsed into claims of divine forebears in the second generation. Glaukos and

---

[20] As e. g. Mireaux does, *Ibid.*. p. 55.

[21] Contrary to Mireaux, cf.*Ibid.*. p. 31.

[22] Denys Page, *The Homeric Odyssey*, pp. 145-6, citing Alcaeus and Aristotle.

Diomedes, in a famous encounter in the *Iliad,* discovered while bragging of their antecedents that their grandfathers were guest-friends and decided not to fight each other.[23] The absence of "family trees" among self-assertive "nobles" raises doubts that they either knew their ancestors or, if they did, could claim any distinction on their behalf.

The Dark Ages, as a catastrophic century, found ancestors in short supply. So also communities. Homer "does not talk a great deal about tribes and groups and clans and sects and varieties of idealistic associations, whether pacific or belligerent. What Homer does is to confine himself to the immediate family of the warrior in question."[24] Only a short paternal link is stressed, along with guest-friends. This is exceedingly strange. It is not at all like "primitive peoples" whose lives are bound into communities of blood served by totems. Nor like a bureaucratic society. But by the "dawn of history," in the next century, we find definite blood lines as the basis of organization of the Greek polis. Apparently, though missing in Homeric times, they are quickly reestablished in the succeeding generations.

The warriors stayed away from their "homes" so long that we could question whether they had any. They remind us of Vandals and Vikings who left home never to return. Odysseus played the pirate - looting, killing, raping. For the sake of Athena, he had to be brought home, there to face and slay a horde of suitors of his "long-suffering" wife. His shepherd slave, Eumaeus, was armed against other shepherds and wild beasts. Marauding was frequent, if not from one's neighbors then from pirates and foreign warriors. Slaves abounded, of various nationalities, one may note. It was a society where every man's hand was raised against his neighbor. *Homo lupus homini.* "The bearing of arms, particularly lance and sword, on all solemn occasions of civil life, was the distinguishing feature which, more than any other, marked the separation of classes in Homer's time."[25]

In battle one encounters a frenzied behavior whereby fear is whipped up in order to gain courage. Eliade's words apply to the heroes: "The frenzied *berserker,* ferocious warriors, realized precisely the state of sacred

---

[23] *Iliad*, VI.

[24] John Cowper Powys, "Preface to Homer and the Oether," p. 146, cf. Mireaux, 124-5.

[25] Mireaux, *Daily Life in the Time of Homer.* p. 137.

fury... of the primordial world."[26] In a famous scene of the *Iliad,* Achilles went so berserk that he battled the river, the River-God and the gods themselves. Ajax went mad and finally committed suicide.

A frank, hollow, extreme braggadoccio characterized the best and the worst of the fighters. The glorification of destructiveness seems interminable. Apart from a chosen few, the women are subjects of aggressive degradation and measured by head of livestock; yet some time before, in Minoan, if not Mycenaean, civilization, women had achieved high position and status. More information about Mycenaean women is needed before we can claim what we guess to be true: that the degradation of women was not a trait of the Indo-European but was the outcome of catastrophically induced aggression.

Certain undercurrents of attitude haunt the passages of Homer. The boasts of the warriors are often about the conquests and destruction of towns. The similes of Homer are overwhelmingly rural and pastoral. May we surmise that the heroes sacked many a half-destroyed town? There is a pervading sense of splendors of the past being gone and citations of armies, cities, and wealth appear to be grossly exaggerated. This pretentiousness is not that of nobles, or of a people who had lost something they once knew, did not own, but had given them their character.

One senses also the general lack of awareness, a "mind-blown" stupidity, a calloused morality.

Am I reading feelings into Homer's poetry that are not there? Perhaps. But the interpellations of morality in the *Iliad* and *Odyssey* are mostly those of the poet. Are these traits not typical of "primitive man?" Definitely not. It is only by getting one's concept of primitive man from Homer that one can believe so, for usually modern "primitive man" is gentle, aware, and only occasionally "possessed" or obsessed. The Homeric warriors are not primitive types.

The "guest-stranger" concept of Homeric times is intriguing too. The Homeric peoples had an ambivalence towards outsiders. Deep mistrust alternated with sometime hysterical acceptance. Apparently, a person entering the precincts of an unknown community, one such as Odysseus, for example, would not know whether he would be maltreated or well-treated. This ambivalence appears to have gone beyond logic or normal

---

[26] *The Myth of the Eternal Return,* p. 21.

behavior.[27] Odysseus was warned by Nausicaa that he should avoid being seen in Phaeacia because of the general mistrust of strangers. Yet she also assured him, that if all went well, he would be royally treated. And so he was. The forms of human relations, like the world itself, were shaky. Augeas, "the king of the Epeians, treacherous to his very guest-friends, not long thereafter saw his own rich city, under stark fire and the stroke of iron, settling into the deep pit of destruction. Augeas was himself dragged to the edge of steep death, nor escaped it."[28] It was for double-dealing over the cleaning of his stable that Augeas incurred the wrath of Hercules which destroyed his city and him.

We should say that this same Hercules is an active participant in many of the events of the dark times and one day it may be confirmed that he is an alter ego of the planet Mars. He destroyed Troy once before its destruction by the Achaeans of Homer. He destroyed Nestor's Pylos once. He is often berserk, a paragon of the crazed survivor, and was deified upon death.

Hercules (or Heracles) had progeny, the Heraclids. They were so many that they seemed to be whole bands of people. More than that, they have been identified with the Dorians whom scholars believe to be the Greek ethnic strain that devastated the Mycenaean kingdoms and carried on their primitive development during the so-called "Dark Ages."

For example, Rhys Carpenter[29] is to be discovered on a magnificent *tour de force* aimed at proving that long term intense climatic change from wet to dry caused the Mycenaean civilization of the "14th century" literally to collapse and permitted the starving country folk to sack and burn the centers of civilization in search of necessities. The country and islands were practically abandoned, and only with time did a better acclimated population begin its rise.

Carpenter encounters many obstacles, only two of which need be mentioned here. He is confronted by *sudden* disaster; yet it is apparent from his own words and in meteorology that climatic disaster can only

---

[27] Cf. Finley, *The World of Odysseus.*, pp. 115-20 et passim. Sociology delineates a "stranger" concept and says it is always observable; but it is a quantitative ambivalence that has a norm which is here far exceeded.

[28] Pindar, "Olympian Ode 10." (Loeb ed.) It would seem that Augeas and his city were swallowed up by an earthquake or volcanic fissure.

[29] *Discontinuity in Greek Civilization* (Cambridge, Eng.: Cambridge Univ. Press, 1966).

be sudden and quite destructive if an immense external source produces it. Second, everywhere he turns he sees terrible incendiarism (or, rather, he turns everywhere to avoid seeing the terrible incendiarism that destroyed Mycenaean civilization).

We cannot help but thank him, however, as one must thank practically every strainer and stretcher of the Dark Ages. For he describes in many an incident the takeover of Mycenaean areas by the Heraclids, whom he obligingly postulates as Mycenaean refugee families returning a couple of generations later at the head of mixed bands of other ethnic Greeks, especially Dorians. The Heraclids, in our theory, are crazed survivors, sons, naturally, of Hercules, who is identifiable in myth with Ares or Mars, even though he sometimes fights Ares. The Heraclids are borne back in the name of the God who destroyed their kin and culture.

"How unsettled and mobile were all these heroes," writes Mireaux,[30] after he has devoted a book, like Finley, to discovering a social order that would make sense. "The heroic world of the epics appears in our eyes as something mobile, effervescent and tumultuous."

They depended upon the seas but were bad sailors. There was no class of specialized sailors. Everyone was a "sailor." Maritime ventures were not materially distinguishable from piratical excursions. We can imagine what confusion and fear drove them over the seas to found their many colonies, for the period 750-600 B. C. was the great period of colonial expansion. The journey from Crete to Egypt took five days and nights, "a terrifying venture for such poor navigators as were the Greeks of Homer's time."[31]

They were meat-eaters: cattle, sheep, and wild game, animals of the uplands. "For Homer fish is a detestable food, while Hesiod does not even deign to mention it. Never is fish eaten at the Homeric repasts."[32]

Probably around 687 B. C. Gyges the Lydian overthrew the Heraclids of Maeonia in Asia Minor, and struck the first coins. Actually they were not the first coins, but the Greeks had largely abandoned coinage. Homer mentions a gold talent of fixed value, reports Mireaux, but exchange was almost entirely in kind rather than in money.

---

[30] Mireaux, *Daily Life in the Time of Homer,* p. 241.

[31] Mireaux, *Ibid.* p. 249 and 242-5.

[32] Mireaux, *Ibid.* p. 146, citing *Od* XII, 329-32, IV, 368-9.

Gift-giving was often a spectacular affair. It was more a system of exchange than a pleasant supplement to normal exchange like bonuses or birthday presents. The things given seem often to be for re-giving, to be untouched and unused, even homely objects like linens, and the metal gifts seem all too frequently to have semidivine or divine "makers" which, as false pedigrees conceal humble origins, may have concealed their origins in loot and theft. Their description, too, conveys an awesomeness, as if they were not familiar objects to the childhoods of the gift-exchangers. They are described as pirates would speak of their misunderstood loot of pots and laces.

Altogether there is an incongruous mixture of ethnic names, events, artifacts and practices in the works of Homer. Names that are "centuries old," and not to be heard again in history, occur. Chariots are used, not as battle-wagons, but to convey warriors to places where they would descend and fight. Their use was partly forgotten or had not been familiar to the types who owned them. T. B. L. Webster[33] shows that Homer is indebted to Minoan and near East influences in plots, style, and references. He is influenced by the archaic Mediterranean culture. He is very Mycenaean, Webster concludes. But in all of his speculations, Webster does not speculate upon the important chronological puzzle: If it is proper to imagine that all of these influences happened so "early" and Homer came so late, why not speculate as well that all of these similar bits actually existed almost within the living grasp of the poet? At one time, many scholars believed that Troy and the Trojans were poetic inventions. Then Schliemann discovered "Troy" or something that corresponded to indications found in the poetry. His site at Hisarlik has revealed in successive excavations a number of "Troys." It appears now that the Troy of levels VI and VIIa may have been Homer's Troy but it also appears now that the Trojans were akin to the Greeks and that the Trojan War(s) pitted Greek against Greek. Homer probably stressed differences between Greeks and Trojans as a splendid device, first, to convey the battle of the gods, and, second, to give the disarrayed and scattered Greek communities a common *Weltanschauung* - a common religious, political and cultural outlook on the world.

Moreover, now we permit ourselves another conjecture: The besieged Troy was a congress of allied forces containing Greek and non-

---

[33] *From Mycenae to Homer* (1964), p. 197 et passim.

Greek forces, clustered survivors, who could be called Greek or Anatolians, who might provide characters with connections as far away as Etruria and send an Anatolian like Aeneas to seek kin in Italy after the wars (as Virgil says).

The Trojan Wars were plural, most likely, during the Martian period. Armies may have come and gone; the occupants of Troy may have changed several times. The artifacts dug up could be interpreted as coming from a mélange of cultures - Greek and Anatolian. The revolution of heaven and earth is the heart of the primordial myth and the epic poem. The Homeric epics are no exceptions to the rule. An old era was being destroyed and a new one was arising.[34]

The *Iliad* and the *Odyssey* used various dialects of Greek blended by the genius of the bard. Homer used metaphors of the clearest and most ordinary kind, to the exclusion of far-flown and fancy comparisons. Words expressing "fire" abound, for example. His poetry seems to be addressing audiences of low verbal ability; or they might have understood a mélange of dialects and phrases, a *lingua greca* like a *lingua franca* or both. On the other hand, his similes are prolonged and complicated, dealing with rural and pastoral comparisons. Obviously, Homer was not primitive, nor inexperienced, nor bereft of imagination; nor were his confraternity of poets, nor their audiences. Why should this mélange be used, and not, say, a single preferred dialect like the Tuscan that Dante's genius made to become the preferred Italian tongue? A reasonable answer would be that there was then only a gathering of tongues: the audiences were related, widespread, itinerant, and diffused.

More significant is the *non-use* of a sacred, liturgical language. If there had been a Mycenaean dead language, like classical Greek is to modern Greek, or Latin to Italian, then would not that have been the basis for portions of the epic poems? But it was not, not even for prayers. Therefore it did not exist. Mycenaean Greek was probably a living and related set of dialects whose standard expression had disappeared with its ruling class and scribes.

It gives cause for bewilderment. If a sacred language was not understood, that would place the old civilization far into the past; but there are many tie-ins of Homeric and Mycenaean cultures. Conversely, the fact might indicate that the old civilization was either foreign (which

---

[34] See Mircea Eleade, *The Myth of the Eternal Return,* chap. IV.

it was not) or largely destroyed (which we think was the case).

The linguistic mélange (with its numerous catch-phrases of all Greek sub-cultures), which was Homeric Greek, was "instant prosody." There had been no time, no more than a couple of generations, to build an epic language. Yet such an epic language would surely have evolved smoothly and uniformly over the several centuries of any "Dark Ages." What emerges therefore is a people and culture exploding in space and time, whose language, that of Homer, had not yet caught up with its expanding front.

The Greeks of Homer, to conclude, did not come as an invasion from afar. They consisted of all kinds of Greeks. They were survivors, largely from the rural areas and the interior highlands. From personal experience and hearsay, they knew of the centers of their societies that had been destroyed. They often lacked kith and kin; they lacked communal security; they lacked law and order; they lacked education; they trembled upon the trembling earth.

The experts commonly remark on the unabashed juxtaposition of knowledge and ignorance in the epics. Mireaux has said: "There was decidedly nothing primitive about Homeric civilization." The very sophistication of the poets, like Homer and Hesiod, who told about them, indicates an age whose savagery could easily be penetrated by civilized forms.

For a grandly disciplined, informed, and stylized poet like Homer to write so sympathetically of his subjects, he had to be of their age, and to be of their age required that *their* age be the eighth century.

> The massive destruction of Mycenaean civilization fully attested in the archaeological record, was accompanied by a complete social transformation, in which all the institutions by which men organized their existence were refashioned to meet the new situation... When Mycenae fell, the surviving Greeks, in their new kind of society, had no need for records or for scribes; in fact, on the evidence we have at present, they had no need for the art of writing and they lost it altogether, improbable as that may seem to modern men.[35]

What seems "improbable" to us is that anything but abrupt catastrophe could cause "the massive destruction" in so many places - Crete, Mycenae, and elsewhere. The Homeric scribes, working with new dialects and a new alphabet, did not need centuries of time to accumulate

---

[35] M. I. Finley, *The World of Odysseus* (Middlesex, England: Penguin Books, 1954, 1967, 1972), p. 168.

material on the chaotic life that followed.

Homer did his best to reassure the survivors and to set them on their way again. The incongruences and inconsistencies of material culture, nomenclatures, customs, and attitudes found in his works are not sloppy artistry; they are of the essence of the people whom he was describing. And his work was not an oral conglomerate of centuries, but a description, from two main sources, those of the *Iliad* and the *Odyssey*, [36] with as much consistency as he could import to them, of the suddenly produced cultural chaos of the eighth and seventh centuries. He took as his task the assembly of plots dealing with erratic and fear-driven survivors and inspiring this folk to become "one nation under the gods."

THE CART BEFORE THE HORSE

The contrast with conventional historiography is obvious: Homer flourished in the middle seventh century. His writings were an agglomerate of the early century. The pieces of his writing came from different quarters; many from the period -670 to -776, some from times stretching far before (-766 to -1500). The people active in his writings were from the crushed cultures of -776 to the beginning of his own lifetime.

The Mycenaean Civilization collapsed in a set of natural disasters. The marginal survivors regrouped repeatedly in the following century. They fought bitterly amongst themselves, used what they could manage of the old tools and skills. Homer sang about them and their destroyed culture.

The assumption is tied to a brief time sequence derived from evidences of natural disaster. (See Chart above). The theory of causation seeks evidence of abrupt takeover of a destroyed culture by marginal survivors who cast aside, or employ ceremonially, practices they do not or cannot use or understand. Then they proceed to draw from every source their new synthetic culture.

On the other hand, most Homeric experts nowadays believe that Homer lived a century earlier, that his writings were an agglomerate of centuries before, that the pieces of writings came from different quarters,

---

[36] See pages 134ff below.

some of them as early as 1500 B. C. The people acting in his writings, they believe, are fictional characters referring to real characters occupying a space of 400 to 500 years. Their culture is believed to be a composite of all this time, but is concentrated in a true primitive culture that made savage contact with the civilized world in 1300 B. C. or thereabout, and after half a millennium, arrived at the stage of producing Homer and Hesiod. The Mycenaean civilization weakened and then was ruined by invaders. Centuries of primitive illiterate history followed. The pre-Homerics emerged and found new tools and skills. Homer at this point sang about their deeds. They were learning to sail boats; they disliked eating fish; they were learning to use chariots.

This conventional theory is tied to a time sequence derived from an incorrect Egyptian chronology. The society and behavior of the pre-Homeric Hellenes are viewed in a sequence, according to a theory of causation that has a culture being gradually born. Practices are invented or adopted slowly from abroad.

Thus occurs the confrontation of two theories. The reader has already some means of adjudging it. Other means will follow. But before this chapter is ended, a suggestion may be offered to all those who read and write about the Dark Ages of ancient Greece. The suggestion concerns methodology, or, more simply, logic.

The logic of writing about history, that is, about the sequence of cause and events, is that events are arranged by time and then causes are uncovered. This usually works because the *succession* of events is ordinarily known before the causes are discovered. *Post hoc, ergo propter hoc,* though strictly speaking a logical fallacy, establishes a presumption of cause: After this, therefore (perhaps) because of this. However, the less the evidence of temporal sequences, the greater the possibility of logical fallacies. *Hysteron proteron,* as the Aristotelians called it, or "putting the cart before the horse" is one of them. When a temporal sequence is not known, but a presumption of the sequence is held, then the possibility of the reversal of cause increases. The logical problem that is involved in "putting the cart before the horse" is exemplified in the saying, "If the Brahmin do not pray, the Sun will not set." Wise skeptics know that "If the Sun will not set, the Brahmin will pray." (As a matter of fact, they will pray anyhow, if only because *in illo tempore* the sun did not set.) At the same time, many people, zealous or simply naive, will let the cart be placed before the horse and believe that the cart pulls the horse. In a subtle way, much of the writing about the Greek "Dark Ages" falls victim to this fallacy. Take, for instance, the statement that "the Dark Age Greeks were poor sailors." This fact is usually interpreted to mean that these Greeks were evolving from land animals into seafaring animals; they had not learned yet to sail. But these Greeks had no reason to be good sailors because they were raised as herders and warriors. Seamanship had disappeared with the washing away and destruction of the seacoast settlements. Or take the fact that "the Greek warriors before Troy misused their chariots, dismounting from them instead of fighting from them." This fact is usually interpreted to mean that they were just learning of the chariot from a superior culture with whom they were now coming into contact. But their chariot subculture had just been destroyed with the palaces, and the survivors had not been raised as chariot warriors but used chariots because their "betters" had used them.

"The government of Phaecia was a typical emerging primitive state heading towards the *polis* of classical Greece out of tribalism." But no tribe stands behind the Phaeacians; they are a colony surviving its mother country and organized more simply than it was.

Or take the fact that "The Achaeans attacked Troy in the name of their gods, and Troy was destroyed." To most, the statement means that the Achaeans destroyed Troy. On the contrary, "the gods" destroyed Troy and the Achaeans occupied it. Not, "the wrath of Achilles elaborated into "the battles of the gods," but rather "the battles of the gods reduced to the wrath of Achilles."

Finally, considering the Love Affair in this light, the "gods" do not act so that people can have comedy; comedy is played so that the effects of the gods can be controlled.

Further, the dance forms and opera theater of the Love Affair were ancient and Minoan. So asserts Patroni.[37] He points out that the dancing circle and chorus carried from Minoan to the classical Greek theater. But when the Greek theater appeared, he writes, we find the rustic god Dionysus, with a goat-cult of dancers cloaked in skins. The poverty of the means, the few actors, the vagabond origins of the Thespian theater, all showed - still according to Patroni who follows the Dark Age theory faithfully - that the primitive real Greek theater was not receiving the subsidies of princes, not the interest or participation of Mycenaean high society; it was left to the rural folk. Again "the cart before the horse." In

---

[37] *Commenti Mediterranei all'Odissea di Omero* (Milano: Marzorati, 1950), pp. 250-2.

the general destruction of societies, the art of the survivors made its way quickly forward. The elite and its sophisticated art forms were destroyed; folk art (not primitive art) dominated the scene. An analogy with the problems of geology is tempting. When folds and faults occur, the principle of superposition is thrown off and the effects are baffling to explain. So in history, when temporal evidence is scarce, the principle of *post hoc ergo propter hoc* loses its ability to guide one. Then, in geology, one says of a layer of shells and pebbles: "This land was raised from the sea", while another will say, "This land was once flooded with shells and pebbles."

A rather lengthy example may be excused, especially since it is the last. After describing what appears to have been a solid and regulated archaic system (which led me to suspect my theory), Mireaux[38] concludes:

> Thus one is led to believe that the (lack of) care for agriculture, and the dispersal of a peasantry so firmly rooted in the soil, must have brought about, in most of the cities, at a quite early stage - and no doubt as early as Homeric time - the dissolution of the primitive brotherhoods of youth and soldierly companionship, and the breaking up of their community-centres. Nevertheless, even if the traditions of a life in common and an armed confraternity were growing looser, they were not yet so obsolete that they could not still color the lives of the rough peasant classes, guiding them and instilling into them the old ideals of honor and pride; for they still knew that their lands were only theirs as long as they could defend them, with helmet, buckler and javelin, after an appropriate training and a traditional initiation received at the hands of their elders.

In this quotation and all of the chapter containing it, Mireaux first establishes the existence of a rigid (old) order, which he calls "primitive," because presumably he believes it to have *followed* the Mycenaean culture over the centuries.

Then in the same breath, as above, he speaks as if this order *preceded* the Homeric order which was a breakdown of it.

That is, he reverses the logic of his own evidence. He moves back and forth uncertainly, reversing precedence and effect, and, of course, cause and effect. It is more likely that the "primitive order" he describes was the collapsed remains of the Mycenaean order that had persisted into the eighth century and was retained especially long by the Spartans who clustered fearfully in villages rather than committing themselves to

---

[38] Mireaux, *Daily Life in the Time of Homer,* p. 124-5.

a great *polis*. This order could only be feebly reinstituted by the Homeric crazed heroes. But a new civilization, which developed out of the Homeric age, moved in all directions; it quickly blended new and old forms. The Love Affair was an effort, on the literary front, to establish the new age by mastering the trauma that came with the end of the old age.

CHAPTER EIGHT

THE TWO FACES OF LOVE

The Aphrodite of the light Olympian-age character plays opposite her usual star in the Love Affair, Ares. Her husband, Hephaestus, earns little affection from her, and, though the story is not mentioned here, she is the mother of three children by Ares. She is one of the few ever to have expressed love for Ares, and in "The Battle of the Gods," in the *Iliad,* she goes to his aid in battle and is roundly smacked by the Goddess Athena.

If we look into Homer for the precise astronomical referents of Ares, Aphrodite, Hephaestus and Athena, we are disappointed. Homer does not say that the three sky bodies - planet mars, Moon, and planet Venus are represented by them, not in the *Iliad,* nor the *Odyssey,* nor in the Love Affair. How then are we to assure ourselves that we are on the right track when we allocate among them several celestial bodies? We cannot be certain - not now, nor in ancient times, if we follow the record. Our difficult task of astral-mythical correlation is to be made even harder by the requirement that we show that Aphrodite in the Love Affair is, if not certainly, then most likely, the Moon. However, we shall proceed to the task, taking four steps. First we inquire whether Aphrodite was tied to the Moon in Greek, Near Eastern and other sources in primeval and ancient times. Next we ask whether Aphrodite was the name of entities other than the Moon. Further, we ask whether she was possibly both the Moon and another entity. Finally, we ask whether Aphrodite stood for the Moon specifically in the Love Affair, in the song of Demodocus.

A MOST ANCIENT GODDESS

The Aphrodite of whom we speak is an old goddess. Always speaking in relative terms, "old" means coming into recognizable form and identity before Jupiter, Venus and mars, probably *after* Uranus, and possibly early in the age of Saturn - using the Greco-Roman Eastern Mediterranean theogony and names as points of reference.

A quotation "On the worship of Venus-Urania throughout the East," from the work of a famous scholar,[1]

> "She was the 'Queen of Heaven, ' the Moon... she corresponded to Minerva, and in Greece to the original Aphrodite, who became at last the mere personification of beauty and voluptuousness."

In the work of another scholar, Jane E. Harrison,[2] we read a passage from the *Danaides* of Aeschylus, and we are told something of the jurisdiction of this Aphrodite - words put into her mouth by the great dramatist:

Lo, there is hunger in the holy Sky
To pierce the body of the Earth, and in the Earth too
Hunger to meet his arms. So falls the rain
From Heaven that is her lover, making moist
The bosom of the Earth: and she brings forth to man
The flocks he feeds, the corn that is his life.
To trees no less there cometh their own hour
Of marriage which the gleam of watery things
Makes fruitful - Of all these the cause am I.

---

[1] Appendix to Herodotus, *Histories*, Bk III.

[2] *Epilegomena to the Study of Greek Religion and Themis,* Cambridge, Eng. 1921, reprinted IIyde Park, N. Y. : University Books, 1962, p. 176.

These lines seem to convey what we would expect of a lunar goddess. We are moving far back in time. In a passing reference, Mircea Eliade writes of a "regime brought about by Aphrodite and later governed by Zeus, in which the species are fixed, there is order, balance, and hierarchy."[3] I have carried the birth of the Moon back in solar system history to an astronomical catastrophe occurring even before the Age of Saturn. We hear Theopompos quoted by Plutarch:[4] "From Kronos and Aphrodite all things take their birth." So Aphrodite is moved back to the time of Kronos.

Back of Zeus, stands his father Kronos, and back of Kronos, *his* father, Ouranos. Hesiod (8th century?), the earliest Greek source of all, places Aphrodite with the earliest great god of the cloudy skies, Ouranos (Uranus). The motherless Aphrodite is daughter of Ouranos, and Eros - a figure of love - seems to have been born with her, nor will this divine helper ever leave her.

A little while after Hesiod wrote, Homer worked, and Homer alludes to a second Aphrodite Pandemos, daughter of Zeus by Dione, aided by Eros Pandemos.

Cicero, a typical confusion emerging out of his elegant prose, has Hermes as husband of the Uranian Aphrodite who is given Hephaestus as a husband and Ares as a lover. A third Aphrodite is the sister of Hermes and daughter of Heaven and Die. Finally, a fourth Aphrodite emerges as a Syric-Cypriot wife of Adonis, by the name of Astarte.

We have almost nothing to say of the latter two personae. It is enough to discuss Aphrodite Urania and Aphrodite Pandemos, if indeed they amount to two distinct goddesses. If the former is the Moon, there is no reason to make of the second also the Moon. Rather, this latter may even have been the planet Venus, who as the goddess Athena, was born out of Zeus' forehead, lacking association in such case with either Dione or Eros. Proclus, much later, but still authoritative, has this second later Aphrodite also born from the sea like the first.[5]

The first goddess, Aphrodite Urania, was born in the throes of the destruction of Ouranos by his son Kronos (Saturn), who severed his

---

[3] *Patterns in Comparative Religion*, p. 77.

[4] *Isis and Osiris*, LXIX.

[5] Plat. *Kraty.* 1-116.

father's genitals with a sickle of jagged flint and flung them into the sea. From the foam of these organs arose Aphrodite, a foam god, literally foam-born (aphrogenis), the "one who is generated from foam."[6] Only three words in Greek are known to carry the *Aphr*-root: "foam" (aphros), "recklessness," and "sexually stimulating." All are obvious associations with Aphrodite's birth and character.[7] This will become more significant when we ask why Aphrodite Urania cannot have been Athena, or Ishtar, or another goddess.

TURBULENT BIRTH IN MYTHS & REALITY

The later myth might have both confusing and clarifying elements, confusing in its resemblances to the Uranian episode, clarifying in that, if it were Athena-Venus which was involved, foam-covered seas are understandable (" Beaufort 10" in navigation has the surface of the sea foaming, hence sperm) and a turbulent setting in which Aphrodite-Moon (does Dione relate to Diana?) was destructively involved and Zeus' activity might have been construed as an attempted (and actual) ravishment of the Moon in the days of the birth of Athena seven hundred and more years before the Love Affair. The Homeric "Hymn to Athena" reproduced in chapter X chants of the foaming seas resulting from her birth.

"Sea" foam, we can see, had reason to be brought in a second time on a later date. Of the name "Aphrodite" itself, a case can be made for its being of an origin earlier than the planet Venus, because of the temporal precedence of the Moon and the definite designation of Urania, an impossible name for a later deity; long before historical nations began, Ouranos was a *deus otiosus*. The goddess Amphitrite Thalassa (" of the Sea") shares this epithet with Typhon and his paredra, "making one being with foam-born Aphrodite," according to F. Nork.[8] Here is another indication that Aphrodite Pandemos is late-born and accompanies the birth (and death) of Typhon.

---

[6] Hesiod, *Theogony*, 196.

[7] Using the Liddell-Scott *Greek-English Lexicon,* Oxford: Clarendon Press, 7th ed, 1968.

[8] *Etym., Symbol. Mythol. Wörterbuch*, 1844, reference kindly supplied by Dr. Zvi Rix.

We employ the scenario of Aphrodite Urania in *Chaos and Creation* and *Solaria Binaria* to approach the reality of those days. Uranus is a giant luminescent planet that fissions in the earliest days of humanity. There occurs a separation from the electric arc or "tree of life" which humans saw reaching up to the god-planet. A major fragment from the nova takes cometary form. In the severance from the tree and in the cometary form, a castration of Ouranos is perceived. When the Moon is seen to arise from the disturbed Earth, it is perceived as born out of the turbulent seas, out of the froth, and the connection is made with the genitals of Ouranos, from which foam-born Aphrodite Urania is generated and rises into the sky.

The bloodiness ascribed by myth to the foaming scene would refer to the ruddy color of the turbulent elements and to the horrific analogy of the divine actions; the same color relations would occur upon the much later occasion of the mythical fall of Typhon and the birth of a new goddess. Many thousands of years separate this catastrophic primordial scenario from the fully sublimated painting by Botticelli of a tender, beautiful Aphrodite riding upon the sea-shell. In Sumerian mythology, the god of the aether, Enlil, who can be compared with Uranus, separates the interlocked Earth Mother and Father-Nammu, and then creates the Moon god, Nanna.

Among the thousands of verses of the *Rig Vedas* of ancient India there is an allusion to the birth of the Moon, which is not among those presented in my other works but was culled by J. Ziegler during his study of the Vedas. The Moon is "the Prudent (Moon)... allied by birth to Heaven and Earth in kinship. The Gods discovered in the midst of waters beautiful Agni (the Moon) with the Sister's labor. Him, Blessed One, Seven strong Floods augmented, him white at birth and red when waxen mighty.... Then they, ancient and young, who dwell together, Seven Sounding Rivers, as one germ received him."[9]

Ziegler has also identified as Moon-names of the Rig-Vedas : Pusan, Indu, Two-Mothered Sun, Pavamana, Sura, Wanderer, Red Bird, Lord, Bull, Vaisvanara, Maghavan, Brhaspati, Brahmanaspati, Kutsa, Sindhu, Sage, Shining One, Agni and Indra, and probably many more. We note how other gods are called by Moon-names or there is a confusion, as with Agni and Indra. The same duplicity may occur in the Mediterranean

---

[9] J. Ziegler, *The Vedas* pp. 233-4 (1983, unpubl. mss)

area.

John Bentley, writing of India, supports us from his peculiar point of vantage: in the war between gods and giants, "the goddess Sri, or Lakshmi, was then born, or produced from the Sea."

> The Venus Aphroditus of the Western mythologists (is) emblematic of the lunisolar year; therefore she is called the goddess of increase, abundance, etc. She is the daughter of Durga, and the Proserpine of the West; and, considered as time, she is the same as her mother. Metaphysically, she may sometimes represent the Moon.[10]

Later on, we shall see that Bentley's support has its problems. He may be confusing two Aphrodites (Moon and planet Venus) and Hindu mythology, it seems, may have the same problem as the Greek.

In geological terms, however, and according to a view that I present at length in the Quantavolution Series, the Moon has recently arrived upon the sky. It was assembled electro-gravitationally from a vast explosion of crustal material from the Earth. It began to orbit the Earth, always facing it, within the traditional era of a cultured humanity that recorded the events through legend later on. Inasmuch as a number of ancient authors declare that there existed, still intact, cultures that claimed existence prior to the Moon's appearance, there was a "Proselenian Period" before the Moon existed.[11]

Among the Proselenians, doubts existed; the Moon may have come into position earlier but, owing to a thick canopy of clouds girdling the Earth, it may have merely come into evidence at a later time, and therefore the Proselenians witnessed the coming of the Moon as an emergence from behind a cloudy barrier, after it had been present in the nearby sky for some time.

Around the world, the moon was more often attributed female gender for several reasons that can be touched upon only briefly here. A matriarchal system may have come into being at times and the Moon was deemed female. Or the rough coincidence of the normal menstrual

---

[10] *A Historical Review of the Indian Astronomy* Part I "The Ancient Astronomy" (1825; reprinted 1970, Osnabrück: Biblio Verlag).

[11] A. M. Paterson, "Giordano Bruno's View on the Earth without a Moon," *Pensée*, (winter, 1973), pp. 46-7; I. Velikovsky, "Earth without a Moon," *Ibid.,* p. 26. Both writers, at least then, believed that the Moon was recently captured. The present author decided upon the Earth-fission model in the years that followed, cf. *Chaos and Creation, Lately Tortured Earth,* and was supported by Earl R. Milton, cf. *Solaria Binaria.*

period of women and the cycle of lunar phases - 28 days, 36 days and perhaps other periods as well, in various calendar ages - could have produced numerous speculations, "confirmations," institutional and ritual tags for the measure of time and religious behaviors. The Moon would thus become female because of its behavior according to the menstrual cycle? Yet, we think, could not a male Moon have commanded and ordered the menstrual cycle, according to the mythmaking mind? Only Venus, of the planets, is often female. The others and the Sun are regularly male. A number of qualities are associated with the Moon and these are also associated with the female sex. The chief among these is a role in fertility. But could not the qualities have been ascribed to the Moon after they were developed in females? Not altogether, of course, because certain qualities are found so universally among women that they would appear to have originated in a common source such as the Moon. One refers here to the function of women in spinning and weaving. Do these derive from lunar behavior?

ENCYCLOPEDISTS & THE MOON GODDESS

Robert Graves refers to "Selene the Moon, alias Aphrodite" and develops the lunar traits of Aphrodite extensively. "The Athenians called Aphrodite Urania 'the eldest of the Fates' because she was the Nymph-Goddess, to whom the sacred King had, in ancient times, been sacrificed at the summer solstice... Aphrodite is the same wide-ruling goddess who rose from Chaos and danced on the sea, and who was worshiped in Syria and Palestine as Ishtar, or Ashtaroth.[12] She was regarded as a queen-bee. "She destroyed the sacred king, who mated with her on a mountain top, as a queen-bee destroys the drone: by tearing out his sexual organs." As Cybele, Phrygian Aphrodite of Mount Ida, she accepted "the ecstatic

---

[12] Graves, I, 49. We disagree that Ishtar was the Moon, at least finally, for she is clearly Athena and Planed Venus, cf. Velikovsky. Further, on Aphrodite as the Moon, see the conclusion of this chapter.

self-castration of her priests in memory of her lover Attis."[13] Concessions, suggests Graves, to the need to grant her masculine powers as society moved under the influence of Jovian patriarchy.[14] Thus could society employ the fantasy of bisexuality to further a political cause.

The Scythians, it is asserted in the *Encyclopaedia Britannica* (16-44) worshipped "Artimpasa (Aphrodite Urania), goddess of the Moon." The famous Encyclopedia of Pauly-Wissowa tells us that Philochorus, "resting on the oldest conceptions of nature," finds a duplicity in Aphrodite and the Moon (p. 2738). It refers to Horace speaking of dances to Aphrodite in the night under the Moon (Horace, *Carm.* I: 45). It pitches the Lemnos myth of a marriage between Aphrodite and Hephaestus against a Theban myth of her marriage to Ares, which are then merged in the Song of Demodocus (p. 2769); the Orphic hymns stretch far back of the Homeric period of the Eighth and Seventh Centuries; the image of Aphrodite here seems lunar rather than planetary, but we realize that the same Mistress of the Heavens title is given to Astarte in Syria, who is probably more planet Venus (with Ananna) than she is the Moon. Also, as Astarte is seen by some as Aphrodite barbata (bearded), still Pauly-Wissowa can find at least that the ancient authority Philochoros again calls the bearded goddess a Moon figure.

Numerous writers besides Graves, among them Winthuis, Jeremias, and Rix, have stressed an original bisexuality of ancient deities.

> The primordial All-Mother of ancient tradition is a man-woman, or a woman-man, virgin not in the physiological but in the cosmic sense.... A naive androgynous symbolism for the primeval mother, forming a part of the doctrine, is apparently shown in the oldest temples to the Virgin Mother, when the All-Mother is represented with a beard... Astarte may appear in a masculine

---

[13] Graves, I, 71. Unity with the goddess excited anxiety over violating the incest taboo and brings on sacrifice of kings and priests. "As Goddess of Death-in-Life, Aphrodite earned many titles which seem inconsistent with her beauty and complaisance" - Melaenis (black one), Scotia (dark one), Androphonos (man-slayer), and Epitymbria (of the tombs). At Cyprus she would sometimes wear a beard, and was also portrayed as "bearded and having the male member, but clad in a female dress and holding a sceptre," 1 George Hill, *A History of Cyprus* (Cambridge: University Press, 1972), Vol. I, 79-80, citing Macrobius (Sat. III, 8) and *Fragmenta Historica Graecorum* (1878-85), Vol. I, p. 386.

[14] Graves, I, 73. When Plato (*Epinomis*, lines 99-101) gave the name Aphrodite to the planet that we call Venus, he said that he was using the name of "a Syrian lawgiver" and in the next statement uses the pronoun "him" in referring back to it. He could mean the "authority" or "in the name of" the Syrian.

form... sometimes with the characteristics of the masculine sex. Certain authors have even offered the hypothesis of an androgynous Ishtar.[15]

There are many of such androgynous representations of Aphrodite, as in Cyprus where the goddess wears a beard, female garments, and seems bisexual. Pilgrims to Paphos there received 'gifts of a phallus and salt,' the latter standing probably for the sea-froth and semen of which the goddess was born. In Rome, like New York City, anything could be found, including this, too.

The case for bearded Aphrodites representing the planet Venus occurs partly because the ankh (shown below), the *crux ansata* or 'cross with a handle,' is associated with both the planet and with a number of representations that must be regarded as the goddess Aphrodite. The ankh is an ambivalent symbol that denotes bisexuality, a combined phallus and vulva. The cometary references seem clear, for a comet's generally round nucleus and straight-out long tail convey in the sky a genital meaning. Insofar as the history of the planet Venus is known, and that may well be from its beginnings, the ankh has been a sacred symbol and one appropriated for the planet Aphrodite-Venus.

Athena is not without bearded associations. Male, bearded serpents were to be found on a pediment of the archaic Athenian Acropolis. These would have been representations of the dragon who was Typhon, and also a part of Athena as cometary Venus. The larger question to be dealt with later on, is whether Athena had a double, a male duplicity, a god of prominence.

The *Dictionnaire des Antiquités* is more confident than Pauly-Wissowa of the lunar identity of the goddesses Aphrodite and Venus. It recognizes the duality of the Uranian and Jovian Aphrodites which grew close with time or may even have been originally the same. (91 fn1) We quote here two passages from the extensive article on Venus:

> She came from Asia where almost all of the Semitic peoples worshiped a lunar deity representation of fertility and animal fecundity. Artakatis-Derketo at Ascalon, Mylitta at Babylon, Ishtar in Assyria, and above all, Astarte among the ancients.

From Cyprus and Phoenicia, the goddess moved North to the shores of the Black Sea, Northwest across the Cyclades, West to Cytherea, to Sparta, to Sicily, Carthage, Latium.

---

[15] Personal letter to the author from Dr. Z. Rix.

Aphrodite Urania is identical to lunar Astarte of the Semites, who appeared at Carthage under the name of the Celestial Virgin. The relations of Aphrodite with the night star are further implied in the myth of Phaeton whom the goddess seized to make guardian of her temple. Phaeton is, in effect, the star of the morning and evening, whose vivid brightness naturally associated it with the Moon whose brilliant acolyte it appeared to be. This star, among other names, is also called the star of Venus, and the assimilation of the goddess to this double star contributed, at Cyprus and Pamphylia, to the idea of an androgynous Aphrodite.

It is to be noted that this authority not only awards Aphrodite and Venus to the Moon, but also Ishtar and Astarte, two goddesses that a number of writers, the present author included, assign confidently to the catastrophic comet-planet Venus. Are we to win one position only in order to surrender another, perhaps more important in the total picture? For much of the best material on the history of the disasters of the mid-second millenium B. C. comes out of the histories of Ishtar and Astarte.

Sophie Lunais tells us that lunar cults are more ancient than solar, that the Moon was worshiped more than the sun, that Diana came to be identified with the Moon and so, too, Artemis, and of course Hecate, Selene, and Luna, but despite all of this, "curiously the mythology of the Moon is practically nonexistent."[16] Her surprise is not surprising, considering that often myths of the Moon do not come forth labeled clearly as such, and that in the book is to be found no reference to Aphrodite! Most of the mythology of Aphrodite is lunar mythology. Diana and Artemis were late arrivals as Moon goddesses, she reports; certainly later than Aphrodite, we add. We could further add that, if moon mythology is not abundant in the Latin authors, it is because Aphrodite tended to monopolize it, and in art as well.

Reports Graves: "The later Hellenes belittled the Great Goddess of the Mediterranean, who had long been supreme at Corinth, Sparta, Thespiae, and Athens, by placing her under male tutelage and regarding her solemn sex-orgies as adulterous indiscretions."[17]

Graves continues: the Moon, to whom "the sun yields precedence"[18] in early myth has three phases - the maiden of spring, the nubile nymph

---

[16] Sophie Lunais, *Les Auteurs Latins -Recherche sur la Lune,* I, Brill: Leiden, 1979,99.

[17] Graves, I, p. 18. I.

[18] Graves, I, p. 12.

THE TWO FACES OF LOVE

of summer, and the crone of winter, to correspond to her three phases: new, full, and old. She could also be identified with Mother Earth's vegetative year, who produced first leaves and buds, then flowers and fruits, and then a withered barrenness. "She could later be conceived as yet another triad: the maiden of the upper air, the nymph of the earth or sea, the crone of the underworld - typified respectively by Selene, Aphrodite, and Hecate. These mystical analogues fostered the sacredness of the number three, and the Moon-goddess became enlarged to nine when each of the three persons - maiden, nymph, and crone - appear in triad to demonstrate her divinity." (We note, in passing, that the council of Phaeacia numbered nine men, who measured the magic circle of the dance and whom we have also associated with a nine-day week.)

Aphrodite was the nubile female, par excellence, declares Graves. She wore the Golden Girdle of the Moon, whose magic would incite concupiscence in any man. In addition, she could stand in the place of the "General Chairwoman," from time to time and from place to place, as the Great Goddess pro-tem.

By the time Demodocus sang, Aphrodite was officially of the family of Olympian Gods, a daughter of Zeus, a relatively specialized god of desire, and the moon by inference as the dark time of trysting and loving. She is fickle, light-hearted, willful, beautiful, golden, perfumed, and anointed, with, of course, all the powers of her station in respect to humanity and an invulnerability in fact to terrible retribution from her father or sisters and brothers. She was a seductive, but no longer active, force.

Still, the universal help and harm, of which she was capable in earlier ages and even now, remained impressed upon the minds of the audience of Demodocus. Whatever happened to Aphrodite was of importance and if she might be treated good-humoredly, it would be still with respect, with awe, with ceremony, and behind the protective shield of other gods, who alone could be the causes of whatever embarrassment her shameless character would permit her.

THE COSMIC SPINNER

The most penetrating studies of Aphrodite as the Moon Goddess come from Elmer George Suhr. He entitles one of his books *Venus de Milo, The Spinner; the Link between a Famous Art Mystery and Ancient Fertility Symbols.*[19] A decade later he published *The Spinning Aphrodite; The Evolution of the Goddess from Earliest Pre-Hellenic Symbolism through Late Classical Times.*[20] The Venus de Milo, as is well-known, is a statue without arms. Suhr, reconstructing the statue anatomically and on the basis of more complete representations of Aphrodite, concluded that she was occupied at spinning yarn. A fine picture is to be found on the Berlin lekythos where beside the spinning goddess are Ares and Eros. "The moon... is in full view behind Aphrodite, where it serves as the total center for the whole composition." Suhr associated a whole complex of attributes and functions with Aphrodite: the Moon directly, the shadow of the Moon (its cone), spinning, the vortex theme in myth, the emblem of the spiral, the dew and rain, Klotho, Hecate, Medusa, the omphalos (sacred navel of the world), rainfall (the dropping of threads upon the Earth), the turning of the vault of Heaven, the forming of thunderheads on her distaff with the help of Ares, lunar calendars. She was "worshiped as the dispenser of the divine elixir running through all life, the mistress of fate and fortune, the author of all things fair and lovable." She is generally antagonistic in various manifestations to Athena. She is a long-time enemy of Athena, in the *Iliad* but elsewhere, too.

Aphrodite, Suhr thinks, was reduced in importance during the age of Zeus, but could not be fundamentally deprived of form and function.

> The Moon, which heretofore had played an important part in this program (of cloud, thunder, and lightning) was also relegated to the background. But Aphrodite was too powerful to be lightly brushed aside. As a goddess of love and beauty she became a respectable member of the Olympian family, both causing the other gods much trouble and bringing them countless pleasures by trapping them in the net of desire. Since Zeus was a male, he never took over the spinning equipment as an adjunct of creation; such an attribute was below the dignity of the father of the gods and men. Aphrodite was allowed to keep this attribute and though she remained a powerful divinity, she was pushed aside in Athens, no doubt in the days of Theseus, by Athena, the bachelor girl goddess who became a favored child of Zeus.

That the Moon goddess was a spinner is also to be discovered in Meso-America and Egypt. Hence if Aphrodite is connected with spinning in Greece and the Near East, then Aphrodite is to be connected

---

[19] New York: Exposition Press, 1958, Foreword by Rhys Carpenter.

[20] New York: Helios Press, 1969.

THE TWO FACES OF LOVE

with the Moon, for the Moon and spinning are generally associated.

An article and photograph of the *National Geographic Magazine* (Dec. 1975) describe

> ....The Mayan moon goddess Ixchel, patroness of fertility, weaving, and medicine. Wife of the sun, she consorted with other gods, just as the moon crosses paths with the stars and planets. In this 4 3/4-inch figurine from Jaina Island, off Yucatan, the moon goddess takes a grinning rabbit for her partner.

The grinning rabbit might in other place be taken to be a wolf, a mouse, a dove or another animal such as have been associated with the planet Mars-Ares in Greece, Rome, and the Near East. The Indo-Iranian texts of the Bundahis refer to a planet called "Gokihar" or "Wolf-progeny" as "special disturber of the Moon"[21] while the Slavs beheld a wolf-shaped Vukadlak that devoured the moon (or sun).[22]

Medusa is identified with Aphrodite and with Selene (moon) by Suhr, who points out that Selene was the patroness of generation and "as a friend of Poseidon (one among other reasons) she became offensive to Athena." We bear this in mind when we see Odysseus protected by Athena and murderously pursued by Poseidon, and when we see Poseidon in the Love Affair arranging an easy exit for Aphrodite and Ares out of the vengeful hands of Hephaestus (hence Athena who, we shall see, is tied to Hephaestus and a protagonist and director of the action in the Love Affair).

Suhr speaks of the countless clay cones of Mesopotamia that copy the shadow of the Moon. They rotate upon the face of the dark land, and become a type of menhir turned by human figures of stone. Nannar the moon god of Mesopotamia works hard to keep the cone rotating. The cone emblem is found on a coin of Byblos (Syria) and at the city of Paphos (Cyprus) where a large cone stood in the open court of the Temple of Aphrodite. With regard both to Aphrodite of Cyprus and Astarte of Syria there was a close association with the Moon. "Both are heiresses of the moon god of the city of Ur" with many cone figures.

---

[21] Velikovsky in *Worlds in Collision,* Part II : 3.

[22] *Ibid.,* ch. 4.

CONFUSION COMPOUNDED

We have already given reasons for the oriental associations of lunar Aphrodite so we are not surprised but confirmed at finding her great temple at Paphos, Cyprus, constructed in the Phoenician style (or is it vice versa? No matter here, but relevant chronologies should be approached skeptically). In this temple, we have noted, stood a monolith that Tacitus, the Roman historian, described as "A rounded mass rising like a cone from a broad base to a small circumference." Some scholars think it to have been an aerolith or meteoroid that had fallen and was emplaced in honor of Aphrodite. This, indeed, it may have been. To suspect that the fallen stone may be set up in deference to a cometary Venus or would be a meteoroid associated somehow with Athena is certainly permissible. We know of a Palladium of Troy, a probable meteoritic stone, associated with Pallas Athena,[23] who is herself identified with the planet Venus. Other meteoroids have been associated with other gods. In the present instance at Paphos, and following Suhr's earlier theory, we would have more reason to see in the meteoritic cone an accidental resemblance to the Shadow Cone of the Moon, and its many fabricated images going back to the city of Ur. Aphrodite of Paphos would then be, if not exclusively lunar Aphrodite, largely or partly such.

Pliny, the natural historian of Rome, writes that Venus is given the name Lucifer as another sun bringing the dawn, whereas when it shines after sunset it is named Vesper as prolonging the daylight, or as deputy of the Moon, and he credits the discovery of the twin property of planet-Venus to Pythagoras of Samos, 142 years after the founding of Rome. Others besides Pythagoras are also credited with the discovery, Parmenides and Ibycus of Rhegium among them.

One implication of this remark, corroborated broadly in Plato, is that planet Venues did not occupy the same course after the incidents that we are tracing in the Love Affair. Planet Venus arrived to be deputy of the Moon following the disastrous scenario in time.

At some period when the planet Venus was emplaced in its modern

---

[23] See Harrison, *Epilegomena to the Study of Greek Religion and Themis,* Cambridge, Eng. 1921, reprinted Hyde Park, N. Y.: University Books, 1962, p. 87, who finds "Pallas" in the "Palladium."

orbit and coming to be recognized as such, in its morning and evening manifestations, there may have been a movement in Greece to call it Hera, for Hera it was called by some. Perhaps the astronomers, more in touch with oriental thought, won out with their name, Aphrodite.

Another source of confusion turns up in the pages of Robert Graves, where he distinguishes the animals of the Moon, Selene, and Aphrodite as those that 'parted the hoof' in the manner of lunar crescents so that the lunar symbol occurred as two facing arcs, contrasting with the single simple disc of the sun. The sacred cow that directed Cadmus (from Ugarit, facing West) to the site of Thebes was so branded on each flank.

At Denderah a red bull was sacrificed formally as Typhon. Temples there for Isis and Aphrodite were found, as well as shrines for Seth-Typhon. Cows, young bulls, bulls, red bulls: to whom does each category belong, to what gods, in what aspects? There were more sky-bovines than bovine species to assign to them. It will be a long time before the pattern is fully discovered. At Denderah, there is something of Aphrodite as the Venusian goddess implicated in the mid-second millennial events. Cloven-hoofed animals are not alone of the Moon, whatever may be the inclination of the symbol of the double-facing crescents elsewhere. Just as Lucifer is the light-bearer of the morning, but is also the Prince of Darkness, Satan, Seth - the light that brought darkness, the darkness of wanderings in the wilderness, of Egypt following the Great Light?

What, then, should one do with the many indications from Egypt, the Near East, and Western and Northern Europe that the Planet Venus is associated with the cow and even the young bull (as in the Revolt of the Golden Calf in Hebrew Exodus)? It would appear that we are dealing once again with mysteries of the succession and amalgamation of divinities in the course of experiencing and forgetting, mnemotechnology. Especially because of the ultimately close physical association of the Moon and Venus and the skies, the facile mirage of celestial horns, and the shapes that comets take, we can reason that Aphrodite would be party to and victim of a confusion between Moon and the Star of the Moon. Hence, Symbols of the one may develop some distinction from those of the other, but an overlapping occurs, enough to tell of the merger of gods, a merger perhaps supremely important in preventing the human mind from taking sides against itself. That is, the very confusion that sets us to arguing is the therapy enabling us to live mentally with historically opposing gods. And such is carried into the sublimations of the arts. "There is something for everyone," "everyone" being the society seeking consensus (therefore a consistent history) and the individual seeking personal sacred integrity.

A MATCH OF SOURCES

The time has come, it appears, to switch perspectives, to show how it might be argued that Aphrodite is also tied to the planet Venus, thus rescuing the several goddesses of the planet Venus from capture by the Moon.

Perhaps following Plutarch, St. Augustine went as far as to assign the archetype of the comet-planet Venus, Athena, to the Moon

> As for Minerva (Athena), they have given her the responsibility for the arts of mankind; but they have not found her a star to be her habitation, and so they have identified her with the upper region of the ether, or even with the Moon.

We can do without this sort of help. This is as unlikely an assignment as any identification can get in mythology and I join Peter James in dismissing it. But James' adamancy on the balance of the equation remains to be dissolved. It lets him turn around and accept Augustine's comment that Aphrodite won the Judgment of Paris about which goddess should represent Venus (the golden apple), "but as usual Venus wins. For the overwhelming majority give the star to Venus."[24] Is it not once more likely that Aphrodite won the star of Venus, that is, the planet that attended the Aphrodisian Moon? The Greeks, he insists, regularly applied the name Aphrodite to the planet Venus, and addressed prayers to that body as the planet associated with her. They could not really be thinking of the Moon in all of this.

> If Velikovsky and de Grazia are right, then Lucian of Samosata, Ptolemy, Aristotle, Plotinus, Diordorus Siculus, Manetho, Sappho, Bion, the Emperor Julian, Nonnus, ... and ... the ancient Greeks were all wrong.

My list of debatable sources here is perhaps as long and may be longer. Several of the star witnesses are contradictory and can be controverted. Augustine mentions two groups, one awarding planet Venus to the goddess Venus, another insisting also that Venus is the Moon. Other witnesses can be called: where are Hesiod, Homer,

---

[24] Citing *The City of God,* VII: 15.

Plutarch, Cicero, Hyginus, Augustine, Proclus? And where are the modern encyclopedists?

They may do no worse, or better: James of course knows them well; I have already joined him in discussing Plutarch and Augustine. But to take another example, Hesiod is the earliest source extant to refer to the transformation of Phaeton, felled by Zeus for threatening the destruction of Earth, into a star. Hesiod writes of "Phaeton, a man like the gods, whom... laughter-loving Aphrodite seized and caught up and made a keeper of her shrine by night, a divine spirit" (987ff). Clearly in line with what we are saying the proto-planet Venus was said to be captured upon her fall from the skies by Moon-Aphrodite and thereafter employed as her divine priest. In a second example, I cannot understand why Sappho is forced to take sides. She sings:

And may Hesperus lead thee full
willingly to the place where thou
shalt marvel at the silver-throned
Lady of Wedlock.

Here, clearly, planet-Venus is performing as the acolyte of the Moon. Nor, to take another instance, is Bion less than a Moonie. The pastoral poet addresses the

Evening star, which art the
Golden light of the lovely Child of
The Foam, which are the holy
Jewel of the blue night.

Here again we are permitted to regard the Moon as lovely Child of the Foam, Aphrodite, whose acolyte is the Evening Star. I suggest that the passage and the poet are ambiguous, and would not rely upon it for support or denial in the argument.

The ancient source Nonnus speaks of an astrologer who "looked especially for Ares and spied the wife robber over the sunset house along with the evening star of the Cyprian." Is the evening star "the Cyprian" or "of the Cyprian;" if "of the Cyprian" then the evening star is the planet Venus and the Cyprian is the Moon, whether present or absent. The modern source Jean Richer (*Géographie Sacrée du Monde Grec*) speaks of "... Cythere, whose Venus was foremost a lunar goddess."

On the other hand, Cicero is often confused, too. Cicero writes that "Diana they identify as the moon... while the name Luna is derived from

Lucere, 'to shine;'" and he says that Diana to the Greeks is Lucifera (the Light-Bearer) and is one of the seven planets or wanderers. Diana is generally involved with the Moon, it is agreed, and with menstruation and childbirth, hence the Greeks were making an erroneous transfer unless they carry the Moon as a wanderer and planet which in fact was often done; so Lucifera could be the Moon as well as the planet Venus of the morning. I prefer to renounce the lunar argument here, and to let go of Cicero, rather than to assert it as evidence. The best that can be said is that Lucifera is a feminine brightness that can be ascribed to the Moon as well as to its primary reference, the Morning Star.

James would cease to "strenuously deny that Aphrodite had anything to do with the Moon," perhaps, if he were to realize how large a contribution his own work has made, first, to my being able to reinforce the Moon identification of Aphrodite and, secondly, to arrive at my final theory on the matter, namely that the two bodies - Moon and planet - interacted physically, became confused in history and myth in certain regards (though not in many others) and were to be found, in the end, to have played now one role and then another. I have shown that their alternation of roles occurred elsewhere; I would only insist that Aphrodite is quite capable of the lunar role I assign to her (and believe that subconsciously the Greeks assigned to her) in the Love Song of Demodocus in Book VIII of the *Odyssey* of Homer.

Peter James proposes another theory - or sub-theory - on the issue, suggesting that a lunar Aphrodite can be totally excluded from consideration if only we imagine that warlike Athena was early granted the Morning Star (Phosphoros) while peaceful Aphrodite was given the Evening Star (Hesperos); thus both goddesses might be accounted for and the Moon excluded.

No less an authority than Kugler can be called on to state James' position on the double nature of Ishtar, hence planet Venus, in his work, *Sibyllinischer Sternkampf und Phaethon* (1927, p. 14) he says of the Babylonian Ishtar: "Venus-morning star there represented *Ishtar-Kakkabe*, 'Ishtar of the Star', and is thought of as 'masculine' - in distinct contrast to Venus-evening star, the *Belit-ile*, 'Queen of the Gods,' the goddess of love and motherhood."

In examining a rock relief of the Hittite pantheon, James discovered that the Venusian planet Shaushga held a double identity and preceded the Moon god on the one side and the Sun god on the other. She also wore wings. She must be here the planet in its morning and evening aspects.[25] This indicates a young (Velikovskian) age, not an old (Jamesian) age of the rocks, if one believes that the planet did not settle into its morning-evening routine until the period of the Love Affair. Still, one should acknowledge that the double goddess and the Moon are distinctly different.

Steven Langdon, another authority, has it that the morning star was called in Babylonia "the male Venus" and the evening star the "female Venus", with Ishtar, of course, as the word for Venus; there is "Ishtar of Agade" and "Ishtar of Anech", for morning and evening manifestations of the planet.

We can go so far as to say that Athena was Venus in her cometary phase, ending in her status as the morning star during the early years of the new status of the morning star. We cannot well imagine the second because of definite statements associating Hesperos with Moon-Aphrodite. We accept, too, that Lucifer was planet-Venus and the morning-star. Such were Ishtar and Astarte, and other gods.

At the same time, although the Aphrodite of the morning was not the Aphrodite of the night, the morning-planet-Aphrodite was working her way into many of the traits of the night-moon-Aphrodite, so that goddesses of the morning star could ultimately possess traits genetically possessed by the Moon goddess - lovingness, peacefulness, sexuality, Queen of Heaven. S. A., Bedini, too, sees this process as occurring - that Ishtar, for instance, guaranteed contract among men together with the Moon God Sin. She was goddess of love, fertility and war. She took qualities from the Moon with her when she moved fully to occupy the morning and evening stars, Venus.[26] Also, long after and for many centuries of the present era, many Arabs worshiped the morning star as both Lucifer and Aphrodite, never mind the evening star.

The scum of the salty foaming sea, held in revulsion by Egyptians, was again two foams, the original Aphrodite-Moon foam of the seed of Ouranos, and the later Aphrodite-Typhon foam transferred from the mid-second millennium. The latter foam came about, the Egyptians thought, from the falling of Typhon (the cometary tail of proto-Venus)

---

[25] Kugler, *Sibyllinischer Sternkampf und Phaethon (1927)* I : 2, pp 3-4.

[26] S. A. Bedini, p. 23, in Bedini, Werner von Braun, and F. L. Whipple, *Moon: Man's Greatest Adventure* (New York: Abrams, n. d., ca. 1970).

into the sea (after Zeus had struck him with a thunderbolt, according to the Greeks), this according to Plutarch. There are in sum numerous reasons to explain the confusion, to assign the name to the planet, and to retain it for the Moon for all the purposes that we have in mind here.

HOW TO NAME A PLANET?

We know that the Moon had names - Selene, Luna, Sin, etc. - which an astronomer or educated layman could apply, whether in Greek or Latin; but the planet Phosphoros and Hesperos had only this double name, implying two distinct bodies, and the Greek intellectual reformers needed a name for the planet that would denote a single entity, a point that they were trying to get across to their public.

They could not and would not take away Moon's name and affix it to a planet. But Aphrodite had long since left the Moon in a conscious sense though she was stubbornly, obsessively the Moon in the subconscious. The literal minds - such as Pythagoras, Socrates, Plato, Aristotle, Plotinus, Diodorus, Manetho, Pliny and Cicero were less (or differently) imprisoned by their subconscious: "Let the planet be called Aphrodite, after the famous goddess." Today we name a new planet Neptune or Pluto; such is astronomical tradition of naming; it can be false to history, unless saved by subconscious memory. Aphrodite was still Aphrodite in a host of connotations, memories and expectations - and she had a wandering star named for her. All the other planets had names of gods, new names, though the names had long traditions behind them - Zeus, Kronos, Ares, Hermes. Now the Romans too would call them Jupiter, Saturn, Mars, and Mercury. As for the Moon, it already had names enough.

But what did the Greeks call the planet before it received its new name? It is said Phosphorus-Hesperus. What was its name when, as our scheme calls for, it was raging through the heavens as a new blazing comet? Perhaps then it was called Phaeton, Typhon, Pallas, Baal, El, the Archangel, or "Daughter of Zeus," or "Athena," or perhaps "She" and then "He," or "The Thing," "It," or why not "the God." Hundred of appellations can be found for it around the globe. What did the Mycenaeans call the planet? No one yet knows. Under such conditions, it would be foolish to be hooked by a name assignment, to neglect

The Two Faces Of Love

natural and human history, and to become illogical in the face of other types of evidence, especially when we are fairly confident that the name was deliberately imposed upon the planetary body by highly sublimated intellectuals.

Does this mean that the Greeks and Romans then stopped upon applying he word, and never added their prior traits of goddess Aphrodite to the planet? No. As soon as an object is called by a name with a history, the history begins to flow onto the name. Further all that was previously attached to the object continues with it.

Suppose nowadays we were to decide that the asteroidal belt, whose materials are being discovered in ever greater detail, had to be called by a name, and hence called it the "Belt of Mars." Suppose that subsequently some traits of the ancient god were evidenced in the asteroidal belt and some students decided to call it "the Belt of Apollo." This does not make Apollo out of Mars, or vice versa. It brings confusion. Soon the word "belt" would be dropped, and just the names would be used. The "Mars Program" and the "Apollo Program" would be erroneously associated with the planets. After a century or so, only some priests of NASA would be able to explain the history, and, if NASA were dissolved, practically no one would know the story. And, after a sky-war in which civilizations were shocked and reduced to subsistence level, only a cultist now and then would revive the terms. Where would truth exist under such circumstances? Probably where truth exists under present circumstances concerning the ancient history of Venus and the Moon.

In the case of the planet Aphrodite-Venus, some of what was Aphrodite in the collective mind attached itself to the new Aphrodite. Furthermore, some that was in Astarte, Ishtar, Isis, and a dozen other Eastern relatives, began to be transferred over to the name Aphrodite.

In the end, the goddess Aphrodite changed. She was now two psychic entities, Siamese twins, in the categories of the mind. Concurrently, the gods that have lent their qualities to the new member of the planet-family, borrow her qualities of old; they take on the history and rights of the Moon. This reverse borrowing results in dubious but understandable claims that Ishtar is the Moon, Astarte is the Moon, even Athene is the Moon (Plutarch, Bedini, etc.). The confusion that must always occur in the association of great gods with natural objects and events here was compounded and intensified by the transference of Aphrodite to an actually antagonistic planet.

We must reckon, too, that a new god may be given an older name in order that humans may prove to the god that "we knew all along who you were, even if it seemed not so. We did not have to await your coming to destroy us before knowing of your eternal being." (" Therefore, planet Venus, cease and desist from your threats to the Earth and Moon.")

On one occasion, depending upon prior conditions such as the background of the subject, the subject's felt needs, and the information and setting provided the subject, the god who appears is a selection of one set of divine expectations. On another occasion, the god who appears may be different. In *God's Fire,* I explain how impossible is true monotheism, and that even Moses was in a realistic psychological sense a polytheist. The same reasoning may be applied here, where Aphrodite is now one god and now another. It is unscientific and pedantic to charge that a name is all that there is to a complex and subtle mental operation.

After the name Aphrodite is given to the planet, the Greeks began revising their religious history. Planetary conjunctions of Venus and Mars were of course known. So now Lucian of Samosata could claim that it was the juncture of Aphrodite and Ares that creates the poetry of Homer, and probably means by her the planet and not the Moon. So Eratosthenes and others. But this is not a proof of what Homer meant or, regardless of what Homer meant, that Aphrodite was not the Moon in the reality behind the poem and psychically in those who heard the Song of Demodocus chanted. Especially are these reservations proper if Athena is conceded to stand for the comet Venus, whence it may be truly said that the war is between planet Venus and planet Mars, but certainly, since Aphrodite and Ares were allies, the epics of Homer could never have been plotted on the liaison or juncture of Ares and Athena. So insistent are the ancient claims of the classical age that the same planet was at a late time discovered to be not two but one, and therefore given a name, that of Aphrodite, that we must believe so and allow that in the mind of Homer and Demodocus, Aphrodite did not posses that planet, except as the Moon. Several generations had lived and died between the last Battle of the Gods and the willful emplacement of the name of Aphrodite upon the planet. By the time of Plato only vague memories stirred of the original behavior of this doubly duplicitous body and of its dramatic roles in the skies of times past.

Revivals occur. Suhr writes that "the association of Aphrodite with clouds, the moon, spinning and fertility was more popular in Greece after Alexander had opened up the channels for a free exchange of ideas with the East than before, but this we may consider a revival; Aphrodite was known and worshiped, even in Athens, in very early times."

There is no suggestion that Aphrodite of the Love Affair is trespassing upon the identity of Ishtar. Ishtar is goddess of the morning star and also of the evening star in the usage of a removed culture. Aphrodite of the Greeks is made to be the goddess standing behind Phosphorus and Hesperus and their duality. Meanwhile she remains goddess of the Moon. Plato mentions a Syrian law-giver as the source of the name. But after considering this surprising suggestion for some time, I think now that Plato may have been of the opinion that a Syrian lawgiver with the advice of the court astronomers gave to the planet Venus the name of Ishtar or Astarte or another such name. In following this learned and authoritative source, the Greeks applied the old name Aphrodite to the planet. Once to the Europeans, the Western hemisphere had no names - or rather, numerous names. A geographer published a map drawn by an Italian navigator, Amerigo Vespucci. It was the map of Amerigo, describing a vast land. What was the land called? Not the "country of Amerigo" but, eventually "Amerigo," Latin masculine Americus, for a feminine country becomes "America."

THE ROMAN VENUS

We ought not settle the Aphrodite identity without a parallel investigation of the word "Venus." Malcolm Lowery conducted appropriate etymological research. Its root, he discovered, contained the senses of seek, desire, want, wish, and winsome, while its relative venire (to come) also relates to the same root, that includes the word "to go" in Greek. Velilovsky follows Cicero's idea that "Venus" meant "the goddess who comes to all things" and extended it to mean "newly come" to fit his theory.

Lowery effectively discusses Velikovsky's speculation and limits Cicero to a possibly very old truth about the word, a truth established long before the time when the goddess would have been attached to the planet Venus. An implication here is that the goddess called Venus may earlier have been attached to a conception of a goddess like Aphrodite, even lunar, before the planet Venus was identified.

Lowery may err in his innuendo that the Roman Venus was "unlike the Greek Aphrodite, whose name, meaning 'foam-born,' was subsequently applied to the human activity of which she served as patron, namely love-making, "born in and from sperm." If the modern, vernacular of the English-speaking world uses the word "come" to designate an orgasm, there is reason to suppose that the less sexually restrained ancient Greeks and Romans could employ the same word in their goddess of coming and thus allow to the Latin word its obvious root meaning.

Lowery misunderstood his own contradiction, for he writes that "the layman may find the range of meaning here attributed to one root something of an obstacle to acceptance of this reconstruction: achievement, supposition, habit and delight are, after all, rather a distance from seeking or desiring." Rather a small distance, we should say. And, once again, we see an old goddess at work, a lunar goddess, a pre-planet-Venus goddess at work, an Aphrodite of the Love Song of Demodocus.

Some etymologists say that the word "Venus" is of an unknown Italian origin but crept out of fertility and bucolic functions onto the skies, where it may have become a mistress of heaven but ultimately became the planet Venus, when the Greeks named their planet Aphrodite.

The Greeks have no letter "V". The letter "B" is used instead. The intermediate Greek-English Lexicon of Liddell and Scott offers only two words beginning with "ben." One is "benthos," poetical for "bathos," meaning the "depth of the sea." This is not too removed from the lunar role, for the Moon rules the night and the night seas, and was born from the sea.

The second meaning is "Bendis" which is a name of the Thracian Artemis, found in Lucian. This is more suggestive to us. For if Aeneas and the Trojans of Northwest Anatolia brought their gods with them, Bendis may have been among them; Thrace is not far away. And if Bendis is Artemis; and Artemis, we know, is the Moon; and if Bendis is a progenitor of Venus, then Venus, too, is lunar, and there is good reason to tie her to Aphrodite as Venus.

The faithful Aeneas, on this way to found settlements in Latium, that later spread to Rome, may well have founded a town in Thrace, as he did

Aphrodisia in the Southeastern Peloponnesus (Gulf of Boiai) and other settlements elsewhere. This shows not only how disorganized and turbulent were the eighth-seventh century decades of Mars-Ares, but also how Aphrodite may have come to Italy, there to become identified with Venus, who thereafter came to be identified with the later Jovian Aphrodite, which came then to be connected, in the wake of Greek insistence, with planet-Venus. We note, however, that the Aphrodite of Aeneas was she of the *Iliad* and *Odyssey,* and of the Love Affair, enemy of the Athena-Venus-Aphrodite goddess therefore and holding to the Moon in history and traits, except that now her name superficially will be taken over almost entirely by the planet Venus.

Or, as some believe, Venus may have come out of the Etruscan Pantheon, whence she may too have arrived as Bendis, for we think that the Etruscans came from Anatolia, as we shall argue later; further the island of Lemnos, between Troy and Thrace, contains Etruscan inscriptions, and, as we develop the argument, is significantly connected with Hephaestus, a principal character of the Love Affair. Aeneas was a son of Venus, that is, Aphrodite, and Romulus a son of Mars. Julius Caesar claimed the same descent.

If we did not believe that substantive connections may have existed between Aphrodite and the Moon, we should not be so concerned with demonstrating the linguistic associations. In our case, the allegation that Aphrodite was not thought to represent the Moon to the audience of Demodocus is tantamount to refusing much of the theory of this book. It is not the same as asking whether the Venus of Willendorf is really the planet Venus, or Aphrodite, or whatever; this is a conventional term invented for a class of small, crude prehistoric stone sculptures of obese females, and is little else than a playfully applied name, which we hope, will not throw our descendants into confusion a thousand years from now.

Those going before Plato knew Aphrodite as a goddess, and probably as a lunar figure, although this latter may have become subconscious. "A new ferment was introduced by the first knowledge appearing with Plato of the oriental significance of Aphrodite as a star."[27] It would seem that the Greeks, especially the astrologers among them, were now to call Hesperus and Phosphorus the stars of Aphrodite, and were thereafter to

---

[27] Pauly-Wissowa, p. 2772.

live with two sets of symbols and references intermingling and causing confusion.

There were enough similarities to permit the duplicity to endure to our day. Both were "foam-born." Further, each in her own way was "One who wanders over the foam," (Aphr-Oditi). Both were strongly female, even while male on occasion. Both were beautiful, in their own way. Often they traveled the night skies together. Whether referring to the planet or the satellite, both could be "of Aphrodite." Both might be called the "Queen of Heaven." Both had been heavily involved with Mars-Ares, and in destructive behavior with regards to Earth. Both were in the Olympian family and council of gods, one as Moon-Aphrodite, the other as Athena-Aphrodite, but who was to say or needed to say, after Hesiod's time, which heavenly body the two goddesses possessed? On the other hand, each goddess - call one of the Moon and the other of planet-Venus - owned peculiar traits that were never to be reconciled or assimilated one to the other.

The possibility that "foam-born" could be rationalized for the birth of the Planet-Venus-Aphrodite should not obscure the importance of this difference. Being foam-born from the Uranus incident means from the seed in the genital and blood foam, not a mere roughing of the waters that would occur with the passage of cometary-Aphrodite.

Another important distinction was occupational. Athena-Minerva-Ishtar-(Aphrodite) never lost her military and craftsman-like qualities. Greek and Roman warriors marched into battle led by these but not by Aphrodite. Why not Aphrodite, if she were among them? On the other hand, Aphrodite-Moon never lost her connection with the motions of the spinning complex in the domestic occupation that emulated the motions of the universe.

Yet another kind of difference persisted in the realm of love. Aphrodite-Moon generally portrayed what today's vernacular would call "straight" sexuality, while Aphrodite-Ishtar-Athena would be assigned to "kinky" sex. The former was the marrying type, the latter an independent and ambiguous lover. Eros helped Aphrodite-Moon, and Suhr has placed this child-god in the closest association with her; he helps her spin and weave to attract "straight" lovers. It is possible that Eros, though as old as Moon-Aphrodite, merged with Hesperus, the Evening Star, and carries this association as well. Eros certainly resembles the later cherubs that float around the Mother of God in Roman Catholic paintings.

The stimulation of fertility belongs to Ishtar-types as well as to Moon-Aphrodite, yet not so much so, and this must be a quantitative judgement for the moment. Virginity is a technical word and should not be confounded with the idea of concupiscence. But consider that Athena-Ishtar is celebrated for her virginity and in one startling portrait is carrying her babies in a basket. "Not only was she never in woman's womb," wrote Helene Deutsch, "but she herself apparently had no womb, for when she carried children, it was in a basket."[28] Such marsupial behavior is hardly the symbol of fertility for womankind. Planetary Aphrodite is *semper parata* like the U. S. Marines. Granted that planet-Aphrodite or Venus was once a comet that lost its tail, then the aura of sexual "kinkiness" around Athena-Ishtar-Aphrodite makes sense: bisexuality, unisexuality, technical virginity, androgyny, vestal virgins, castration - these cluster around the cometary Aphrodite and relate to the phallicized comet that loses its male organ in a sky-conflict and becomes a special type of female. She is not sexually stimulating, at least not to a conventional male. Moon-Aphrodite is more languid, less aggressive, usually "there when you need or want her." Athena and her planetary counterparts are artists appearing one moment here, the next moment gone.

The materials assembled here help us to understand that the nations at some point were observers of a great change in the sky, an implantation upon the human vision: a single body of double aspect and less terror.

A cometary Venus was greatly feared in the period 1500 to 700 B. C. and the Moon god had been heavily worshiped long before then. We will suppose, therefore, a competition of these two gods, female, for a long time before the disastrous natural events of the Eighth and Seventh centuries that involved Mars. By the process that might be called divine succession, the god of cometary Venus was the more terrible in this period of 700 year and took over a number of traits and much of the obeisance given previously to the Moon goddess. The Shaushga, Astarte, Annana, Anat, Minerva, Ishtaroth, Ishtar, Isis, and Aphrodite figures would have become largely proto-planet Venus in their connotations, orientation, and imagery. The Aphrodite idea would have moved from lunar to cometary, carrying a conglomerate of old and new traits.

---

[28] *A Psychoanalytic Study of the Myth of Dionysus and Apollo,* New York: Int'l U. Press, 1969.

When, however, the catastrophes of the Martian age reduced and confounded the pre-existing civilizations - Mycenaean, Trojan, Near-Eastern - a readjustment of the Pantheon had to occur. New relationships had to be invented within the family structure of the gods. Mars, for one, had to be granted a larger role. Proto-planet Venus was at a new peak of activity, but was apparently tamed by the god of Mars.

When the disasters subsided, the skies had to be resurveyed; a new astronomy occurred. After some decades, astronomers discovered, first, that two new bodies existed, a Morning Star and an Evening Star. The former was quickly re-identified as old cometary Venus, on a new regular and unthreatening orbit. Soon thereafter the Evening Star was declared to be the same planet-star. Then came the fateful attachment of the old names, once ambiguous and now still ambiguous, to the planet in both of its manifestations. Goddess Aphrodite once more became strongly planet Venus, with lunar attributes. With the passage of time, Aphrodite became a more ambiguous figure, because peace had settled upon the heavens; she was once again lunar, a peaceful spinner, a sensual lover. To some, psychically, she was the planet Venus; to others she was the Moon and the planet was "of Aphrodite the Moon;" to others she was the god of night and the lunar heavenly spaces. So she was a complex "herself," the goddess, rather like the Emperor of the Holy Roman Empire, which, they say, was neither "holy" nor "Roman," but he could act either way on occasion.

After all of this complicated research and reasoning, it is hard to recall ourselves to the present issue and to its vulgar denouement. The question is still, "How did the Phaeacian sailors, women, courtiers, adolescents and priests imagine the heroine of Demodocus' Love Affair?" As in a modern public opinion poll, the gravest questions of world concern have to be reduced to extremely simple questions. Here our respondents (in Phaeacia, Naxos, Athens, or Syracuse of about 650 B. C. before the Scientific Revolution of Thales *et al.*) are to be interrogated, with (I think) the following results:

> There are those who say that Aphrodite stands for the Moon (Selene)?" Do you (indicate the response closest to your opinion): agree-15%; maybe-25%, disagree-10%; no opinion or don't know-50%.

Next, of those (10%) who disagreed, the question is asked:

> Who, then, does Aphrodite stand for?" Athena-3%; Hera-5%; Hesperus-32% Phosphorus-10%, No opinion or don't know -50%.

That is, I would estimate that even on the conscious level, there is a tendency to tie Aphrodite to the Moon. The high level of unconcern and ignorance as to the question would signify that the Love Affair is making no demands of ordinary people to extract subconscious materials and bring them into consciousness. Both this figure and the 25% of "maybe's" would indicate that many persons mixed up Aphrodite with the Moon, Athena, Artemis, Hera, *et al.* I would maintain that on the subconscious level, the identification with the Moon would be much more common and intense. I have tried to describe earlier what the subconscious contained, and will try to express this subconscious mood in a later chapter.

It does not matter that elsewhere and at other times and among other people, the name Aphrodite signifies the planet Venus. Indeed we have been pleased to contribute to an understanding of her plural personality and worship. On the basis of this chapter and of other congruencies and support found throughout our work, we conclude that for the purposes of this book and in the scene of the Love Affair Aphrodite acts the role of the Moon and is so understood by the audience. Aphrodite represents the Moon in the drama and, insofar as the drama represents a memory, then Aphrodite acts out this memory.

CHAPTER NINE

THE RUINED FACE
OF A CLASSIC BEAUTY

In the *Iliad*, Aphrodite leads her wounded lover Ares off the field of battle after he is pierced by the spear of warlike Athena-Venus, and in so doing is herself struck.

The poets and historians of ancient times may have known more than we do of disasters among the planets. "That the Moon was attacked and scarred by the comet Venus was known to the Greeks and described graphically by Nonnus." So writes Peter James, and we quote the fine passage from this historian of late ancient times, Nonnus:

> "Many a time he (Typhon) took a bull at rest from his rustic plowtree and shook him with a threatening hand, bellow as he would, then shot him against the Moon like another moon, and stayed her course, then rushed hissing against the goddess, checking with the bridle her bulls' white yoke-straps, while he poured out the mortal whistle of a poison spitting viper." But Titan Mene would not yield to the attack. Battling against the Giant's heads, like-horned to hers, she carved many a scar on the shining orb of her bull's horn; and Selene's radiant

THE RUINED FACE OF A CLASSIC BEAUTY 117

cattle bellowed amazed at the gaping chasm of Typhon's throat."[1]

The fable bespeaks cosmic cyclones, where earthly and celestial effects are simultaneously visible and apparently connected by an uncontrolled raging dragon-god.

THE INNOCENT ASTRONAUTS

The Moon, as a round rock in the sky, was a manifestation of the Goddess Aphrodite. What happened to it happened to her and what happened to her, in many cases, happened to it. We turn, therefore, to geology and astrophysics and ask what, if anything, happened to the Moon in the time of Homer. The Moon is old, as all matter and energy may be said to be old - even infinitely old if one considers that "matter" and "energy" are convertible events and that neither can become space or non-being. That is not a point to be disputed.

The question is whether the Moon, as a chemical agglomerate, pursued its present set of motions at the time of which Homer wrote. Moreover, was its chemistry the same after that time as it was before?

The moon is enveloped by a crust of igneous anorthosite to the depth of 35 kilometers, "which must have resulted from melted rock of at least twice that depth."[2] Lunar rocks were discovered to have undergone heating and bubbling, probably more recently. A large part of the soil consisted of tiny glass spheres, probably resulting from the evaporation of boiled lunar rock that collapsed back upon condensation in the cold. Some trace of organic, aromatic hydrocarbons were found in lunar sample returned by the astronauts of Apollo XI. Carbide rocks were found on the lunar surface. Rocks of the moon also revealed magnetic properties, a remanent magnetism that could not have been implanted by the moon's own weak magnetic field and certainly not at any time since the rocks solidified from a molten or gaseous state. The equipment implanted on the moon by astronauts of Apollo XII returned to its monitors on earth a record of moonquakes, averaging one a day. Lunar

---

[1] *Dionysiaca,* I, 213-23, trans. W. M. D. Rouse (Loeb Library).

[2] Neil P. Ruzie, "The case for Returning to the Moon," *Industrial Research* (July, 1973), pp. 48-54, p. 51.

rocks were found to be rich in argon and neon; the larger the ratio of surface to mass, that is, the smaller the rock particle, the more of these gases was contained in it, leading to the conclusion that the source of the gases was external. Some unusually radioactive "hot spots" were observed.

It thus appears likely that the Moon experienced devastating events within a period of time into which the Love Affair might have fallen. Conventional theorists of lunar history have been relieved of a number of expectations, founded on the belief in a three to four billion years old object that, since then, "has been a remarkably quiet body suffering only the occasional large meteorite impact. Subsequent modification of the surface features has been mainly erosion due to the impact of small meteorites, cosmic rays, and particles from the sun. This is in great contrast with the earth's history which has been one of continued volcanic and mountain-building activity up to the present day."[3]

RADIOACTIVE CLOCKS

Nowadays, such statements are not to be heard. It is difficult to conceive how such could even have been written in 1972 in view of the lunar quakes and the other discoveries recited two paragraphs above. But the author of the quotation, Derek York, was holding fast to what others were telling him about the general situation and was supporting his faith by work that he had been hired as a specialist to do: radioactive clockwork. He used three clocks: the uranium-lead, the rubidium-strontium, and the potassium-argon methods of determining the ages of rock samples picked up and returned to Earth by the astronauts.

York offered, against Velikovsky's proposition of a recently molten lunar surface, alternative explanations based on the fact that all three tests showed the lunar surface to have been last molten 3.6 billion years ago at least. In each case, a determination of the amount of the first chemical element that radioactively decayed into the second element was used to estimate age, since physicists believe that we know the rate of such transmutation and can rely on its constancy over all conceivable

---

[3] Derek York, "Lunar Rocks and Velikovsky's Claims," II *Pensée* no. 2(May 1972), p. 18.

time spans. York therefore argued that either

> (a) this part of Velikovsky's thesis is wrong. (b) Velikovsky is right but the four Apollo landings and the Soviet Luna 16 landings were in areas which escaped the 'catastrophes' referred to by Velikovsky. (c) There is something seriously wrong with the radioactive clocks or our reading of them.

In reply, Velikovsky cited two additional "commonsense" tests in his favor. Geologist examining the samples of Apollo XI recorded "the extremely fresh appearance of the interior of all crystalline rocks, in spite of their microfractures and high potassium-argon age."[4] Moreover, noting a widespread *glazing* of the lunar surface, T. Gold, writing in *Science* had conjectured upon "a giant solar outburst in geologically recent times" that glazed lunar surfaces less than 30,000 years ago."[5]

Velikovsky mentioned here yet another prediction of his, earlier in time, that gained in validity when the Apollo 15 team discovered that the outflow of heat below the surface was almost three times greater than expected by those who believed that the moon originated gaseous and then became molten: those who thought the moon had always been thoroughly cold could make nothing of this internal heat at all.

Specifically with regard to the challenge of the tests, Velikovsky argued that lunar rocks would be argon-rich (and therefore seem very old) because they would have captured, while molten, some of the argon of the atmosphere of Mars. (In 1974, Russian reports spoke of a Martian atmosphere of argon in the 10th of percent.)[6] As for the reading of the uranium-lead test, the explorers had apparently sampled rocks not only poor in lead but in all *volatile* elements: bismuth, cadmium, thallium, indium, etc. He surmised, therefore, that the volatile elements had escaped their rock housings in a period of high heat and melting, such as the episode in Homer that occupies our attention.

The third radioactive clock appears to be the most absurd of the three, since rubidium vaporizes and migrates from its housing with strontium even under the conditions of present-day temperatures of the lunar day (+ 150 degrees Celsius) and the continuous bombardment of surface rocks by hydrogen ions from the solar wind. A period of

---

[4] "When Was The Lunar Surface Last Molten," II *Pensée,* no. 2,(May 1972), p. 19.

[5] *Ibid.*

[6] James B. Pollack, "Mars," 233 *Scientific American* (Sept. 1975), p. 110.

electrically and gravitationally induced heating such as occurred in the Love Affair would have greatly reduced the rubidium present in the tested rocks. Velikovsky and Wright[7] are not alone in their criticism of these tests. We cannot close these brief passages without referring to the brilliant critique offered of these and other clocks by Melvin Cook in his book, *Prehistory and Earth Models* 1966. In brief, what York regarded as impossible was true. "There is something seriously wrong with the radioactive clocks..."[8]

The one test that Velikovsky asked for was to determine the degree of thermoluminescence of lunar surface cores extracted at about three feet of depth to avoid contamination of the test by the effects of normal solar heat. The more the time that passes after a heat-up of over 150 degrees Celsius, the more luminescence is stored and given off in a laboratory re-heating. When the tests were performed on cores gathered by Apollo XII between 4 and 13 centimeters underground, it showed "anomalies resulting from disturbances 10,000 years ago." Such disturbances had to be thermal, that is, events of great heat upon the moon. Velikovsky thought that increased radioactivity may have promoted a quick-aging effect on even this test and suggests sampling from sites that are least radioactive.

We return now to the problem of the remanent magnetism in the rock samples brought back from all Apollo missions. Velikovsky's theory of the Mars-Moon encounters required that such fossil magnetism be traceable in the rocks, and it was found. Robert Treat has written the history of the affair, from which we quote:

> Scientific deliberations grew in intensity after the third (Apollo IV), and the fourth (Apollo XV) missions testified to the bewilderment of astrophysicists. It transpired that sometime in the past the moon must have been heated in the presence of a strong magnetic field. The best guess was: 'It is a thermoremanent magnetism acquired when the specimen cooled in the presence of a magnetic field.' Other possibilities were weighted. Was the inducing field due to a close approach of the moon to the earth? "In this model the hard remanence suggests a distance of closest approach of 2 to 3 earth radii," But this is 'an uncomfortable proximity to the Roche limit....' The moon would have been broken into pieces if it ever approached the earth so closely. Another team of scientists found that the magnetization "shows a well defined curie temperature at 775 degrees Celsius": the lunar surface must have been heated above this

---

[7] Also in *Pensée* (May 1972), loc. cit.

[8] *Ibid.*, p. 21

temperature in the presence of a magnetic field and must have cooled off thereafter.[9]

Surface marring, "hot spots" of radioactivity, high past heat, and encounter with another large celestial body spell devastation. Fresh-looking rock, high thermoluminescence levels, "hot spots" seismic movement, and below surface heat spell *recency*.

The "recency" suggested by our interpretation of the explorations of the moon is "under 10,000 years." The world-wide historical and legendary record strongly indicates about 2,700 years. There is good reason, therefore, after having passed the 10,000 year barrier, to proceed without hesitation to the 2,700-year point.

THE RILLES OF MOON

The recent devastation of the Moon is the subject of an analysis also by Ralph Juergens.[10] He focused especially upon its hundreds of wavy rilles, its canyons and its craters. The craters are sites of explosions. Some, like Aristarchus, are still warm. The rilles cleave the surface and often seem to feed into the craters, going up-ground to do so with whatever they might once have carried. The craters seem to have exploded after the rilles reached them, since debris obscures the ends of the rilles.

Juergens examinations of the rilles shows that they cannot have been produced by water erosion; they flow uphill and have no deltas. Nor can they have been produced from the collapse of underground tubes that once carried lava; for the margins of the rilles reveal upturned strata and empty bottoms; Nor can gas explosions have created the rilles, for they are exceedingly tortuous; and they are not vented holes. Only electrical currents, declares Juergens, could produce the jagged trenches. The currents erupt, heat up the land and excavate it, and cause secondary melting in the rille valleys. They move as streamers upwards. A return

---

[9] "Magnetic Remanence of Lunar Rocks: A Candid Look at Scientific Misbehavior," II *Pensée*, no. 2 (May, 1972), p. 21-2.

[10] "Electrical Discharges and the Transmutation of Elements," IV *Pensée* 3, (1974), pp. 45-6; "Of the Moon and Mars, Part I," IV Pensee 4 (1974), pp. 21-30.

stroke explodes the ground and creates a crater.

What caused the rilles to erupt and the craters to burst? On the basis of his general theory of the electrical nature of the solar system, to be explained later, Juergens posits that Mars and Earth-Moon each held (and hold) massive electrical charges of negative valence. These charges, on the close approach of the bodies, repel each other. But if the bodies are approaching with great momentum, the repulsion is not sufficient to divert them entirely. The charges are driven to accommodate. By "accommodation" is meant that, if there is any possibility of a reversal of charges on one or both bodies, the negative electrons will "flee" from each other. Assuming that Mars, with an atmosphere, and a larger surface, more readily permitted its electrons to flee to regions far removed from the nearest points of contact, positive ions would congregate and set up an anode-cathode relationship, that is, a situation matured for an exchange of thunderbolts. The rilles ditches erupted by a rapidly moving and charge-accumulating current. Craters are the spots where the exchange of opposite charges, attracted for discharge, occurred, usually at prominences of the two bodies. A map of the major rilles of the moon shows a concentration of them in the general area of the great crater, Aristarchus. Emanations of radon-222, whose parent element is radium-226, were detected from Aristarchus. The rays are several times more intense there than in areas farther removed, indicating a local source. Radium 226 isotopes decay rapidly. In 1620 years, half the element is transmutated; that is, it has a half-life of 1620 years. "If the radium were produced by an electric discharge to the Aristarchus site some 2700 years ago, more than 25% of it would still be there, emitting radon -222."[11] Lightning strokes of 100 billion volts can constitute a high-energy projectile capable of creating heavy elements such as radium-226.

It should also be pointed out that visible light, as well as heat, has been observed from time to time, from Aristarchus and other sources. Again, a sign of recency.

Glass found that glass ejecta along the banks of the Hadley Rille and procured by the astronauts of the Apollo 15 and 17 expeditions exhibited significant peculiarities in comparison with other moon glasses. Tests on one sample showed that cooling rates of 1000 F/sec. were necessary to

---

[11] Juergens, "Electrical Discharges...," *op. cit.,* pp. 45-6.

form the glass. The researchers considered the possibility that volcanic eruption might have caused the glass to form, but the cooling rate was too fast. So they conjectured meteoritic impacts. However, for meteorites, the glasses are too uniform and are not splashed or shattered. Furthermore, meteorites would not line themselves up along a rille valley, if such is the case here. Juergens conclusion is acceptable.[12] The glass is a product of an electrical current that melts instantaneously, explodes simultaneously, and withdraws its heat immediately along the meandering course of the rille before streaming upwards from the ground at the end of the rille.

The surprises that the Moon holds for scientists are not ended. Because of the nonexistence or prior extirpation of life forms that would have ingested radioactive carbon, there appear to be no possibilities of applying Carbon 14 tests to Moon material. Still, the electrical mechanical behavior of the Moon and Moon-space are coming to be better understood. The Moon's several spherical asymmetries deserve pondering. Unmanned excavating apparatus may bring back more material for analysis. Moreover, ancient records and myths are still largely unanalyzed.

The "beauty of raiment" with which the Graces "clothe her body" and the "refulgent ointment" with which they anointed the Moon, once her love affair with Mars was ended, may refer to a shift to a position nearer Earth; the month of 29.5 days replaced a longer month.[13] Greater brilliance indicates that the change was in orbital radius, rather than in orbital speed.

It is also possible that the lines of Homer may be a reference to a chain of colorful low mountains whose origin has baffled astrophysicists. Juergens has suggested that, if the theory of electrical discharges is credible, the explanation of these anomalous protuberances may lay in a simple and surprising theory of cosmic welding.[14] They are Martian material electrically heated and exploded, which fastened electrically upon the surface of the Moon.

To the wishful eyes of men, women, and children of the eighth and

---

[12] "Of The Moon..," *op. cit.,* pp. 27-8.

[13] Velikovsky, *Worlds in Collision,* pp. 342-4.

[14] In a communication to the author, October 1973.

seventh century, Aphrodite emerged more beautiful than ever from her escapade with Mars. Perhaps it grew less lovely thereafter, for Plutarch was speaking of its craggy appearance seven centuries later.[15] The astronauts and geophysicists of today have to report the disillusioning fact that the face of the classical beauty was ruined.

---

[15] "The Face of the Moon."

CHAPTER TEN

HE WHO SHINES BY DAY

Not satisfied with setting up the production of the Love Affair, Athena, the virtuoso of Olympia, must play a leading role in it. Will it be masculine? Athena has been known to play such roles. Actually, she ends the *Odyssey* playing the male role of Mentor, Counselor of State. By now we know that gods can readily become transvestites. Hercules, for all his impressive masculinity, dresses and behaves like a woman when he lives at the court of Omphale, Queen of Libya. More strikingly there is the beautiful Aphrodite who sports a beard as the so-called Cyprian Aphrodite.

A *major* role is intended. In the Love Affair, there is only one such role for her that is logical: that is Hephaestus. Athena, the goddess of the Planet Venus is Hephaestus, also the planet Venus. No one appears to have said so, but the evidence is strong to that effect.

Velikovsky and the scholars associated with him have presented evidence that Pallas Athene was the god of the planet Venus, that the planet appeared in the sky sometime before 1500 B. C., that she behaved as a comet, traveled on an eccentric orbit that brought her perilously close to Earth, and that around 1500 B. C. and on several other occasions caused tremendous destruction here. The foundations or refounding of the city of Athens may be of this date,[1] just as those of Rome were concurrent with the raging appearance in the skies of the planet-god Mars 700 years later. References from a number of cultures lead one to believe that, as the Greek theogony put it, Athena sprang from Zeus fully-armed with a shout.

> Athena sprang quickly from the immortal head and stood before Zeus who holds the aegis, shaking a sharp spear: great Olympus began to reel horribly at the might of the bright-eyed goddess, and earth round about cried fearfully, and the sea was moved and tossed with dark waves, while foam burst forth suddenly; the bright Son of Hyperion stopped his swift-footed horses a long while, until the maiden Pallas Athene had stripped the heavenly armor from her immortal shoulders.[2]

Hephaestus, some said, had to split Jove's aching head with an ax to help him give birth.

THE EPITHETS OF VENUS

Velikovsky, James and others offer numerous connections between Planet Venus and Pallas Athena through analogies of birth, traits and deeds. They further offer persuasive cross-identifications of Athena and Planet-Venus with the corresponding divinities of the same planet from other cultures, among them the Hebrew, Egyptian, Babylonian, Chinese, Mexican, and American Indian.

Graves, for example, lays out in detail the material on Pallas, whose primary myth-ensemble is as foster-sister to Athena. Pallas means simply "youth" or "maiden." Athena and Pallas were raised on the shores of Lake Triton in Africa. While playing at armed combat Athena

---

[1] Stecchini, *op. cit.*, p. 145. The destruction of Thera-Santorini about 1100 B. C. would have overwhelmed the Attic shores, even if it had occurred as a solitary catastrophe (Cf. S. Marinatos, whose writings on the subject began on Minoan Crete, XIII *Antiquity* (1939), p. 425); Velikovsky interprets the myth of Solon concerning Atlantis as occurring around 1500 B. C. (W in C, pp. 146-8). Plato refers to Athens after Atlantis as a remnant civilization, peopled by illiterate survivors. I believe that Solon's Atlantis was sunk about 4000 B. C., but that Plato, not knowing of the disasters of 1500 B. C., telescoped the two catastrophes in his mind, and made them more ethnocentrically Athenian.

[2] "Hymn to Athena" XXVIII.

accidentally killed Pallas. In grief, she placed the name Pallas before her own. The incident is symbolic of the world tragedy of that time. An immense Saharan lake, called Triton by the ancients, suddenly disappeared, leaving a great desert and some marshes, with the dry beds of rivers and streams. A flourishing civilization subsided with the lake, a civilization that perhaps dominated the Mediterranean and surely represented a pre-Hellenic, matriarchal culture, whose women wore the same garments and aegis of Athena, even down through many centuries following the catastrophe.

The destruction provoked and wrought by Planet Venus probably encompassed in North Africa not only the Egypt of the Exodus but the recently explored Saharan "Libyan" culture. And if, as Velikovsky argues convincingly, Phaeton, which plunged somewhere along the longitude of the Red Sea, was a part of Comet-Venus, Planet-to-be, then Pallas was the earthly destructive force of comet Venus in North Central Africa. Stecchini, from his studies of the architectural measurements of the Parthenon, the crowning temple of the Virgin Athena on the Acropolis of Athens, offers a confirmation. The Temple was erected in the glorious late period of empire. The Athenians, subconsciously true to remote history, set their Pallas Athena pediment facing directly and accurately towards the marshes of present-day Tunisia, and portrayed on the pediment the birth of Pallas Athena.[3]

In the manner of legend, an alternative myth is offered. "Some Hellenes say that Athena had a father named Pallas, a winged goatish giant, who later attempted to outrage her, and whose name she added to her own after stripping him of skin to make the aegis, and of his wings for her own shoulders..."[4] Hardly a "maiden" and hardly a maidenly reprisal. Perhaps, as Graves suggests, the myth came from an ancient story of one of Athena's many combats. But, more interested in what force can have carried this underground myth, we would suggest that this "fake Pallas" is a diabolic representation of Zeus; the physical contacts of Athena with the Father of Gods are numerous. And humans, as already argued, have ways of getting back at the gods who caused them so much fear and suffering.

"Pallas" may also designate Athena as a comet before it lost its

---

[3] Telephone communication of October, 1973.

[4] Graves, I, ch. 9, p. 45.

appendage. Visually and astronomically, it should be recalled that everyone speaks of the "tail" of a comet, whereas this "tail" sometimes moves in directions parallel to the "head" and "coma." The ancients often were excited by the image of the comet "tail" as a phallus. Hence Athena would be phallus-Athena before Pallas was destroyed and she became a proto-planet without a penis. In Sanskrit, palas means Phallus. The altars of Athena were called Palladia, as at Troy. The dropping of the "ph" (j) sound takes away the sexual "fire."

One would proceed farther. The "goatish giant" who attempted to outrage her has additional dimensions. He may stand for Hephaestus who, in another legend, attempted to rape Athena at his smithy and was repulsed. So that Athena's killing of this monster corresponds to the professed Hellenic triumph over the powerful proto-mediterranean religious culture. The mythic mind can support this idea along with the contradictory apotheosis of Athena as the ideal castrating female of psychoanalytic theory.

Hephaestus has a resemblance to the Etruscan smith-god and death-demon, Tuchulcha, who dispatches people with a giant hammer. Tuchulcha is assisted by a winged demon with snakes,[5] So that the composite suggests a god-monster like Typhon, a devastating winged dragon who, like Seth and Lucifer is sent crashing into the underground, there to fulfill his destiny.

The Love Affair lends support to the quadrilateral relationship: Hephaestus/Tuchulcha: Greeks/Etruscans. There one hears Demodocus singing that the cherished home-island of Hephaestus was Lemnos. Also, he has Ares speaking disrespectfully of Hephaestus having left to join his barbarous-speaking Sintians of Lemnos. (By "barbarous" is probably meant non-Greek.) Now recently some inscriptions found on Lemnos have been identified as Etruscan,[6] even though they are not yet deciphered. Etruscan has been connected also with Hittite and Minoan (Linear A) by Barry Fell.[7] New information has appeared, too, placing Etruscan relatives in the area at the same time as the Love Affair. These people of Lake Van are not only culturally close

---

[5] See Dennis, *Cities and Cemeteries of Etruria*, II, frontispiece.

[6] Patroni, 6 *Commenti Mediterranei all'Odissea di Omero* (Milano: Marzorati, 1950) p. 244, fn. 3; Cambridge Ancient History, Vol. II (1973).

[7] Occasional Publ., Epigraphic Society, Vol. 4, no. 77 (Sept. 1977), Harvard University.

but close in blood types to the Etruscans.[8] The Etruscans feared and were obsessed by this Hephaestus-Tuchulcha. They offered human sacrifices frequently: the planet Venus, says Nicolo Rilli, was a favored object of such bloody supplications.[9]

It will be a long time before the identities of the gods of one and all cultures are clarified. The sublimation of God requires a smokescreen of confusion and the allocation of ambivalence. If a god has been given too much of good, a balancing evil is allocated, and vice versa. The interplay of names and epithets is part of this process, but more unconsciously, the neural equivalents must function. Basically such is the meaning of the practically universal theological belief: "God cannot exist without the Devil."

Athena was a "glorious goddess, bright-eyed, inventive, unbending of heart, pure virgin, savior of cities."[10] She was brilliantly beautiful, a great warrior; she enjoyed the confidence of Zeus to an extent unequaled by any other god. In the *Iliad* (iv, 74), she sweeps down upon the Trojan plain like "a shooting star," trailing fire. She was furthermore the most creative god, mother of invention, teacher of the arts and sciences. It is bizarre that we should find her the female counterpart of Hephaestus. But that she was, of course, an evil destroyer as well, emerges from many an earlier description. She was, in the Greek mind, a desexualized good-bad mother. Many deeds ascribed to her directly and indirectly would make lame and slow Hephaestus appear quite harmless and capable of exciting laughter of a grim sort. She in fact, as a planet, broke up the Jovian order of the universe and kept it in confusion until the eighth century, when Zeus, through Homer's and Hesiod's work, deserved to the full his reputation as the law-giver. At least so far as Greek myth was concerned, and we cannot go farther here.

CONGENITALITY & HOMOLOGY

---

[8] G. A. Wainwright, "The Teresh, the Etruscans, and Asia Minor," IX *Anatolian Studies*.

[9] Conversation with the author, 1966. Cf. his *Gli Etruschi a Sesto Fiorentino* (Firenze: Tipografia Giuntina, 1964), where the Etruscan obsessions with lightning, flood, and fire are treated.

[10] Homeric "Hymn to Athena," no. xxviii.

> Athena's birth from Zeus is expressly related to the birth of Hephaestus. A quarrel between Zeus and Hera had been mentioned in what preceded the fragment (of Chrysippus), and in consequence of this quarrel, Hera gave birth to Hephaestus without Zeus' aid, and Zeus lay with Metis and swallowed her. But she conceived Athena, and Zeus gave birth through his head. That Hephaestus' birth was a complement to Athena's, and connected with a quarrel between Zeus and Hera, is also implied in (Hesiod's) *Theogony* (924-9), but the logical order of events has been destroyed.

So writes West in his *Commentary on Hesiod's Theogony* (pp. 401-3). We need not agree that Metis was the mother of Athena, because Athena is not only called *parthenos* (virgin) but also *parthenogenous* (the offspring of a single sex).

West (with others) suspects that the quarrel may have arisen over the capacities of the sexes. Hera and Zeus disagreed concerning whether man or woman achieved more pleasure in sexual intercourse. Teiresias, called to arbitrate, declared that the pleasure is woman's in the ratio of ten to one. Hera, a poor loser, blinded Teiresias and Zeus gave him the gift of prophesy as a consolation. Then each defied the other and gave birth parthenogenously. Hera to Hephaestus, Zeus to Athena. In a striking parallel, Hera also bore parthenogenously the monster Typhon, who was also sent crashing to Earth by Zeus.[11]

Plato has Critias (109 b-d) declaring that Hephaestus and Athena are of the same father. They are of the same nature. "In the days of old the Gods shared out the earth among themselves... Hephaestus and Athena, for instance, being brother and sister... obtained this our land as their joint portion... They raised its aboriginal population to the status of a great nation." It was protocatastrophic Attica, much larger in extent, before the disasters that ended an epoch. When Poseidon (god of deluges and waters and chief god of Atalanta, the Moon) struggled to possess Attica, he had to contend with both Hephaestus and Athena.

We find in Robert Graves' *The Greek Myths* these words:

> Hephaestus and Athene shared temples at Athens, and his name, if it does not stand for *hemerophaistos*, 'he who shines by day' (i. e. the sun), is perhaps a masculine for *he apaista* (shortened in Stesichorus: *Fragment 97* to *aista*), 'the goddess who removes from sight,' namely Athene, the original inventor of all

---

[11] Slater, *The Story of Hera and the Greek Family*, (1968) p. 130; see Apollodorus i, 3, 5; Homeric Hymns to Apollo; Hesiod, *Theogony* 924-5.

mechanical arts.[12]

Graves, like most authors upon whom we depend, did not ascribe *real* celestial behavior to the gods and demigods, planetary or otherwise. When a celestial reference is forced upon Athena, the Sun or Moon or other bodies are called upon. This has resulted in the Sun, workaday Helios, being elevated to a divine status such as he never achieved in the minds of the ancients. If the minds of scholars had not been embraced by uniformitarian principles, that is, the ideology of science of the nineteenth and early twentieth century, they might have asked, as for instance in this case, why "shining by day" should be the exclusive prerogative of Helios or, at least, why bother to name a god by this trait which is so ordinary and expected? Every ordinary thing shines by day as well.

A nearby cometary body, meteorite, or planet, especially if it is incandescent, as was Athena (Hephaestus), will shine like the sun, and supplement the brilliance of the day to a painful degree until clouds intervene, mercifully in some cases, destructively in others if they shower down red waters, brimstone, ashes, and noxious gases. She and he have a habit of disappearing. They blind humans; and they cover up deeds. Both are great dissemblers.

As for the alternative base of his name, we can rephrase what was just said: His name again would be a name of Athena, for the action implied is the beclouding of the human vision. Who might shine brilliantly and also block vision - contrasting behaviors? A cometary intruder in the skies is one answer, and there are not very good alternative answers, especially when the details of both behaviors are collected. An enormous volcano will shine brilliantly in the daytime as it erupts, and afterward darken the vision of humans. But one volcano does not inspire a whole people in communication over thousands of miles to create a major god. Hephaestus is, for that matter, god of volcanoes and fire, but this is not his sole or even major life-activity.

Graves reports (I, 51-2) that Hephaestus seems to have been the title of the sacred king as solar demi-god. We have alluded to the former; for "solar" we insist upon "Venusian," because the sacred kings of the ancient Mediterranean flourished concurrently with Cretan and Minoan civilizations and were both well-remembered and hated as an institution

---

[12] Vol. I, p. 87; 23: 1; cf. I, 393.

by the misogynist Hellenes, for whom kings were not to be periodically set up and sacrificed by queens.

Hephaestus ruled with Athena over the realm of arts and crafts.

> Sing, clear-voiced muse, of Hephaestus famed for inventions. With bright-eyed Athene he taught men glorious crafts throughout the world - men who before used to dwell in caves in the mountains like wild beasts.[13]

"Athena was frequently linked with Hephaestus, as in the simile in which a comparison is drawn with a goldsmith, 'a skillful man whom Hephaestus and Pallas Athena taught all kinds of craft (techne).'"[14] Hephaestus was the Smith-god,[15] suggests Graves, to be found in many distinct cultures. We understand that Hephaestus is a technical genius, like Athena. He is more circumscribed; he is a Master Electrician, a fabricator of thunderbolts. Often he is portrayed as lame; sometimes the smiths were lames, says Graves to prevent their wandering far from their proprietary city. This is all very well. We recognize the need for towns to retain their smiths, even as we recognize[16] that the smith was one of the few "strangers" to be invariably welcomed in their wanderings, along with poets.

However, one must acknowledge that just as there are sacred kings who are put to death annually, there may be "sacred smiths" who have to be lamed in order that they behave like the god whose skills they possess. "Smith-god" surrogates, like "sacred kings," were also anciently killed in sacrifice, every 20 years, says Graves, to correspond with a solar-lunar calendar conjunction; we are entitled to question whether it may be a Venus-Moon conjunction, the 20 years being a playback of time of modern calendar reckoning, but we find no grounds presently to challenge the periodicity and its source.

Which leads us to the general problem of the lameness of Hephaestus, the god and the Planet. There is more than one legend of the source of his disability.

---

[13] Homeric Hymns, no. XX, in the Loeb edition of Hesiod. The "men" referred to are possibly the catastrophized victims of this same pair 700 years earlier.

[14] M. I. Finley, *The World of Odysseus* (Middlesex, England: Penguin Books, 1954, 1967, 1972) citing *Odyssey,* 6, 232-4.

[15] *The Greek Myths,* I, 51-2.

[16] Cf. Finley.

One legend would have it that Hera chose a monster to conceive of Hephaestus and, naturally, the offspring was ugly and deformed. So she cast it from heaven.

A second is that Hephaestus defended his mother, Hera, for leading a revolt against Zeus and Zeus cast him from Mount Olympus to Earth, crippling him. Here we find Hephaestus as the monster, Typhon, that part of Athena the planet that was struck by a thunderbolt of Zeus while it was wreaking destruction upon Earth, and crashed, some say near the Red Sea, others say upon what is now the Sahara, burning and drying up the area and pushing the waters of the Great Lake Triton into the ocean.

To pursue the parallel, instead of the monster Typhon, it was Hephaestus who came crashing down and, presumably, he picked himself up, physically the worse for the experience, and rejoined the Olympian party of gods when the father of the gods graced him with his pardon. Vase paintings show Hephaestus mounted upon a mule (symbol of sexual barrenness), plodding back up to Heaven, escorted by Bacchus (Dionysus), satyrs, and bacchantes.

Both descents of Hephaestus-Athena from the skies precede Homeric times by 700 years. Krates of Pergamon explains that Zeus was determining the measure of the universe by means of "two torches moving with the same speed:" the Sun from east to west, and Hephaestus from Olympus to Lemnos. Hephaestus struck Earth as the sun was setting. The measure of a new age of the world was taken.[17] Graves points out that Hephaestus has affinities with Prometheus,[18] Talos, Daedalus, Icarus, and Minos.[19]

Graves further illuminates the emerging picture in giving us further details of the birth of Athena Tritongeneia. "As Zeus walked by Lake Triton [the great Saharan Lake that disappeared]", say the priestesses of Athene, "he was seized by a headache and he howled until all heaven echoed. Hermes ran up, divined the cause, and persuaded Hephaestus (or possibly Prometheus) to take a wedge and beetle and make a breach

---

[17] Giorgio di Santillana and Hertha von Dechand, *Hamlet's Mill* (Boston: Gambit, inc., 1969), pp. 273-4; cf. 73-4. This book contains on page 272 a design from ancient China showing twin deities, male and female, dragon footed, surrounded by constellations and carrying a plumb bob, square, and compass, reproduced in *Chaos and Creation* and *Solaria Binaria*.

[18] Graves, *The Greek Myths,* I, 149.

[19] *Ibid.,* 1, 315-6, 172.

in Zeus' skull, from which Athene sprang, fully armed, with a mighty shout."[20] So Hephaestus was involved in Athena's birth.

Hephaestus has enough reason to be lamed. However, a marvel of myth, like creative works in general, is that several levels of meaning can be simultaneously conveyed, both consciously and unconsciously. If Athena is a virgin, and ushered in legions of virgins in many parts of the world (as Peter Tompkins relates in *The Virgin and the Eunuch,* citing the Vestal Virgins of Rome, among others), not to mention their contraries, the sacred harlots of the temples, then how would Hephaestus portray the analogous quality? By being a eunuch, a *castrato,* one would reply. But a god, not, in any event, a Homeric Hellenic god, could not suffer this indignity unless, like Ouranos, he was Deus Otiosus, that is, permanently removed from the scene.

The lameness, we are bound to suggest, was a genital lameness. To match Athena, Hephaestus had to be unsexed. The crippled feet would represent this to the unconscious. Psychoanalysts find such to be the case in their analyses of dreams. We note again how Hephaestus in pictured riding a mule, a barren animal, on his way back to heaven after his fall. Also, the Roman Hephaestus is Vulcan; Vulcan is represented by several Roman authors in the form of a phallus in the hearthfire,[21] an image that joins together Hephaestus' fire, and the comet's severed phallus-tail.

Slater stresses not so much the idea of Hephaestus' lameness as a symbolic castration but "what might be called his 'interpersonal' self-castration. By this I mean his withdrawal from the lists of sexual and marital rivalry, his role of clown - in a sense, his resignation from manhood."[22] Consistently, he is rejected both by Zeus and Hera, for he was also cast into the sea by his mother, Hera.

Now again, one may ask about the marriage of Hephaestus and his famous marriage bed, that four-posted imitation of the four-pillared sky he was wont to occupy with Aphrodite in the Love Affair. It was on the

---

[20] *Ibid.,* p. 46.

[21] Ovid, *Fasti VI,* 627; Pliny, 36.70; Ling, I, 39; Plutarch, *Lives,* Rom., 2; Pauly-Wissowa, *Realenzyklopädie* article on Tullius, Ocrisia, Tarchetius; Frazer, *Golden Bough;* II, 198; O. Gruppe, Griech-Mythologie (1906), p. 1311. (Citations kindly supplied by the late Dr. Z. Rix, Jerusalem.)

[22] *The Story of Hera: Greek Mythology and the Greek Family* (1958), p.130.

instigation of Zeus, once, perhaps as a bad practical joke, that Hephaestus when Athena arrived to be fitted for a fine suit of armor, made the amorous advances upon her, which she repulsed. Apart from marking a further association of these two parthenogenous gods, mulishly incapable of offspring, the tale stresses Hephaestus' unluckiness in love. Aphrodite is his "better half," fully sexed, unlike Athena; he wants her (the Moon) but also rejects her, for he cannot cope with her.

Aphrodite has not been known to copulate with him recently, although in a dim past there was a marriage and contacts resembling sexual relations. But now, in the Love Affair, the bed is cold. Aphrodite's children come from others, including especially Ares. Hephaestus may be the indignant husband, but he is impotent in sexual affairs and it is perhaps because of this empty show of dignity that the gods Apollo and Hermes laugh.

Hephaestus' advances upon Athena were strangely fruitful, says another account. As he gazed at Athena, he ejaculated and his seed fell upon Gaia, "the Earth," from whom Erichthonios (Auriga) was born. Athena succored the infant when Gaia rejected him. He was half-man and half-serpent; later on he became King of Athens and instituted her worship.[23] Once more we find interconnected Athena-Hephaestus - sexual incapacities, the serpent Typhon, destruction visited upon Gaia, and the Athens connection. Dr. Z. Rix of Jerusalem, a medical doctor and mythologist, writes me on January 26, 1975, that:

> "Hephaestus is the primordial father whom Freud recognized again and again in his patients' dreams. He is cometary Venus who struck by Jupiter's lightning fell from heaven. Many mythological narratives recount the event of Lucifer's, Phaeton's, and Typhon's (the Egyptian devil's) fall. It is comprehensible that the onlookers wished that the forbidding figure should lose its tail - conceived as male attribute - with which it threatened to annihilate the whole population of the earth."

Again, Dr. Rix calls my attention to the deity, Nephthys (in Egypt, Nebti), who is wife and sister of Typhon. She is the seashores: Typhon is the sea, according to the ancient Egyptians. This same Nephthys is pictured in various Egyptian sources[24] together with Isis (the Egyptian Athena), lifting the sun-ship at dawn. Surely this is additional evidence

---

[23] *Ibid.,* p. 264; Graves, I, 25b, c, d, 1, 2. Erichthonios means "wool-strife-earth" or, possibly, "from the land of heather," but the heather-country meaning may picture the former meaning.

[24] Cf. Pauly-Wissowa, "Nephthys," Vol 53, p. 100.

of the connection Athena-Hephaestus, corresponding to Nephthys-Typhon. Herodotus mentions that there were numerous temples to Hephaestus in Egypt.

At the same time, such is the overlapping that readily occurs in the memory of the gods as the ages pass, that foam-born Aphrodite later is said to be created, not by Uranus, as we assert, but by the seed of the drowned Typhon that becomes the salt-foam of the sea. Now one may perceive how some confusion between Athena-Aphrodite-Urania and Aphrodite-Planet Venus arose: the former sprang out of the sea earlier from the fallen member of Uranus; the latter arose later from the seed of the fallen Python. Probably the new myth was grafted upon the old.

On still another level of suggestibility is the profile that the hobbling smith in the sky would provide. It is easy to see in many artifacts the shapes that celestial bodies like meteors and comets take. Nevertheless it may be of some value to mention that a comet in a typical apparition is an angel with wings and flowing gown, a head with horns, a helmeted head (Athena), a long-haired one (coma means hair in Greek), a phallus with testes, and even a head with two massive arms - "Hephaestus of the two strong arms," Murray translates the phrase, and then, curiously, notes that other scholars translate the phrase as "Hephaestus of the lame legs." We wonder at the possible original sight of the mighty-armed bronze-smith trailing his feeble legs like the tail of the comet, and at the etymology that could cause such an alternative construction. In connection with the language of the Love Affair, to be treated below, additional symbolic issues will be discussed.

Finally there is the sentence: "The slow catches the swift; even as now Hephaestus, slow though he is, has outstripped Ares for all that he is the swiftest of the gods who hold Olympus. Lame though he is, he has caught him by craft." Once more the synchronization of reality into a plausible plot seems incredible. To take part in the cosmic drama, as it probably occurred, Hephaestus (as Planet-Venus) would make his planetary approaches at a great distance and behind Moon and Mars, which would put him actually a half-million miles distant from the pair with a gravitational-electrical effect sufficient to repel the Earth's magnetic envelope and cause their liberation. Under the circumstances, Hephaestus would move with apparent slowness, and would, *mirabile dictu,* be in accord with his crippled condition.

So it was then, that Pallas Athena, Hephaestus the strong-armed

Smith, and the planet Venus are locked in unconscious identity in the human mind as indissolubly and unbreakably as Ares and Aphrodite were by the invisible net.

ATHENA'S LAST BATTLES

Velikovsky summarizes the late history of the protoplanet that became Venus in the following words :

> Venus, which collided with the earth in the fifteenth century before the present era, collided with Mars in the eighth century. At that time Venus was moving at a lower elliptical velocity than when it first encountered the earth; but Mars, being only about one-eighth the mass of Venus, was no match for her. It was therefore a notable achievement that Mars, though thrown out of the ring, nevertheless was instrumental in bringing Venus from an elliptical to a nearly circular orbit. Looked at from the Earth, Venus was removed from a path that ran high to the zenith and over the zenith to its present path in which it never retreats from the sun more than 48 degrees, thus becoming a morning or an evening star that precedes the rising sun or follows the setting sun. The awe of the world for many centuries, Venus has become a tame planet.[25]

The planet now called Venus, identified with the goddess Athena (and later with Aphrodite) in Greece, Minerva in Rome, Tistrya in Iran, Ishtar in Babylon, Baal and Lucifer-Mazzaroth in Judea, Hathor in Egypt, and Quetzalcohuatl in Toltec Mexico, was to become only the morning and evening star, an ever-pleasant sight, if, at the sight, people could rid themselves of its historical connotations. The planet circle nearer to the horizon, and, because it did not approach Earth closely again, was smaller in apparent size. Isaiah proclaimed (14: 12-13):

> How art thou fallen from heaven,
>
> O Lucifer, Son of the Morning! How art thou cast down to the ground
>
> Who did weaken the nations!

Still human sacrifices were offered to Venus, the planet, when she approached closest to Earth on her famed journey. Still she was the greatest goddess of Athens and the fountain of some of the world's greatest literature. Still, in the sixth century, Jews evading the Babylonian captivity and settling in Egypt rued their abandonment of Venus-Baal for the abstract single God. At the same time, the Greeks were

---

[25] *Worlds in Collision,* p. 259.

circulating a legend of Cadmus who had killed a dragon, a son of Hephaistos, no less, and the devilish lame Hephaestus had laid upon Cadmus and his descendants, including Oedipus, a curse; thus was the sin of castration punished in hereditary succession,[26] and the sin of Oedipus foredoomed. And walk down any street where astrologers tell fortunes or pick up any book on astrology, and see that the deeds and spirit of Venus are still part of human nature, speaking now literally, and not even of the unconscious role she plays in our religious rites and our forms of thought and behavior.

But in those days when it was visible to mankind that "the star Venus pursued Mars and inflamed him with an ardent passion," as the geographer-astrologist Erastosthenes wrote in the third century, B. C., (thinking probably of the planet as the Aphrodite of the Love Affair, in the confusion which we addressed earlier) what happened to Venus is marked upon her today. From the encounters with Mars, of the eighth and seventh centuries, we seek positive evidence, and that is difficult to find.

Velikovsky has been proven correct in several of his judgements respecting her seven-hundred-year reign of terror. It is now known, as Velikovsky claimed beforehand, that Venus is a hot planet, whose surface attains 9250 Kelvin without explanation except by a recent origin (from Zeus) and/or a recent heating-up.[27] Although only more simple compounds have until now been found, her fifteen miles of dense clouds may contain some of the chemicals that could have mixed with the Earth's upper Atmosphere under electrical discharges to make and precipitate the ambrosia and manna that tradition says preserved various early peoples wandering in desolation and darkness.[28] We know an ever-enlarging fraction of what the surface of the earth and archaeology can tell us about the catastrophic events of her pre-Martian period. We are aware of, and shall soon understand better, how the horror of her visitations affected the human mind.

But precisely because of her erratic, destructive, and self-destructive,

---

[26] Anton Ehrenzweig, "The Origin of the Scientific and Heroic Urge," 30 *International Journal of Psychoanalysis* (1949), 115.

[27] See Eric Crew, "Thermal Equations of Venus," 3 Society Interdisc. Stud. Workshop 4 (Ap. 1981) 1-4.

[28] See *The Lately Tortured Earth* and *God's Fire* surveying recent research on these matters.

earlier history, it is difficult, more difficult than in the case of Mars, say, to pinpoint her presence by the scars left upon her by the Love Affair. Let us look again to the song of Demodocus and see whether Hephaestus-Venus signals any possible effects of its role.

Velikovsky has gathered historical, legendary, and geographical evidence to the effect that the shortened tail of the cometary proto-planet was effectively destroyed in the Mars encounters. Hephaestus trails his legs; that may be indicative of the tail. He also manufactures his gossamer trap in a shower of sparks and lays it about the trysting place of Mars and Moon. These actions may signify the shedding of cometary material in great quantities, producing meteoric effects of high visibility and destructiveness. Some of the voluminous debris here portrayed as sparks off the anvil and netting for the trap may be what supplied Mars with the troop of "terrible ones" that stories from Greece, Palestine, India and elsewhere described, a host of terrifying images in the sky and real storms of missiles and gases.

As a result of the Martian encounters, several gods of planet Venus became lesser gods, the Fallen Lucifer and the Etruscan Tuchulcha, an underworld god. In the Love Affair, Hephaestus does not win his case: he has been the victim of the crime of cuckoldry. He has discovered the culprits. He has captured them and turned them over to the police and to the great judge. Yet, instead of retribution and triumph, he receives indifferent admiration for his technical skill, a jest from a policeman that he would commit the same crime if he could, jeering laughter, a bail that may or may not be paid, and a bail-jumping by the criminal. The great judge does not even put in an appearance. Indeed, how Lucifer is fallen!

Does Hephaestus change his ways? Does the orbit of Venus change from the elliptical to the circular to some degree, in the course of the Love Affair? This is difficult to say. He is wont to visit the barbarous-speaking Sintians of Lemnos. He starts back to see them, but doubles back again to view the lovers caught in his trap. This may signify an axial tilt of Earth. (See Chap. XIII.) Does Hephaestus ever return to Lemnos, as the others return to their familiar places? Probably not. Like many an old warrior, the time has come to write his memoirs and live off his past deeds. Still heated up but without a tail, the planet is braked as it has been for some time by its own viscous surface, but more speedily. Then it is struck and forced into an inner orbit by the combined energy of Earth and Mars. Thus it may have achieved the circular orbit it has maintained since the regularization of Venusian movements. Records, newly ascribed to the eighth century in Babylon, appear to show that by the seventh century Venus was approaching a circular orbit and, by the sixth century, it is definitely revolving on a near perfect movement.[29]

Not only was there an orbital change in this period, but also a rotational deceleration of the earth was experienced. Velikovsky shows that the day grew longer, at one point, and then shorter. Also, the Moon changed its orbital speed. Also an axial tilt was experienced. Can these possibly be accounted for from a small treasury of poetic lines?

Hardly. As the next chapters will show, many motions can and probably do change at the same time. We may solve some of the problems in the future, but at this time, we can only point to two indications of such change. The Sun, Helios, appears to have behaved erratically. Patroni, we recall, thought that the Sun had to send a messenger to inform Hephaestus of events in his brazen palace. This might literally indicate a tilting of the earth's axis momentarily, and twice, as a matter of fact. During such tilts the Sun and Venus, as seen from the Earth, would apparently come closer together and then resume their distances. However, electrical solar flares of great magnitude might have stretched out from Helios to give the same impression, as Kugler surmised.

The second indicator of changed position in the story would be the freezing of the action at its climax. Hephaestus roars his anger to the skies. (Was this when, in the Battle of Troy, Athena "uttered her loud cry. And over against her spouted Ares, dread as a dark whirlwind, calling with shrill tones to the Trojans"?) The gods stand with him at the threshold. Ares and Aphrodite are paralyzed in their trap. The Sun may be gone. There is a definite and portentous pause here. It could be the climactic conjunction of the four bodies: Earth, Mars, Moon, and Venus. It could be a moment when "the sun stood still," or more likely, when the night lengthened and the day refused to come. But what a night! The sky would have been more lighted up and colorful than ever by ordinary solar day.

Finally, Planet-Venus may be searched for some signs of surface and atmospheric damage that might be attributed to the Love Affair. It is easy to say, and undeniable, that since Venus suffered such an experience

---

[29] Lynn Rose, "Babylonian Observations of Venus," III *Pensée* no. I (Winter, 1973), pp. 18-22; C. J. Ransom and L. H. Hoffee, "The Orbits of Venus," " Ibid., 22-25.

also with Earth, Moon and Mars, then it would have to exhibit the same effects as they did, given, of course, the differences in its composition. An already hot planet would be heated up more, but other effects could cool it. More of its atmosphere would be dissipated to a larger planet and some gained from a smaller planet that possessed any, but this would depend, too, upon the composition, atomic weight, electrical discharges and pressures exerted.

More recently, an important set of observations of the surface of Venus was made by the use of radar.[30] In August of 1973, American astrophysicists announced that they had penetrated the hot dense clouds by radio waves, which were then able to probe features of the unknown surface. They discovered the equatorial region to be marked by craters of large diameter, dozens and hundreds of miles wide. But these gave shallow soundings. A crater of one hundred miles diameter appeared to have a basin whose depth was only a quarter of a mile. We should expect a depth of several miles.

If Venus were incandescent in 1500 B. C., it will have been cooling up to the present. Originally, any exchanges of material that might have occurred in its encounters with Earth and Moon would have been promptly concealed by the sinking and melting of the foreign bodies. Over time, the temperature of the molten surface would have reduced to that of today.

It is conceivable that by 776 B. C. the surface temperature might have solidified to a point that would register the imprint of a large body falling upon it through its dense cloud formations. Of course, the foreign body would itself become heated, but if it were large enough it might not disintegrate before striking home. If the craters had been formed by electrical explosions, again the soft terrain would have shortly reduced their depth. Shallow craters would, then, be explainable either by explosions alone or by an exploding body, and would tend to support the theory of Venus' cometary history, and the theory of its exchanges with Mars, Earth and Moon of the eighth and seventh centuries.

In 1975, Soviet scientists landed an apparatus upon Venus, named Venera. Venera endured the hostile environment long enough to register brisk winds and to photograph, in a surprising amount of natural light, a

---

[30] E. Driscoll, *Science News,* 4 August 1973, p. 72; Andrew and Louise Young, "Venus," Scientific American, 233 (Sept. 1975), pp. 70, 78.

shambles of sharp rocks. The rocks were described as seemingly "new." They are probably new. Whether the area in which they were found was struck by planetary debris or by electrical discharges, a splattering of foreign and indigenous rock would have occurred in and around the craters. The great heat, the heavy winds, and the high atmospheric pressure (90 times that of Earth) would very shortly have metamorphosed any terrain of sharp rocks. Volcanism, of course, would not throw off sharp rocks, but lava and tephra. Therefore, Venus may now exhibit the scars of very recent events.

Such were the effects of Athena's last battles. As if to commemorate the occasion, planet-Venus resonates periodically with the Earth. On April 23, 1966, P. Goldreich and S. J. Peale reported to the American Geophysical Union the surprising discovery that every time Venus passes between the Sun and the Earth it turns the same face towards Earth. T. J. Gordon, rocket scientist and author, wrote: "This type of resonant motion resists outside disturbances; once locked, the motion tends to remain locked. When did the Earth capture Venus' rotation?"[31] Might it not have been on or about 687 B. C.?

---

[31] *Ideas in Conflict* (New York, 1966), p. 37.

APPENDIX TO CHAPTER TEN

LOGIC OF IDENTIFYING RELATIONS SUCH AS "HEPHAESTUS IS ATHENA"

We are pursuing a set of identifications in this book. We say Hephaestus stands for Athena, for instance, and Athena is also the planet Venus, and the goddess of the Greeks. She is also Hathor, Ishtar, Lucifer, and Minerva. Some aspects of a lunar deity have also affected her identity. To a remarkable degree the validity of this book depends upon such identifications. In this chapter, for example, everything said which favors the identification of Hephaestus with Athena-planet Venus *ipso facto* supports a separate Aphrodisian identity for the Moon. We must be careful of the word "is," short of writing a volume of philosophy on the question. For "is" can never mean some absolutely simple "is." It has to mean something that never quite "is" no matter how close two things are to being the same.

One scholar who appreciates this process in which mythologists commonly engage is Philip E. Slater. In his book on *The Story of Hera: Greek Mythology and the Greek Family* (1958), we read:

> To demand an exclusive interpretation is equivalent to insisting that a Spanish peasant, a tropical flower, the Hudson River, an oyster, and the fountains of the Villa d'Este are identical because they contain H2O. It tells too much and therefore tells us too little of what we need to know precisely... A myth draws material from events in the history of a group, but orders it according to the desires and stresses common to those participating in the culture of that group.

An extreme example can be offered. Suppose we say A is H, or A is O. We intend by these two statements that: A and H refer to one and the same thing; A and O refer to one and the same thing; and H and O are the same. Even so they differ - these A and H and O - by the fact that they are named differently, and, however complete their shared identity, they are called by a different name. And *every* name has some connotation, some affect-load in the sensing organism. Now let us proceed to the other extreme, and declare: *A* is quite *non-B*. We will, no sooner than we are told this, tend to affirm an identity of *A* and *B*, namely that the two are associated in the same sentence, capable of undergoing the same logical analysis, have qualities that are comparable, and further that he who says so has some ulterior motive which joins them in his mind

From these examples we are led to various surmises, pertinent to the Love Affair. One is linguistic. One symbol can excite stimuli by being related logically and empirically to a predicate. It must be also related illogically, through sheer conditioning by "irrelevancies."

We can imagine this seemingly foolish conversation:

1st speaker: "See the planet."

All: "Yes."

1st speaker: "It is Athena."

2nd speaker: "It is Lucifer."

1st and 2nd speakers: "Athena is Lucifer."

3rd speaker: "I sacrifice when the planet arises. You must sacrifice too."

4th speaker: "I sacrifice only to the god Hephaestus who helps me make sturdy plows."

3rd speaker: "My planet represents the invention of the plow."

1st speaker : "Athena invented the plow."

1st, 3rd, 4th speakers: "All hail to the plow, the planet and the gods Hephaestus and Athena. Preserve our way of life."

2nd speaker: "Lucifer is cast down by God."

All others: "Lucifer is cast down but restored to heaven by his father, Zeus. If you don't believe it, we shall hate you."

2nd speaker: "Lucifer is not Athena or Hephaestus. Lucifer is the devil cast down."

All others: "Go to the Devil! Hail the gods of Olympus! '

Let us proceed with speakers (1, 3, 4) whom we recognize now as a group of the Olympian Culture. We find in them: "*H* is *A*" meaning

    a. *H* is identical with *A*

b. H is related to A

c. H represents A

d. H symbolizes A

e. H & A share similar relations to L

in each case with respect to:

1) Speakers 1, 3, 4 for certain subjective functions, but

2) H and A are separate for other functions serving speakers 1, 3, 4.

That is, Athena is Hephaestus and vice versa when and insofar as they share similar qualities (traits and behavior) in the minds of any person or group.

Athena is Hephaestus when the effects of Hephaestus and Athena produced on any person or group are similar.

Athena is Hephaestus when their names are used interchangeably.

Athena is Hephaestus when their names are not used interchangeably, because to avoid the interchange permits the fulfillment of and resolution of a cognitive dissonance. That is, where what must be said about the one psychically precludes that the same be said about the other.

For understanding both natural and social relations, all forms of "is" must be taken into account.

When a Q-behavior of A produces changes in X that H also produces, then A is HQ and H is AQ. When a speaker affirms (or denies in such a manner as to affirm) that A and H are the same, in respect to Q, this is evidence also that AQ is HQ.

When the behavior of a body X activates A and H with similar effects $AQ(X)$ and $HQ(X)$, then A and H are also given an identity.

When similar X effects are observed upon A, H, L, S... n, then we can say that A has psychological and organic existence in the group $(A, H, L, S... n)$.

To say that A "is" or has existence apart from $(XQAG)$ and $(YQAG)$, we resort to a second group $(abc... n)$ and observe whether $(XQVg)$ and $(YGVg)$ are observable. If yes, then this is a confirmation. If $(XQVg)$ and $(YQVg)$ are different than $(XQVG)$ and $(YQVG)$ then we must investigate whether the two sets of effects are reconcilable according to the logic of each group, G and g. That is, discover whether Q is the same, despite the different logics of G and g. This is essentially what we do when we inquire whether the planet Venus known to modern observation *(G)* is the same as the planet Venus known to the ancients *(g)*.

Carl Sagan is only reciting a phenomenon well-known to ethnologists when he says: "legends and myths, handed down by illiterate people from generation to generation, are in general of great historical value."

From the remnants of what has been handed down, we are here trying to discover a history in which "Who is Who?" and "Who is what?" are central questions.

CHAPTER ELEVEN

THE BLASTED CAREER OF THE MIGHTY SWORDSMAN

A Homeric hymn addressed Ares:

> "who whirl your fiery sphere among the planets in their sevenfold courses through the aether wherein your blazing steeds ever bear you above the third firmament of heaven."[1]

Ares had many names and epithets in and among the peoples of the world. He is Mars of the Romans, Nergal of the Babylonians, Gokihar (and Indra) of the Hindus, Odin of the Teutons, Huitzilopochtili of the Aztecs, and the Archangel Gabriel of the Jews. In Babylonia, writes P. F. Gossmann, he is Nergal, and also Era, Irra, and Death.[2] Odin had over fifty names and epithets. This Gokihar of the Hindus was "born of the wolf," was a "special disturber of the Moon," and became involved

---

[1] *Hesiod, the Homeric Hymns and Homerica,* trans. H. G. Evelyn-White (Cambridge, Mass.: Harvard U. Press, Loeb edition, 1950), p. 433.

[2] *Das Era-Epos* (Wurzburg, 1956).

in *yuddha,* which in ancient Hindu astronomy meant a clash of planets in conjunction.³

THE QUALITIES OF ARES

Ares, scholars typically assert, was the simplest character among the Olympian gods. Ares means in Greek "male warrior." Eris, "strife," is his sister. He is bloodthirsty, ruthless, warlike, fleet, ruddy, and, of course, well-muscled. He is drunken, quarrelsome, impetuous, and a favorite lover of Aphrodite; he had a number of children by her and other women.

"Rushing Stars" often appear to the vision as swords. Ares seemed especially prone to the sword. Velikovsky expounds the theme of the sword in the international background of Ares. He quotes a hymn to Nergal:

Shine of horror, god Nergal, prince of battle,
Thy face is glare, thy mouth is fire,
Raging Flame-god, god Nergal.

Thou art Anguish and Terror,
Great Sword-god Lord who wanderest in the night,
Horrible, raging Flame-god...
*Whose storming is a storm flood.*⁴

Of the Scythians, Solinus wrote: "The god of this people is Mars; instead of images they worship swords."⁵ Herodotus tells that they sacrificed human beings and poured their blood upon the sacred sword.

The Romans, sons of Mars, perfected their sword, a short, straight, double-edged steel weapon with an obtuse-angled point. Their drill, their fighting formations, and their tactics were based upon the sword in the hand of the legionnaire.

---

³ *Worlds in Collision,* p. 256.

⁴ *Ibid.* p. 261.

⁵ *Ibid.,* p. 263.

The male-chauvinist Greeks and Romans made Mars out to be a handsome athletic lover. He both vanquished and loved Aphrodite-Venus. The sword is a phallic symbol by an easy stretch of the imagination: a "dashing young blade" and "a swordsman" are used in vernacular epithets today of the sexually eager pursuers of women.

Homer, pro-Athena, grants her the victory over Ares in his epics, but around the world, Mars is victor more than vanquished because planet Athena never threatened Earth again after the age of Mars. Ares was called "Alloprosallos" because he fought indiscriminately, without principle, "on one side or the other."

We have pointed to Odysseus in his wanderings as the representative of Athena in her planetary behavior over the centuries. It would be well to investigate Hercules as the representative of Ares, performing an analogous set of tasks. Although his exploits find him sometimes assisted by Athena and in opposition to Ares, he is said to be Mars himself by Eratosthenes and Varro, the ancient commentators. Hercules, son of Zeus, wanders and is directed over much of the world. He destroys Pylos; he captures Troy in a preview of the Trojan War. At times he goes mad, explicitly so. His stories often do parallel the probably older Babylonian Gilgamish, but his exploits are sometimes transferred to the western regions where the Greeks have gone in large numbers. Indeed Hercules is engaged in measuring the new dimensions of the world.

Hercules spawns the Heraclids who are identifiable with the Dorian invaders (re-invaders) of post-Mycenaean Greek places in the period following the planetary disasters visited upon earth in the eighth and seventh centuries. More than Odysseus, Hercules is one of our crazed heroes of the catastrophic generation, just as his godhead is a cause of the catastrophes.

Gods, like people, have different reputations depending upon whom you ask about them. Priests, poets, and people - all have a say. Gods have a good side and a bad side. In the case of Aphrodite - sheer beauty and concupiscence may pass for good in the later Greek lexicon, whereas sheer irresponsibility denominates evil. In the case of Ares, physical beauty combine with swift force on the good side; ruthless destructiveness highlights the bad.

The terrible presence of Mars attended the birth of Rome and warranted him a longer and more fateful career than the Greeks could afford him. The Hebrews, striving for monotheism, incorporated the visitations of Mars variously - now as a divine intervention of the Lord (and the archangels) against the army of Sennacherib, blasting it to death, then again as a divine retribution for a collective "immorality" that the population and its rulers appeared to exhibit prior to each natural or human disaster visited upon them.[6]

Good and bad traits of a god are, hence, a combination of what happened alike to a set of cultures, what happened differently to them, and whether in either event what happened chanced to be good or bad in its contemporary historical circumstances.[7] Also, the fear of offending a god brought about the coinage of multiple names and related gods, so that good and bad epithets might be buried in obscure and "innocent" references.

THE FATAL WOUND

Let us examine more closely the present and possible prior condition of the "blood-stained stormer of walls" as the *Iliad* called Ares. The state of Mars today is known not only by means of transcribed legends, but by telescopes and space explorations.

Ancient history, myth, and theology have advised what to expect in general. They suggest that Mars underwent severe electrical encounters and some exchanges of material involving Venus, Moon and Earth. Its satellites entered the picture as the Steeds of Mars, the Maruts, etc., terrifying "animals" or "angels" indeed, if we heed the ancient accounts. J. Ziegler, a physicist interpreting the Hindu Vedas, finds the "Maruts" to be electrical phenomena, or at least short-circuits and resistors for cosmic electricity.[8]

The two satellites of Mars are rough rocks of small size. Today they are called Phobos (fear) and Deimos (rout), names given to the steeds of Mars by the ancients. There is some likelihood that, although they are

---

[6] *Worlds in Collision,* Part II, Chapter 1.

[7] See the author's *The Divine Succession* (1983).

[8] Manuscript kindly lent to the author for reading, 1982.

invisible now, the ancients may have recognized them.[9] Legend has it that they are the sons of Aphrodite. Hence we must raise the possibility that they were engendered in the Love Affair, the lovers' last encounter. Just as some mascons of the Moon may have been welded upon it by interplanetary thunderbolts, the sons of Aphrodite and Mars may have been exploded from the Moon and carried off by their father. They were part of a frightful bombardment of debris and ball-lightning which Earth suffered in the days of the Vedas and the Hebrew Prophets.[10]

Velikovsky wrote in 1950 that an atmosphere, now residual, existed on Mars and that organic carbons may characterize the polar caps. Soviet sources now report that a considerable proportion of the thin Martian atmosphere is of argon. Recent photographs indicate that the polar caps, which advance and retreat seasonally, are composed of solid carbon dioxide with possibly some ice beneath.[11] In *Solaria Binaria,* Milton and I speculate that all planets have had experience with life forms. That the surface of Mars was devastated beyond recognition and beyond any remaining possibility of "higher" forms of life is consistent with the legendary damage done to the warrior god, and also with the legend concerning the removal of Venus from an orbit that threatened Earth.

As was remarked in Chapter Six, a heavy contamination of the carbon constant was noted to have occurred in the 8th century B. C. This might result from several causes, granted the near presence of Mars in the sky. Electrical and geological disturbances on Earth and material and atmospheric exchanges among Earth, Moon and mars are suggested. Electrical charges can assemble and disassemble molecules of many different types. As a smaller planet, Mars was much larger than Moon and might devastate it, but be equally devastated in turn by Earth. In the heavens, even more than among men, the larger force strips the smaller.

The present features of Mars are becoming known and even give hints of what it might have lost 3200 years ago. First its geosphere. The mariner IX flight (1972) that provided year-long observations by camera in orbit provide evidence that, in Velikovsky's words (1950), "Mars has

---

[9] Velikovsky, *Worlds in Collision,* 279-80.

[10] *Ibid.*

[11] Bruce C. Murray, "Mars from Mariner 9," *The Scientific American,* January, 1973, p. 60.

been subjected to stress, heating and bubbling activity in recent times."[12] Also that hot spots of presumed radioactivity would be found as evidences of electrical exchanges.[13] The cracks of Mars, concentrated upon one face and along the equator, appeared quite fresh to the readers of its photographs. Little erosion has occurred. It was as if, some said, a highly vigorous water system had carved itself onto Mars' face and then all the water had been instantly removed.

How fresh is "fresh"? No one will speak up, unless one has a prior theory (the Velikovsky position). The uniformitarians are hesitant.

"One week?"

"Impossible, we would have photographed it."

"One century?"

"No, we would have observed something going on through our telescopes."

"One-two-three thousand years?"

"Events of this magnitude even then would have caused apparitions that are neither recorded nor geologically possible if not observed."

"Apparitions were observed in the eighth and seventh centuries B. C. respecting Mars."

"That is astronomically impossible."

"Well, how fresh is fresh, then, do tell?"

"Fresh is millions of years. It has to be."

"What happened then?"

"We don't know, but we know that you cannot know either."

As Eugene Rabinowitch, physicist and editor of the *Bulletin of Atomic Scientists* once wrote, historical evidence is "inevitably tentative and often controversial matter."[14]

"I see.. Unlike historical geology."

The "erosion," "volcanism," or devastation of Mars is most impressive, by earthly standards. Its major feature consists of a canyon running along the equator for nearly 2200 miles in a sinuous line that brings the "crack" to 3300 miles. The canyon, called Coprates, is over 300 miles wide near its center, and about 4 miles deep. Proceeding

---

[12] *Worlds in Collision,* 36-5, 367-8.

[13] *Ibid.,* 368.

[14] Actually in a letter to the author, June 23, 1964.

beyond the canyon and various associated faults with the same general orientation, one encounters "volcanoes" of massive diameters and great heights relative to earthly experience. Nix Olympica, previously believed to be a crater, appears now to have a base that is 300 miles wide and a 100-mile peak. The Island of Hawaii, the world's largest volcano, can be easily lost in it, along with Fujiyama, Vesuvius, and Etna.

The response of the scientific establishment to the evidence produced by its own work may have been predicted but is continually frustrating. It is not only that conventional hypotheses are advanced, but that they are exclusively employed. For example, an article by Bruce C. Murray in the *Scientific American* of January 1973 is possessed of full documentation from the flight of Mariner IX and illuminated by all the graphic tools that imagination and skillful hypothetical speculation might demand. The article describes the enormous canyons and craters, and a number of features of the battered Martian hemisphere.

But faced with the facts, the same author reverts to conventional theory. He accepts the eternal, unchanging order of the heavens. He resorts to internal heat and vulcanism. He wonders at the sudden burst of activity that must have erupted upon an earth-like atmosphere and that produced canyons, craters, and liquid flows in dozens of meandering rifts by a single event. Then a sudden freeze, *et voilà,* the present surface of Mars. The author says he cannot believe this could happen but he is forced to believe in miracle. The "waters" that "produced" the vast canyon and rift system are nowhere to be found, nor is there evidence that they existed. Further, the "waters" would have existed solely in one region of the Martian surface.

The claim is made that Mars has no magnetic field, yet the enormous dust storms that howl over the planet go unexplained, too. The cameras of Mariner IX circled the planet for weeks before the dust settled enough to photograph the surface. Now would not cavities miles deep and many miles across, and craters that would contain cosily the great cities of Earth offer a settling place for this dust? How does this dust pick itself up and fly about the planet? And, if it is once up, and accelerated in a vacuous atmosphere, whatever brings it down? It would seem reasonable to assume that the Martian "atmosphere" is capable of regular electrical phenomena such as produce clouds, winds and tides on Earth even if the constituent material is so humble as to be called "dust." In fact, as Ralph Juergens has mentioned, airborne dust is an ideal medium in which to "brew" electrical discharges.[15]

Nor, for that matter, is Murray perturbed by the fact that the carbon dioxide caps photographed at the poles of Mars are a couple of hundreds of kilometers off center. Here, again, is evidence of a tilting of the axis of the planet. The obvious hypothesis is that Mars was intruded upon externally in recent times; and suffered an axial tilt. The polar caps have not had time to reassemble around the true geographic poles.

Furthermore "*Mariner 9*'s pictures also disclosed a most peculiar terrain in the south polar area... It covers much of the south polar region up to about 70 degrees south latitude. The laminated terrain is composed of very thick layers, alternately light and dark, whose gently sloping faces exhibit a certain amount of texture, or relief."[16] These "plates" are perhaps half a kilometer thick and up to 200 kilometers across, with slopes that face outward. They exist only in the polar regions. They have few impact craters.

To our eyes the feature appears as a frosting to a turning cake applied erratically by a baker between filling orders, each layer flowing out and hardening before the next diminished batch was poured over the center. In the wintertime of mars, the error is partially concealed by a coating of carbon dioxide. These laminated plates may well reflect a series of meltings of the Martian surface, produced concurrently with a series of axial tilts. If in the six or seven near passes of Mars with Earth, the Earth's axis tilted twice (or, for that matter, not at all), the possibility of more numerous changes in the Martian axis of rotation would be greater.

However, there is also to be considered, given the thermal melting of the surface, the possibility that a period of axial wobbling from a single blow would produce the "start-stop" effect observable on the poured-out area. The thermal melting itself might have been produced by the rush of electrons to the poles of Mars, when, with a negatively charged surface, Mars approached other like-charged bodies, especially Moon, equatorially; there the electrons would pour out into space inciting discharges upon encounter with the positive ions that had been contained from them hitherto by a neutral belt.

Whereupon we return to the main features of the devastation of

---

[15] Letter to the author, Oct. 27, 1973.

[16] Bruce Murray, p. 60.

"fiery, bridling" Mars: the canyons and crater system. None of the hundreds of Mariner-watchers who have spoken up under establishment sponsorship by the time these words are written have dared to mention an external force. Much more is at stake for the human mind than a scientific theory; Holy Dreamtime is threatened if a disorderly cosmos is recalled. Only a few non-establishment scientists, almost exclusively sympathizers with the ideas of Velikovsky, were quick to recognize how relevant were the materials of Mariner 9 to the theory of an erratic cosmos.

Allan Kelly has described what may have happened to create the gigantic canyon of Coprates. He had written, with Frank Dachille, a seminal book on comets and geology in 1953, and has lately come to regard *close-encounter* as important as *collision* in the carving of planetary surface.[17] An "Intruder (much more massive than Mars) was traveling in the same direction as Mars and in nearly the same direction as the Martian rotation about its axis. This nearly parallel movement of the two bodies provided a relatively long period of time in which the gravitational force could act... As the two bodies approached each other, the gravitational power of the Intruder suddenly came to a focus [we would say "arrived at a sufficient intensity"] on the surface of Mars, ripping off the crust in a swirling motion beginning at the eastern end of the canyon called Coprates." Mars was zipped open. The sinuous "unzipping" we would imagine to be the effect of erratic jostling between Mars and the Intruder.

From the wound crustal material exploded and lava flowed. Possibly the satellites of Mars, with their rough shapes, blew out at this time along with a stream of material that was not recaptured. The metaphor of the unzippering of Mars reminds one of the battle of the gods in the *Iliad*, when Pallas Athena charged Ares and cast her spear "mightily against his nethermost belly," upon which "the brazen Ares bellowed loud as nine thousand or ten thousand warriors cry in battle, when they join in the strife of the Wargod." And Homer adds, marvelously, "Even as a black darkness appears from the clouds when after heat a blustering wind arises, even thus... did brazen Ares appear as he made his way among the clouds towards the sky."

---

[17] The early work was *Target: Earth* (1953); the present account is based upon an unpublished paper kindly furnished the author by Mr. Kelly.

As for the "volcanoes" of Mars, Kelly argues, these number twenty and all except one are found along the same straight line, but at some distance from the unzipped canyon. These Kelly explains as being created by related, gravitationally induced, explosions produced as the Intruder pulled away from Mars.

In the *Iliad* (Books XX and XXI) we find additional details of the fighting between Athena and Ares. Athena screams great war cries (one thinks of Wagner's Valkyrie). Ares comes "spouting" against her, shrieking to his Trojans, and leaps at her with his spear, driving it into her tasseled aegis. She gives ground, but smites him on the neck with a huge rock that "loosed his limbs," or, as we say, "shook him from head to foot." When Aphrodite tried to help him off the battlefield, she too was struck by the hand of Athena and her heart melted.

Planet Athena-Venus was probably the Intruder that devastated Mars. The Earth, while doing damage also, was too remote to have produced the Coprates complex. Yet it may be incorrect to believe that the Coprates complex was a product of gravitational explosion alone. Electrical forces were assisting. True, the point of minimal distance and weakest material strength between two bodies would be the first disrupted area. But to overcome the resistant gravitation of these two points inwards upon their parent body is not all that is needed to cause material dislocation. At the protruding points, the chemical bonding of the material would have to be overcome. That is, a rock is self-contained hardly at all by its center of gravity, but is held together by the chemical ties among its molecules. Otherwise mountains would flow down to the sea like water.

The Coprates complex exhibits the important qualities of the rilles of the Moon, which the electrical theory of Juergens appears to explain. The zig-zag eruptions (also explainable as "wobbling"), the sharp cleavages in the waterless environment, pointy canyon bottoms, "river" valleys that stop in the middle of nowhere instead of by the banks of a sea, and rilles that do not approach "volcanic" mountains close enough to "drain" them of liquid are reasons to diagnose the "blood-stained stormer of walls" as a victim of electrical as well as of gravitational disruption.

Therefore, probably both Moon and Mars were affected during the Love Affair by electrical discharges building on gravitational pulls. These were sufficient to soften and break the chemical bonds of many places on both spheres. Such, at least, is the terminology I am using in this book. Elsewhere, most prominently in *Solaria Binaria,* I join with Earl R. Milton in an exclusively electrical formulation of interactions between large bodies. We find that the concept of gravitation is no longer needed, in accounting for the transactions.

From all over the world, a small collection of peculiar meteoritic stones has been collected over the past hundred and fifty years, half of which were originally seen to fall from the sky, none of them anywhere near active volcanos. Lately, examinations have been made of the rocks by new techniques, and they have been deemed to have originated from Mars. A high content of mineral maskelynite along with crystals of augite, indicates that they were originally igneous feldspar and later were converted by an explosion or impact that did not melt them. Their chemical composition is "unlike that of any known Moon rock," reports S. P. Maran.[18] The clouds of Venus would prevent such material from escaping. The rocks are young with respect to the time of impact (assigned 180 m/y), and they could not be part of the asteroid belt because the asteroids are supposed to be much older and a large one would have to explode more recently producing a great many more small rocks of the same age than have been observed. Io, the explosive Jupiter satellite, is dismissed because it appears to have much more sulphur in its constitution than these so-called SNC meteorites. "The tests reveal that the meteorite's content of neon, argon, krypton, and xenon, and especially the relative amounts of two isotopes of argon and two isotopes of xenon, have an uncanny resemblance to the relative abundances of these gases as measured in the Martian atmosphere by the Viking Landers." There is an equally good match with the chemical composition of Martian soils.

"Mars would accordingly appear to be the parent body of the SNC meteorites," writes Maran, "but how did they get from there to here? Alternative theories are, first, collision, but the heat of such would have melted the rocks when they separated from the parent body, or, second, a glancing encounter with an obliquely approaching body that pulled off rock fragments in its vapor stream without melting them." This problem is not serious, it seems to the present author. Furthermore, to these two mechanical theories may be added electrical effects: lightning strokes can

---

[18] "Rocks from Mars," *Sky Reporter,* 36-9, 38.

pull up material from the ground without melting it; so can tornadoes which are closely related to lightning phenomena; I discuss such matters in *The Lately Tortured Earth*.

As expected, the dates given to these episodes by the investigators are uniformly far older than the mere 2700 years of which we speak in *Moon and Mars*. Still, within their very old framework, the SNC meteorites "represent notable exceptions," to all other extraterrestrial ages, 1.3 b/y instead of 4.5 b/y. Also, the shock waves that produced the maskelynite are dated only 0.180 b/y. In the grossly short-time perspective of the Quantavolution Series, the 0.180 b/y figure would be 2700 y and the 1.3 b/y figure would be between 0.5 and 1 m/y.

As to whether the Earth or Venus was the wounder of Mars, Venus seems the more likely, astrophysically as well as historically. The evidences of change and destruction on Earth, although great, are less than those of its earlier encounters with Venus. Furthermore its motions changed less than did those of Mars and Venus. Tentatively Venus-Hephaestus is designated as the assailant.

More will be said on this subject later on, in pondering "How the Gods Fly." For now, it is proposed that the main encounter devastated Mars - that it was caused by Venus, that an enormously long venting fissure and holes opened up, and that it was recent. Too, the blow was forceful enough to change any and/or every motion that characterized Mars beforehand.

Furthermore, the Martian surface and atmosphere may have been quite different before this particular incident, as before the series of incidents with Venus, Moon, and Earth that Mars experienced. It probably vented poisonous carbon dioxide clouds through the Earth's atmosphere, in association with electrical discharges, resulting in occasional episodes of mass asphyxiation such as I have cited in *The Lately Tortured Earth*. It may also have lost a considerable atmosphere, a soil (that precious few feet upon which all terrestrial life depends) and a hydrosphere (on which all marine life depends).

Apart from signs and remnants of these features, the planet Mars has been reduced to a naked force, resembling what the Greeks thought of Ares as a god, a narrow-minded compulsively destructive force whose solitary spark of sensitivity was reflected in the perverse love that Aphrodite bore for him. But virtue triumphed:

"Behold on wrong
Swift vengeance waits...
... and the god of arms
Must pay the penalty for lawless charms."

CHAPTER TWELVE

THE LAUGHING GODS

When Hephaestus roared out his anguish and humiliation at being cuckolded, he demanded that "Father Zeus and all you other eternal and blessed gods come here to see for yourself this laughable, this unyielding truth." But not all the gods came to gaze upon the trapped "embedded" couple at his copper-floored house. There came Poseidon, Hermes, and Apollo, all three being important Olympian sky gods.

From Father Zeus came only silence. He deigned neither to appear nor to return the bride-price that Hephaestus had paid him. The "gifts of wooing" were unlike the gifts of Ares to Aphrodite; they were injuries received, not injuries given. Most of the gods had "taken their lumps" from the Father, from time to time.

To imagine Zeus upon the scene could only occur to the raving Hephaestus. He is not to be called upon for a laughable matter. Indeed, the presumptuousness of calling upon him is comic. The scene would become too heavy, the literary critic would say, if Zeus should appear. Besides, Zeus was in truth absent. In the tragic setting of the Trojan War, Zeus had been engaged, acting to preserve the balance of power so as to work out the preordained plot, arbitrating, mediating. Still he is remarkably aloof, even there, his thunderbolts remembered by gods and men alike, but held in a kind of nuclear missiles reserve. His deeds were deeply etched upon human memory but physically he was receding into the far skies.

Why then, would Hermes, Apollo, and Poseidon make an appearance?

MERCURY

Hermes does not enter upon the action. As the planet Mercury, he may have been in a conjunction with one or more of the principals, in which event he may have vented some unusual expression. He may have presented an apparition at the time. For the scene may not have had the celestial clarity in the actuality that it achieved in the dancing circle. In a time of storm, of darkness and ashes, of lightning strokes, of different visual and acoustical perspectives - especially at the climax of the celestial disturbances - it is possible that a convocation of the gods was perceived.

Perhaps Mercury appeared as an optical illusion and also as a re-engagement of memory, as both crisis and the memory of crisis struck hammer blows upon the mind and, later on, made demands upon the unconscious to recreate the "pluperfect" along with the "perfect." Venus was there; Mercury *had* been there, too. The climax of tension produces in the mind both memories overlaid.

The fourth day of the month in Greece was sacred jointly to Aphrodite and Hermes, celebrating a game of dice between Moon and Hermes, the outcome of which added five days to the year, bringing it from 360 to 365 days. (The legend is probably of Egyptian origin.) In my book of *Chaos and Creation* (1981), Mercury was assigned a period of heavy worship between 2200 and 1500 B. C., that is, up to the Exodus, when Athena-Venus became the cynosure of Earthly eyes. M. Mandelkehr has more recently informed me of several additional authoritative sources who found Thoth active throughout the Old Kingdom of Egypt, and points out that his ibis symbol existed even before dynastic times.[1]

One should not be astonished by the implication that the planet Mercury had inflicted its presence upon Earth. Other volumes of the Quantavolution Series have explored this possibility in detail. The natural history of Mercury is significantly marked by its appearance earlier as a most prominent god in the succession of gods. Its physical composition and size resemble the Moon's; the two bodies possess, too, with one of Zeus' satellites, an odd angular momentum. Like the Moon, it has suffered heavy bombardment from space.

Called by different names in different cultures, he was represented often by various animals, especially by monkeys, in Egypt for instance, among the Gauls, and in India. Hanuman, the Indian monkey-god, once became as resplendent as the sun and moved whole mountains. The planet is suspected of having played a major role in the destruction of the Tower of Babel; there in Babylon it was called Nebo and emperors carried his name in theirs. A Jewish legend says that the survivors of the disaster and fire were turned into monkeys. The recollection may have arisen from a gibberish, the confounding of tongues, following upon mass electroshock; it may also have pertained to many physiognomic changes by mutations or congenital defects.[2]

As a god, Hermes has more than a touch of the Moon's irresponsibility. He is fleet, perhaps because his solar orbit is shortest of the planets. He is the lucky god of gamblers, the messenger, the robber, the friendly night. He leads downwards into Styx and upwards into heaven (as a planet rises and sets). He guides the flocks. He is a helper, a healer; he is - writes Otto - Priapus, Tychon, and Perseus. He may have inspired Moses as scientist and electrician. He carries a snake-entwined rod, nowadays the symbol of healing medicine. He is younger than Apollo, older than Athena.

---

[1] E. A. W. Budge: *Osiris, The Egyptian Religion of Resurrection*, (Univ. Books, 1961), pp. 81-3; J. Bonwick: *Egyptian Belief and Modern Thought*, (Falcon's Wing Press, 1956), pp. 101-2; R. T. R. Clark: *Myth & Symbol in Ancient Egypt*, (Thames & Hudson, 1959), pp. 124-6; D. B. Redford: "The Sun-Disc in Akneton's Program: Its Worship & Antecedents I", *Journal of the American Research Center in Egypt*, Vol. 13 (1976), p. 57; *Cambridge Ancient History*, Third Edition, Vol. 1, Part 2 Early History of the Middle East, p. 53.

[2] Hugh Eggleton, "Mercury and the Tower of Babel," V Society for Interdisciplinary Studies Workshop 2 (1982-3) 10- 1; and see the present author's *God's Fire, Chaos and Creation*, and *The Lately Tortured Earth*.

He can laugh. His responsibility here is as spectator, apparition, and "extra" brought in to reinforce the climax of the story with more bodies. But he not only laughs. He speaks several significant lines. Asked by his older brother "would you really be willing, despite being tightly netted, to couch yourself alongside golden Aphrodite?" Hermes replies that he would gladly be witnessed by the gods and goddesses and suffer twice as many fetters for the pleasure of Aphrodite's love.

Perhaps, then, he is reminiscing; perhaps once upon a time he, too, had enjoyed the devastating experience.

"Again the laughter arose among the immortal gods." Unless Mercury was laughing at his own joke, Apollo must have been laughing alone. In two places, the poet has more gods laughing that appear to be present and in a laughing mood. It is possible that several dancers are emulating unidentified minor gods or the idea of collective divine laughter.

APOLLO

Apollo, himself, is always a character of ambiguity and mystery. We have an abundant mythology about Apollo, from several cultures, but he has never been placed among the heavenly bodies, except that, for lack of better, and because he is "shining," he is commonly identified with the Sun.[3] But most, if not all, of his Sun-identity comes later in the history of mythology, and much of this ascription is readily traceable to an effort to clear the skies of gods.

Apollo earlier commanded greater respect and fear than did the Sun. He was the god of prophecies, of music, the archer-god, the source and also healer of plagues. He showers rocks and poisonous airs as well as arrows upon humans who have incurred his enmity. He has an aloof, judicious temperament. He does not interfere in the Love Affair but plays the minimal role of lending his presence and posing a question to his younger brother. In the *Iliad*, at one point, he disdained a challenge to personal combat.

If Hermes is a subconscious memory of an apparition which itself is

---

[3] See discussion by R. A. Herring and others in 2 *Society Interdisc. Stud. Workshop* 4 (april, 1980) and subsequent issues.

the subconscious memory of an earlier celestial appearance, Apollo may be the same. But he may be even more so, as I explain in *Chaos and Creation*. Unlike Hermes, who existed in the sky as the planet Mercury, Apollo most probably did not then exist in the sky at all. He may represent a lost planet, a destroyed planetary body of an earlier age. He may be the belt of asteroids between Mars and Jupiter, whose existence has from time to time been premised upon a previously existing body that disintegrated upon the approach of Jupiter or another intersecting mass.[4]

Apollo's traits befit vanishing and disintegrated behavior. Plague, arrows and prophecies have in common a widespread incidence of discrete events upon individuals. In addition, Apollo acts from a distance. Murray, in one of his few interpellations, explains his translation of an Apollonian epitet as "the archer god" by adding "or, possibly, 'the averter of ills. ' The word means literally, 'he who works afar.'"[5] Apollo is a retired and disoccupied god, Deus Otiosus; he is a god who works as a ghost presence.

Apollo has been moved in myth closer to the events of which we speak, for he is the slayer of the monster serpent Python. Python, says Graves, is none other than Typhon,[6] hence to us a form of Hephaestus. But Graves is probably mistaken, for the Python incident seems to have been an earlier analog, following the death of Saturn (Osiris). So we use it here to explain further how the presence of Apollo at the Love Affair climax was subconsciously prompted. The closeness of the names strengthened the suggestibility of Apollo's presence, and originally Typhon may have been named out of a wordplay with echo of the more ancient Python case.

There is yet another hint of Apollo's presence. If he does represent the asteroids, if he does pelt the earth with various small missiles and gases, then the disintegration of the cometary tail of Venus-Hephaestus, not to mention the material exchanges occurring among other bodies,

---

[4] Cf. Fritz Heide, *Meteorites,* 1957, trans. by E. Anders and E. Dufrense. (Chicago: Univ. of Chicago Press, 1946), p. 130, and *Solaria Binaria.*

[5] T. Murray, translator, *Homer: The Odyssey,Op.* p. 281.

[6] Graves, *The Greek Myths.* Apollo used a bow and arrows fabricated by Hephaestus, ibid., 21. a. We must suppose this is an incidental mythical reversal of time. For Hephaestus, we reason, is active later than, unless he earlier participated in, the events of Apollo's life and death.

would prompt the subconscious memories of Apollo and bring him into the climactic scene of the opera.

POSEIDON

Poseidon is present, "yet did not laugh." He is disturbed, impatient, persistent. He wants Hephaestus to set Ares free. He offers to guarantee Ares' just debts as an adulterer.

Hephaestus at first refuses: "Don't ask this of me, Poseidon. You're sure to be sorry if you give bond for a miserable rascal. And how would it be among the gods, if Ares should escape both his fetters and his debt and I should have to bind you instead?"

Poseidon is etymologically "master of the earth." He is the sea and the mover of Earth. Here now, he insists. "Even should he avoid his debt and flee, I shall pay for him." Hephaestus cannot refuse. "It is not permitted me to say 'no', nor would it be proper."

Why? Is this mere politeness, to move the plot along? But a plot in literature is as determined by psychology as falling rock by gravity. Is it respect for a feared uncle, brother of Zeus? Hephaestus once sympathized with a rebellion against Zeus; he is clamorously angry at his parents now. No; the end is foreseen because that is the way it happened in nature. Hephaestus cannot command the planetary gods. They move ultimately in freedom according to their natures.

So the fetters were loosed and the freed pair sprang up and off. Poseidon has reason to feel relieved, although he is still in bondage to Hephaestus.

Poseidon is here a representation of Earth. He is the masculine of the Earth-Goddess. Before the Olympians came the Earth-gods. The Earth Gods were female, as Erinyes in Aeschylus' *Orestes*. In Sophokle's *Antigone,* the chorus chants of Gaia, "the eldest of the gods, the eternal and inexhaustible earth".

Poseidon, says Graves, is lord of the seas and the Earth-shaker, but is always greedy to possess himself of land, if by no other way, then by loosing floods upon it.

The "Love Affair" threatens turbulence for both land and seas. Poseidon is the only god to fit the role, and the plot might have had to be completely redesigned if the role were absent. Besides, the evidence of the ancient accounts and of the calendrists and geologists lend confidence in the designation of Poseidon and Earth.

Michael G. Reade, in a brilliant study of perplexing perturbations registered in the famous "Ramesside Star Tables" of Egypt, has fixed the critical year to which they refer as around -700, about the time of our Love Affair. It would be the time of the Trojan War, too, when Homer says, as Lattimore translates the line (p. 405), Poseidon "shuddered all illimitable Earth, the sheer heads of mountains." We quote Reade's conclusions.

> ...the axis of the earth was forced out of its hitherto normal alignment with the stars at a season shortly after the summer solstice... the displacing force was a sustained one rather than a shock... it was associated with an acceleration in the spin rate of the earth... the effects of the disturbance were in many respects only temporary... the axis of the earth did eventually drift back in the same attitude with respect to the fixed stars (subject to a minor discontinuity in the precession of the equinoxes)..." (IV S. I. S. R. 213 1979- 80, 49.)

Any such disturbance in the motion of the Earth would have caused earthquakes, volcanism, tidal movements, and atmospheric turbulence.

Poseidon has reason to feel surly and "put upon." It is Earth that has suffered devastation in these sky-battles. This is no laughing matter. Earth has had to change its calendars. Its cities have been battered, its plains flooded, its skies filled with poisons and ashes, its magnetic field has been reversed.[7] Earth will chance future disaster at the hands of cometary Venus if Venus will only deliver it from Mars. Besides, the Moon is with Earth. If Hephaestus-Venus lays claim to Moon, that is one thing, a claim long experienced. If Mars now claims Moon, that is another thing, a serious conflict indeed. Already, the Moon may have been drawn away from Earth. It would be noticeably smaller.

Earth-Poseidon is put in the sky, as a sky-god. This should not cause surprise. He was born brother of Zeus and son of Chronos (Saturn), and assigned Earth, when Zeus received Heaven and Hades the underground. Earth was immemorially conceived as an entity, a unity, a being. Further, even the idea of Earth as a space-ship, like the other gods,

---

[7] *Science News* (Penguin Publications, July 1949). Manley discusses the reversal of the Earth's magnetic field as evidenced in Attic and Etruscan pottery of the eight century. The reversals, cited in Velikovsky, *Earth in Upheaval* (1955) p. 283, seem to have been a temporary phenomenon resulting from "The Battle of the Space Sheaths;" See below pages 265ff.

had been developed in a number of pre-Homeric cultures. The sense of the instability, the changeability, the restlessness of Earth affected Homeric and pre-Homeric humanity much more profoundly than it affected mankind more recently.

To the Greeks, as expressed in Plato's writing, the Earth was an organism, alive, as the planets and stars were alive. In conceiving of this state of affairs, modern man might not simply imagine that it was alive simply because it was covered with live plants and animals but that it was full of gods (as Thales said), alive as a whole, breathing and moving as the Mother Earth Goddess. Poseidon, her counterpart, was masculine, but so was the god-earth of Egypt, Geb. This conviction was a sensual impression, not a metaphor and was born out of thrashings, twistings and turnings, and from transformations for which people have today only the barest of sensitivity.

So the song has the Earth siding with the lesser of two evils to retain the Moon, to settle peace upon the Moon-path and thence to tranquillize its own way through the skies.

HELIOS

Helios is not present among the laughing gods and there is no reason why he must be. There are so many differences between the Sun and the sky gods that one must continually suspect mythological claims that assimilate their identities to him.

Helios is an everyday herald, a routine chariot-driver of the sunlight. Whatever importance late historical man may ascribe to his life-giving powers, he did not contribute significantly to the development of the human mind and soul in the Homeric age. A Homeric hymn begins "tireless Helios who is like the deathless gods," and ends, "now that I have begun with you, I will celebrate the race of mortal men, half-divine."[8]

Something of the passive incapacity of the Sun is revealed in another place in the *Odyssey*. Helios, when his cattle are stolen and eaten by the sailors of Odysseus, exclaims: "Father Zeus and you other happy and

---

[8] "Homeric Hymns," no. XXXI, contained in the Loeb edition of *Hesiod,* p. 459.

eternal gods, I call on you to punish the followers of Odysseus, son of Laertes. They have had the insolence to kill my cattle, the cattle that gave me such joy every day as I climbed the sky to put the stars to flight and as I dropped from heaven and sank once more to earth. If they do not repay me in full for my slaughtered cows, I will go down to Hades and shine among the dead."

"Sun," the Cloud-gatherer answered him, "Shine on for the immortals and for mortal men on the fruitful earth. As for the culprits, I will soon strike their ship with a blinding bolt out of the dark-wine sea and break it to bits." That is, the Sun must keep to his course. Only the great gods fly freely. Helios must use the gods for his needs. Graves reminds us that "Helios was not even an Olympian, but a mere Titan's son; and, although Zeus later borrowed certain solar characteristics from the Hittite and Corinthian god Tesup and other oriental sun-gods, these were unimportant compared with his command of thunder and lightning."

Further, Graves tells us, "The Sun's subordination to the Moon, until Apollo usurped Helius's place and made an intellectual deity of him, is a remarkable feature of early Greek myth.[9] It appears that the herds of Helios are numbered by lunar multiples, that "cattle are lunar rather than solar animals in early European myth," and that "Helius's mother, the coweyed Euryphaessa, is the Moon-goddess herself."[10] "Thessalian witches used to threaten the Sun, in the Moon's name, with being engulfed by perpetual night."[11]

A DIVINE SENSE OF HUMOR

When the gods are no longer near enough to be recognized as dwellers in their celestial homes, the age of philosophy begins. They are assigned to a mundane abode or relegated to astrology and denigrated. A Mount Olympus is provided, together with such local vacation places, you might say, that they favor for rest, recreation, rehabilitation, and retreat. The gods must be kept nearby. It is well enough for astrologers

---

[9] Graves, *The Greek Myths,* I. 156.

[10] *Ibid.,* 156-7.

[11] *Ibid.,* I, 13 citing Apuleius, *Metamorphoses* iii, 16.

THE LAUGHING GODS

to watch remote planets and to bank their fears and hope thereupon, but for most people, displacement of the gods upon more familiar grounds is preferable.

For humanity can suffer great fear, but it is an animal with a formidable physiology for converting fear into intelligence and power. Much of the complexity of theology is the rationalization of how the powerless, the misbehaving and the ashamed can nevertheless infiltrate their will into the almighty and the all-knowing, living a successful perennial paradox. By the time of Homer, men are beginning to strut, to smile grimly, to mutter innuendoes. *Hybris?*

This laughter of the gods has puzzled ages of scholars and schoolboys. However, the gods jest with each other. They do not laugh at pathetic, troubled, insubordinate, vicious or the occasionally happy human beings. Nor do humans indirectly laugh at the gods. The sight of the gods in good humor is still a sacred sight. One of the means that enable the plot of the Love Affair to come off so well is the absence of humans in the cast. This precludes a dangerous conflict of interests; one need not fear the overstepping of bounds.

Which is not to say that the audience is not laughing at the gods. It is, but by the completely safe psychological technique of displacement and projection. The Greek sense of humor, itself derived from the way its theomachy is constructed, writes into the gods' behavior what they would laugh at in themselves and at the same time feels dissociated from that behavior by its imputation to sacred character. Therefore, the audience may have laughed as the dancers and singer spun out the humor; more likely they marveled, were fascinated, and thought of themselves as receiving moral instruction from the gods.

The humor itself - the laughing at the discomfiture of Ares and Aphrodite, at the insulted dignity of the deprived Hephaestus, and at the desirability of committing the same crime if one could (spoken in the very presence of the injured party) - this falls readily into the category of sadistic and savage humor. Except that we do not understand the genesis of humor very well yet.

Two major contributors to the theory of humor are Sigmund Freud and Arthur Koestler. Freud's *Jokes and Their Relation to the Unconscious* explains a joke as the subconscious prevention of a wish from completing its natural aim. For that aim is tabooed or aggressively hostile or tragic. Hence the mind switches onto a parallel track that unexpectedly carries it to a conclusion of minimal threat.

In *Act of Creation,* Koestler insists, besides, that both humor and creativity rest upon hidden associations. These associations are inharmonious. They are wrestled into contact with one another in a double frame of meanings that resolve into a synthesized single frame with a new more acceptable meaning.

Since the whole of the Love Affair proceeds on a double level of meanings, two sets of mental events that lead to humorous resolutions may occur, or six in all, because there are three mentions of laughter.

For the Love Affair, Hephaestus is first to confess the laughable. It is that he should be victimized for his born disabilities. On the overt level, the threat is that he will prove false assurances of fidelity had been given him when he married Aphrodite. The expected and feared result is that he will prove these false assurances and gain an undeserved right. The situation is to be resolved humorously, laughably, as Hephaestus himself confesses in advance, because other people actually will see that he has been denied his rights despite his assurances.

Covertly, Hephaestus is threatening to possess the Moon himself, though rather impotently. The danger is nevertheless that the Moon will go beyond all bounds in losing its free and irrepressible spirit. However, all will gather to see that the assurances are denied of their validity.

There was probably also amusement, though not named as laughter, in calling upon *all* the gods to appear. Nothing would be less funny in the play or more tragic in reality than the coming of Zeus, the father of gods. Fortunately "everyone knows" that Zeus is not likely to intervene in such a ridiculous affair. Hence, humor. In fact, Zeus does not appear. Again, comic relief.

Next, the gods laugh as they see how "swiftness," speeding to its rendezvous, is unexpectedly and ignominiously trapped by "craft." Here the overt thrust of the action is that Ares is bound to steal a love. It is expected that he will succeed. But he is in fact trapped. Covertly, Mars is moving towards the ravaging of Moon and Earth. The fear is that he will succeed. The comic release follows when he is trapped and exposed to view by the public of gods.

Then the gods laugh because Hermes gives an unexpected and amoral answer to a question about himself. Apollo asks whether he would agree to such fetters if he might lie with Aphrodite and Hermes answers that he would accept thrice as many bonds for the pleasure it would give him. Here the thrust is towards repeating the adultery. The expectation is that he will falsely deny it. Instead he affirms it, but does so "harmlessly." The covert parallels are that Mercury too now (as once) is invited to ravage Moon and Earth. The result expected is that the disasters will continue; instead the memory is affirmed while the future possibility is dismissed. There are here, in effect, four types of joke. But in all there are four overt thrusts leading to expected disappointments; four covert thrusts leading to subconsciously feared disasters; and eight triumphs of evasion leading to laughter.

So then a conclusion is manifest, in general, regarding laughter: that the formula of laughter is *ipso facto* satisfied when laughter occurs, but an audience will laugh only when a threshold of anxiety has been reached. Also, laughability (and its companion, the plotting of laughability by a jester) is moral one in which criteria of savagery, vulgarity, virtuosity, and sophistication enter. To know when to joke is to know when to harm; to know how to joke is to know how to dodge the larger harm - which is to say that high wit and laughter become a property of morals and genius.

CHAPTER THIRTEEN

HOW THE GODS FLY

My readers, who thus far have been kind enough to loose me on a long tether, have probably been conducting their own more restrained examination of the events being discussed. I suppose that I can rely upon their achieving a certain respect for the connections shown between gods, skies, Earth, and the audience of Demodocus. Reviewing their own information, they will have recalled that a great part of human activity, especially in earlier times, has gone into watching the skies, relating the movements and events there to human affairs and celebrating the connections by religious observances, astronomical observations, fairy tales, song, and dance. They would readily acknowledge the occasional episodes of conjunctions of planets, earthquakes, clouds of volcanic dust, lightning storms, and cometary apparitions; these they might think are adequate to explain the celestial imitations occurring in the Love Affair. More than this may be in their opinion unnecessary and probably untrue. Indeed, the reader may feel that every step that I take to tighten the correspondence between a sky episode and dramatic poem and dance becomes less believable until finally every step become false. "Let well enough alone!" would be their advice.

I grant that this liberal view may be correct, and that I should be thankful for it and that in pursuing my radical exercise I am constructing a model of the absurd. Nevertheless, I shall proceed, on and on, until if I fail to validate the relationship between the scenarios of drama and disaster, I shall have opened up new lines of thought about ancient history, dramaturgy, religion, human memory, and the psychology of the unconscious. Whereupon, since the cast of characters in the "Love Affair" is composed of celestial bodies, it needs to be explained how they can move about in the skies as they moved in the opera theater of ancient Phaeacia. The movements of the scenario should be translated into astrophysics. One will encounter three major problems. The first, which has been dealt with in Part One and will be treated again later on, is to discover and justify the movements of the plot as being the movements to be traced in the sky. How strictly must one be able to follow the scenario in the sky in order to accept its general validity? Up to a point, it is excusable to perceive a physically impossible movement; myth and dream, in the interest of censoring content and creating an aesthetic experience, may have Hephaestus-Venus, for example, doubling back on the "celestial bedroom" too quickly for any conceivable physics to account for. On the other hand, suppose that Ares-Mars had flown off to Cyprus with Aphrodite there to be reunited with her. This would present an obstacle to credulity, although there are some twenty-eight movements, and "one swallow doesn't make a summer." The whole set of movements must be nevertheless both necessary and possible leaving only an occasional screening anomaly to be justified by causes outside of astrophysics and astronomy.

Secondly, there is the problem of apparent movements of celestial bodies. The Phaeacians, proud of their navigational skills, will nevertheless have set the story on a flat stage, a platform of the celestial map of the vault of heaven emplaced upon the platform Poseidon-Earth. They will have been perceiving apparent speeds, flattened orbits when the bodies were close-in, apparent sizes that would not make allowances for distances in space. How great a problem is presented by the semblances, as opposed to the reality, of vision of bodies in outer space, remains to be seen. Although the best of ancient astronomers struggled to actuate the apparent frame in their observations and calculations, still the Phaeacians may have carried an astronomical sense from extremely ancient times. That the Earth is round has been discovered and forgotten several times. The measured circle of the dance and the Coda Dance of the Purple Ball are suggestive of many early theories of the vault and dome of heaven.

The problem is that of translating apparent motion into acceptable and probable real motions. If one cannot offer an explanation of the movement of the scenario that is respectable, even if controversial, as a working hypothesis in astrophysics, then the credibility of the structure here established will slump. Accordingly, after discussing the movements of the scenario, we shall consider in the section on "Electro-mechanics of the Gods" certain theories of astrophysics under development today, and use them to explain the events of the Love Affair.

Another indulgence is besought. Consider, for a moment, that there are five bodies plus considerable debris whose matter, motions, and positions are to be accounted for. Each body has orbital and rotational motions that provide its angular momentum; it has orbital distances from the sun and the other bodies, orbital speed, and mass. It has volume. It has rotational speed. It possesses an angle to the ecliptical plane, and an axis of rotation at an angle to that plane. It has a magnetic field. These still do not include "minor" eccentricities, such as the fact that the shape of the moon reveals three "remnant" asymmetries, or that the earth is swollen at its equator and flattened at its poles. More ominously, the other planets, notably Jupiter, are excluded from the scenario.

Consider, too, that each property of a body may have an effect, provided it changes, upon all these other properties of its own body and upon any one or all of the properties of the remaining four bodies. The number of possible combinations of changed motions - taken in the bare qualitative sense of change, not as a quantitative set of relations that would give us azimuth readings or particle counts - will be (pardoning the metaphor) astronomical.

From one moment of time to another, one state of affairs may transform into another. It is as if one had come upon a round billiard table with five balls already struck and in motion at each its own speed. Each is of different size, each is capable of a change in its volume; each is spinning at a different rate and angle to the board; each possesses a magnetic field of different size and intensity that is capable of change, plus a changeable electric charge; each is drawn invisibly and is electrically related to the center of the board (the Sun).

If commanded to describe the scene, one might pray to God to restore order immediately by sending the bodies into non-intersecting circle moving around the center of the board according to a single law of gravity and with unchangeable speeds. Failing this, one might invoke the most skillful mathematicians and latest computers to tell us what is happening. But they would be distressed by the lack of data. "Give us some benchmarks," they would plead, "Give us parameters." At which point one would have to offer some fuzzy archaic snapshots with their double and triple exposures saying; "Here you are. We must do the best we can with them."

Thirdly, concerning how the gods may fly, is the problem of power to change all the motions involved in the scenario. Briefly, the gods fly by electrically assisted inertial power, gravitationally maintained. This, too, requires explanation, much more than what can be supplied here.

THE MOVEMENTS OF THE SCENARIO

The group's dance in the measured circle that precedes the song is intended to indicate the celestial and sacred nature of the story. It is not counted here as a spatial event. Nor is the Dance of the Purple Ball that follows the story. In general, the scenes are brilliantly lit, 'Phaeacia, ' 'Hephaestus, ' 'brazen, ' 'copper, ' 'golden, ' 'sparks, ' 'bronze, ' and 'blazing' are among the metaphorical suggestions of light; brilliance is carried as the 28th movement or change.

The "Love Affair" proper gives the following spatial changes. They are listed in the order in which they occur.

1. Secret copulation of Ares and Aphrodite in the house and bed of Hephaestus.

2. Ares gives gifts to Aphrodite

3. Helios moves past their bed.

4. Helios passes and reports to Hephaestus

5. Hephaestus goes to his smithy.

6. Hephaestus places his anvil on the block and hammers out fetters in his smithy.

7. Hephaestus goes to his house and bed.

8. Hephaestus spreads the net from ceiling and bed posts.

9. Hephaestus moves towards Lemnos.

10. Ares is moving towards house and bed.

11. Aphrodite goes from Zeus' presence to house.

12. Ares arrives at house after Aphrodite does, and speaks to her. He reaches out for her hands.

13. Ares and Aphrodite copulate in the bed.

14. Ares and Aphrodite are paralyzed.

15. Helios passes by their bed.

16. Helios approaches Hephaestus and reports to him.

17. Hephaestus moves to the doorway of the house and stops.

18. Hephaestus shouts terribly to the gods.

19. Poseidon arrives at doorway and pauses, disturbed.

20. Hermes arrives at doorway and pauses.

21. Apollo arrives at doorway and pauses.

22. Hermes and Apollo laugh, jest and draw conclusions.

23. Poseidon argues with Hephaestus and gives guarantees.

24. Hephaestus strikes off the fetters.

25. Ares flies to Thrace.

26. Aphrodite flies to Cyprus.

27. Aphrodite is bathed and anointed.

28. Overall and repeated brilliance.

Let us classify these movements, following their temporal sequence in the scenario and retaining their given numbers. When a movement is appropriate to more than one category, it is carried more than once. At this point we shall also change to astronomical names.

1) The first category of movement includes all passages of bodies through space. In astronomical terms, we are speaking of the relative motions of these bodies in the terrestrial sky.

The left-hand numbers correspond to the list of spatial changes above.

FIRST DAY

3. Sun passes Mars and Moon

4. Sun moves and passes Venus

5. Venus moves to a false setting

7. Venus moves to Moon and Mars apparent orbital rendezvous location

9. Venus moves to a second false setting

NIGHT

11. Moon moves to rendezvous location
10./12. Mars moves to rendezvous location

SECOND DAY

15. Sun passes Mars and Moon
16. Sun (approaches) passes Venus
17. Venus moves to apparent rendezvous point slower than Mars
19. Earth moves to rendezvous point
20. Mercury moves to rendezvous point
21. Apollo moves to rendezvous point
25. Mars moves from rendezvous point
26. Moon moves from rendez-vous point

From these movements comes confirmation that the action takes place in the sky. The Sun gives an orientation by pursuing its regular rounds. Although Demodocus does not say so, the elapsed time may be two days; the Sun makes two rounds; better say two days and their intervening night, but the climax (catastrophe) of the scene probably occurs after sunset of the second day. Moon appears generally to hold its course. Venus moves erratically and may not have set during the period. Mars appears to be moving on a near collision course parallel to the Moon-and-Earth solar orbit (the persistent lover) until sprung into a farther orbital track by Venus.

2) The second category of movement includes all decelerating and accelerating events, including pauses, that is, what would be referred to astronomically as *changes in orbital and rotational speed*.

1. Erratic, jostling movements of Moon and Mars in close proximity
6. Venus apparently pauses for discharge remotely
8. Venus apparently pauses for discharges near at hand
12. Mars stops at Moon's house (apparent rendezvous point)
13. Erratic, jostling movements of Moon and Mars in close proximity
14. Longer pause and slowed movements of Mars and Moon as Venus approaches
17. Venus apparently pauses at rendezvous point

19. Earth apparently pauses at rendezvous point

20. Mercury apparently pauses at rendezvous point

21. Apollo apparently pauses at apparent rendezvous point

25./26. Mars and Moon move at opposing adjacent angles from rendezvous point

From this collection of movements, it may be inferred that marked changes in the orbital speed of Mars, Moon and Venus occur. The two sets of encounters tend to confirm the two-day calendar. Earth's rotation is slowed to give a strong impression of the whole action being frozen during the dramatic crisis, when Mars, Moon, Venus (and Earth) are all lined up (in perilous conjunction). Mercury and Apollo, with Earth, join the scene at this point, as archetypical memories from earlier crises being forced upon the scene of the present crisis. If it is objected that the convocation is simply a literary device invented to stress the literary catastrophe, one should recollect the theory that *experience* calls forth devices of literature.

3) The third category of movement involves motions, sounds, and colors that connote *exchanges of energy and/ or mass.*

1. Erratic responsive jostling of Moon and Mars in close proximity

2. Material leaves Mars for Moon

4. Venus increases in size, darkening as Moon passes behind

6. Venus thunders and discharges streams of electrified clouds

8. Venus discharges streams of electrified clouds all over sky and affecting Earth

12. Noises from Mars/Moon as Mars approaches rendezvous; electrical belts stretch out between the two as they near each other

13. Erratic responsive jostling of Moon and Mars in close proximity

14. Venus relative movement halts or slows jostling

16. Sun passes behing Venus, darkening it apparently

18. Giant cacophony apparently from Venus, which also explodes material against Mars

22. general noise

23. Quakes on Earth promised

24. Venus approach suddenly propels Mars and Earth-Moon to resume movement

27. Moon returns to serenity with new face

28. All major bodies (Venus, Mars, Moon) and their atmospheres achieve some incandescence during the experience

The events of the third category include Mars disturbing Moon and Earth disturbing Mars with discharges of electricity and material. Earth slows Mars' rotation causing heating and jostling. Venus showers Moon with the sparks of Hephaestus' smithy. The intervention of Venus behind Mars and Moon causes heightened disturbances.

Terrible noises are heard - electrical, atmospheric and/or meteoric in origin. Incandescences of Mars, the Moon, and Venus (already incandescent for over 700 years) are noted, from which great heat is inferred caused by electrical discharges, crustal frictions from altered motions, vulcanism, and atmospheric turbulence, especially on Venus.

The appearance of the Moon is altered. Its rocks seem new, contain remanent magnetism, and are freshly glazed. For the Earth to magnetize the rocks of the Moon would require that the Earth approach its satellite to at least three and possibly two earth-radii distances, there to heat up and magnetize its surface.[1] This is unlikely to occur in any event because Moon might disintegrate at about that distance from the electro-gravitational force pulling at it. Since in the period of the Love Affair the Moon appears to have been drawn for a time away from Earth, and Mars came between the two bodies, it is likely that while Earth beat upon the one face of Mars, Mars beat upon the Earth face of Moon.

The perspective of the scenario is probably that of an observer in the southeast corner of Asia Minor. Then, as evening came and Earth rotated eastwards, and the bodies were accelerated, they would see Mars-Ares fly northwest to Thrace; Sun-Helios would fly west; and Moon-Aphrodite would spring southwest to Cyprus. Venus-Hephaestus is presumably left in charge of the moonpath from a great distance and follows the setting sun.

Phaeacia was discovered to be a Utopia, but positioned in Homer's mind in the west. Some have assigned it to Corfu. Patroni insists upon Malta. Pocock opts for Trapani. Etc. Notwithstanding this doubt, Phaeacia was recently founded, by Nausithous, the father of King Alcinous, who hosts Odysseus. He took his people on a long journey to the deliberately preferred isolation of Scheria because they had been persecuted by neighbouring giants (more likely, the meteorites of Mars). But Phaeacia is now doomed. Two days after the recital of the Love Affair, as the boat that carried Odysseus home was returning to its

---

[1] R. Treash, *Pensée,* May 1972, p. 22.

harbor, it is turned to stone; a circle of mountains erupts and girdles the town, land-locking it forever.

We can surmise, therefore, that the Phaeacians had witnessed the Love Affair in Southeast Anatolia and had played the drama later on in the West, without realizing that the actions in the sky would have followed a different terrestrial mapping if witnessed from their new home.

ELECTRO-MECHANICS OF THE GODS

Isaac Newton cleared the skies so tidily, and his laws imparted such regularity and tranquillity to the solar system, that, amazed at his results, he imagined that only a God could create the heavenly order. There was born in those times a new *deus ex machina*, a mechanical god, from the laws of gravity, inertia, and angular momentum. But the real historical gods are created out of catastrophes, not from order. And the heavens are as prone to disorder as to order.

Attention is called to two additional facets of Newton's mind, one naturalistic, the other religious. He could not believe that gravitational attraction between two bodies could exist without a medium for transmitting the gravitational force. And, putting aside his *deux ex machina*, he went searching for his real God, the Old Testament God, who brought the Deluge down upon mankind, even seeming to agree with Whiston, his disciple, that a cometary force might have provoked the Deluge.[2]

The latter is an irony that needs no elaboration here. But the former sets one to wondering. That all things are "falling" towards other things with measurable momenta is apparent; also that motion and matter are communicable, *intra se* and *inter se*, seems indubitable; further both seem to be inextinguishable. One must be wary, however, in using general laws of physics and astronomy when questioning the validity of observed events and historical-mythical accounts. The task of reconciling the two kinds of data is so difficult and frustrating, that many a good mind ends up in some dogmatic or empirical monomania. All this is a prelude to

---

[2] Stecchini, in *The Velikovsky Affair,*, pp. 89-105.

saying that the Love Affair portrays cosmic events that require extraordinary explanations. Yet one can take heart from the direction in which the current revolution in astrophysics is moving.

> Much of the new astrophysics is based on non-equilibrium - even explosive - phenomena, rather than the steady state thermal phenomena which have been the primary concerns of astrophysics in the past. It is the violence of the phenomena discovered in the astrophysics of the past fifteen years that has changed dramatically our current views of the universe.[3]

That some physicists are moving closer to a determination that gravitation may be transmitted by waves, and that others are pushing ahead rapidly in electromagnetism and plasma studies likewise enhances the plausibility of the events of the Love Affair.

For the Love Affair appears to have the planets moving in an essentially electric environment, with gravitational movements largely subsumable under the law of the conservation of momentum (inertia), which in turn may remotely have originated as a product of electrical laws. The imagery of the story is conveyed in motions that appear arbitrary, reversible, and erratic - qualities more characteristic of electrical than of gravitational forces. The examination of Moon and Mars has already shown features, such as rilles, that electrical theory can explain.

Ralph Juergens, who has made a special effort to reconcile the much-neglected science of gaseous electrical discharges with the theory of cosmic catastrophism, has recently proposed an electrical concept of the solar system that appears to fit the scenario of the Love Affair.[4] He suggests that the Sun's corona and the surfaces of the planets carry a heavy electric charge of negative value. Interplanetary space, on the other hand, is a plasma, a gas of dissociated positive ions and electrons. This highly conducting medium isolates the electric field of the planetary body; it shields itself from it. The shield is called a space-charge sheath.

"In the space-charge sheath, positive and negative charges collect and arrange themselves in such a way that the electric field of a body with alien potential is contained within a limited region surrounding the body."[5] The electrical composition of the sheath is a function of the need

---

[3] John A. Simpson, "Journey to Jupiter," *The Univ. of Chicago Magazine* (Nov.-Dec., 1973), 6-11.

[4] "Reconciling Celestial mechanics and Velikovskian Catastrophism," II *Pensée* (Fall, 1972), 6-12. The concept is full developed by Earl R. Milton and the present author in *Solaria Binaria*.

[5] *Ibid.*, p. 6.

to segregate itself from the interplanetary plasma and thus the plasma from the charged planet.

The electrified body, however, has to continually receive a current of like charge from the outer environment in order to maintain its charge. This the planets do from solar and galactic sources, Juergens theorizes. Thereupon "when no orbital conflict exists, the system operates serenely under the direction of forces accounted for in conventional celestial mechanics."

However, he continues,

> ... Let us imagine what might occur should two electrically charged major bodies in this system find themselves on intersecting orbit... The stage would be set eventually for a rendezvous at one or another point of orbital contact. Since the space charge sheaths of the bodies would occupy greater volume than the bodies themselves, a collision between sheaths would actually be more likely to take place than a direct, bodily collision.
>
> When the moment arrived for the inevitable encounter, sheaths would make contact. Unleashed electric fields would clash. Almost instantly, forces immeasurably greater than gravitation would be brought to bear on the charged bodies. Cosmic thunderbolts would flash between the bodies in an effort to equalize their electric potentials.[6]

In the present case, Mars, according to Velikovsky's reconstruction of the events of 776 B. C. or thereabouts, was caused to shift its orbit by the planet Venus, that had previously caused periods of cataclysm on Earth. The orbit of Venus grew more round, while that of Mars enlarged. The new orbit carried Mars on a collision course with Earth. In due time, the encounter occurred.

The encounter witnessed in the Love Affair was one in a series that agitated the world in the period between -776 and -687. The first encounter between Venus and Mars may have taken place at a great distance, with a largely visual impression being created on Earth, an impression that the terrible and eccentric proto-planet Venus was following a new course and that Mars too had changed its orbital movement to an eccentric one that brought it periodically - every fifteen years by Velikovsky's reckoning - racing on an elliptical orbit almost tangent to that of Earth. There were six such near-misses in the period between 776 and 687 B. C., until a final encounter among Venus, Mars,

---

[6] *Ibid.,* p. 7. Recently, what are believed to be electrical discharges have been observed between Jupiter and one of its satellites, Io, whose distance is many thousands of miles. The heavens have settle since 687 B. C., but the same natural phenomena may continue in a subdued form.

and Earth brought about the present planetary system by expelling Mars into a new orbit. That Earth may have had the last word may be the inference to be drawn from the coincidences between the rotational period of Mars (approximately 24 hours) and its inclination to the ecliptic (approximately 24°) and those of Earth. For these qualities, "swift Ares" may have exchanged orbital speed and an outside position on the racetrack around the Sun.

Let it be supposed now that the Earth and Moon compose a type of binary system bearing negative charges on their surfaces: the two bodies tend to revolve around each other; but the only sign of this is the perturbation of the Moon, because Earth is so massive relative to the Moon. The same electric sheath, however, (which may coincide with the magnetosphere of the Earth) keeps them in electric balance with the plasma. The sheath is elongated to embrace the Moon as the Moon, pulling the earth around it, ineffectually, because of the great inertial orbital momentum of the Earth, revolves around the Earth. When the sun shines upon Earth, the Earth's magnetosphere streams away from the sun-side to a perceived distance at least sixty times the distance from Earth to Moon.

The approach of Mars, on a generally parallel course to Earth, disturbs the Earth-Moon system. Repelled by both bodies from a direct encounter, it passes between the two. (One argues this mid-passage because of the recent searing of the Earthward face of the Moon and the one-sided searing of Mars, also recent.) Its orbital momentum is also great and there is no question, under these conditions, of its becoming a part of the binary system.

Nevertheless, it introduces a new negatively charged body into the sheath and the sheath undergoes violent adjustment. All three bodies intrinsically repel one another, bringing about bodily vibrations of considerable amplitude (the "sex bout"). The electrical repulsions overcome the gravitational attractions. Earth pushes Mars; Mars pushes Moon, and pushes back at Earth; the Earth's orbit expands slightly. The two sheaths temporarily strive for electric assimilation and equilibrium, although this is doomed from the start by the differential in inertial momentum (including factors of speed and angle). The space sheaths expand enormously into the plasma to acquire the electrical charges they need on their peripheries. They probably invade and excite the electrical sheaths of Venus.

As the sheaths move to assimilation, they invade the negative fields of the body surfaces and cause physical conversions of several types - chunks of matter are exchanged between the bodies (in a sense, "gravity falls apart" as opposite charges momentarily prevail); thunderbolts strike the surface of all three bodies, with immense violence.

Some of these are not typical thunderbolts. They are the weapon of the sky gods, at least of Jupiter, Athena and Hephaestus. Thyestes, a hero of the period, is portrayed by Seneca as asking Jupiter to still his anguish by bringing disaster upon Earth, "not with the hand that seeks out houses and undeserving homes, using your lesser bolts, but with that hand by which the threefold mass of mountains fell... These arms let loose and hurl your fires."[7] Juergens refers to them as of the species of plasmoid, explosive projectiles of electricity consisting of equal numbers of electrons and positive ions, rare examples of which have been duplicated in the laboratory by Winston Bostick. They carry immense electric and magnetic energy at the speed of solar flares.[8]

A simple principle might explain which body will receive the greater damage. Since the electric charge of a sheath is proportional to the surface size of the space-body, the destructive potential of the sheath in reference to a second sheath is proportionate to the surface size of the body contained by the second sheath. This would account for devastation of the side of the Moon facing Mars and Earth and of the side of Mars that locked its face upon Earth. Nor should we neglect the protective capacity of the Earth's atmosphere against all types of bombardment.

The Earth's rotation brought repetition of the incident the next day. Now, however, Venus is much closer than it was on the day before and Mars is greatly retarded. It is said that today Mars rotates at less than half its expected speed. Such may be an effect of one or more of the encounters. Here Venus actually seems to catch up, watch, and then passes by. It is possible that at this point, Mars was driven back by Earth and Venus, and moved into its present outer orbit. That Mars is locked in on Earth in its rotational speed and axial tilt may indicate that its final pass by Earth came *after* Venus had sprung loose the "loving couple."

---

[7] *Atreus and Thyestes* (Miller, trans., 1917), quoted in *W in C,* 217: and cf. p. 272.

[8] Ralph Juergens, *Pensée,* Jan., 1974, pp. 2-4, citing Bostick, 16 *Scientific American* (oct. 1957), 87-94.

Also, when Venus "loosed" them, it perhaps added a push to the Moon that reduced its orbit, restoring the lunar month to very much what it had been before the series of incursions by Mars began, and to its present length of approximately 29 1/2 days. Thus the electromechanical scenario may be synchronized with the year -687, with calendar adjustments that began all over the world after -687, and with the physical description of the Moon following her devastating Love Affair. Concerning the last of these, we recall that Aphrodite emerged more beautiful than ever - bathed, anointed, and astonishingly clothed. That would mean with "new beauty marks" and an aura caused by heat and dust clouds.

In effect, both the destruction and the preservation of the bodies in the encounter are due to the electric environment which lets only a limited collision of spheres take place. At the same time, the electrical theory permits one to explain how planetary surfaces can be torn, exploded, and heated - including in all cases the dissolution of the chemical bonds of matter - without carrying the bodies implausibly close enough to call upon gravitational pull alone.

The primary effects of encounter are the penetration of the atmosphere and surface of the bodies by attracted oppositely charged ions. A secondary effect is the retarded movement (rotational and orbital speed), displacement (oscillations), and orbital shift of all bodies.

The gravitational force, which, if the bodies were nearing in a non-electric vacuum, would draw them together in inverse proportion to the square of their distance, is canceled out by the repellent negative charges on the surface of the bodies which operate with quite opposite effect and force. (They are repelled in proportion to charge and the square of the distance.) The "Battle of the Gods" resolves into a battle of the space-charge sheaths.

The tertiary effects are heating of the bodies and their atmospheres, resulting both from electric particle bombardment and from atmospheric, hydrospheric, and lithospheric shearing friction. New levels of surface crust are developed on all of the bodies, new "scar tissue," new stratigraphy.

The effects upon the biosphere are grave. They have been described time and time again by the ancient observers, by early students of the Deluge such as Whiston, Newton, and Boulanger, by modern catastrophists such as Cuvier, Donnelly and Beau,[9] Lane,[10] Schaeffer, and, in especially systematic form, by Velikovsky.

There emerge, in the perspective of the human race, disasters without number. The gaseous composition of the atmosphere changes (a noticeable thinning and occasional mass poisonings). Large-scale destruction of herds and crops, and of wild-life and forests occurs. Basins are emptied or filled with water. Tidal waves wipe out nearly all coastal settlements (where perhaps 80% of the Greek-speaking population was contained in 800 B. C.). Chasms are opened; volcanoes are created and activated. Surface soils are ripped off by winds traveling at hundreds of miles per hour. Communities are obliterated or disrupted by showers of ash and debris, winds, water, fire, and famine. The apocalyptic vision, historically founded, is renewed.

The stupefaction and manias of the survivors are understandable. Older, similar experiences are reinforced in the memories of the group. That every aspect of human feeling, thought, culture and creativity should be affected is to be expected. To the explanation of these psychological and cultural transformations, the next chapters turn. They continue, at the same time and to the degree possible, with the exegesis of the torrid Love Affair of Moon and Mars.

---

[9] The scenario of geological effects is well-delineated in their book. *Target Earth, The Role of Large Meteors in Earth Science* (Carlsbad Calif.; Box 225, Target Earth press, 1953). See also this author's *The Lately Tortured Earth* (1983).

[10] Frank W. Lane, *The Elements Rage* (Philadelphia: Chilton Books, 1965).

PART THREE:

THERAPY FOR GROUP FEAR

CHAPTER FOURTEEN

THE USES OF LANGUAGE

The Love Affair is not a *double entendre* and was not viewed as such in its ancient production. It is not an opera with two levels of *conscious* meaning. If it were, it would have arrived in our hands in a different version. But the Love Affair does not permit a conscious second level. In order for the drama to have been born at all, it had to become the mask of a historical reality. It had to speak and sound and mean a love story, first and finally.

Nevertheless, upon being created, the story still had to develop in two contradictory directions. It had to retain its hidden meaning, and it had to shed more and more of its hidden meaning. It had to tell the truth and in the same breath deny it. This formidable task of the unconscious was doomed from the start, but yet it is perennially successful.

Such "success through failure" is achieved not only in the Love Affair but in all myth. It is granted to few minds to comprehend the mechanism. Even philosophers build defenses against its comprehension. Some are rigidly obsessed with the attachment of words to objects (nominalists), or with words to operations (operationalists).

Others, their opposites, insist upon the correspondence of words to ideal images (idealists, Platonists); to them the contradiction is anathema. It is intolerable, unphilosophical, confusing, meaningless. To the anthropologist, psychoanalyst, and psychological linguist, however, it is the veriest grist for the mill.

METER & METAPHOR

Homer's 28,000 lines were six-footed, the hexameter, which Paul Maas[1] renders schematically and typically as:

$$\underline{1}\ \underline{\underset{\cup}{\cap}\ \underset{\cup}{\cap}}\ \underline{3}\ \underline{\underset{\cup}{\cap}\ \underset{\cup}{\cap}}\ \left[\underline{5}\ \Big|\ \underline{\underset{\cup}{\cap\cap}}\ \right]\ \underline{7}\ \underline{\underset{\cup\cup}{\cap\cap}}\ \underline{9}\ \underline{\underset{\cup\cup}{\ \ }}\ \underline{11}\ \underline{\ \ } .$$

Each of the six long, stress syllables is followed by two short ones except at the end of the line, where a stressed sound prevails. Besides the stress, there runs a pitch that rises on some of the short syllables. The fifth and sixth syllables present a more variable combination than the other feet; they often embrace a "caesura," a pause or rhythmic division of the melody of the line. "All methods of imposing an order upon discourse by means of rhythm... are on a lower level, from the point of view of metric, than the oldest type of Greek verse, the Homeric hexameter."[2] Unfortunately, little is known about the rhythmic feeling of these measures or how dynamic and tonal accents were introduced as well. Furthermore, "we have no means of reading, reciting, or hearing Greek poetry as it actually sounded,"[3] and can only form a shadowy notion of it. And, to make matters worse, nearly everyone believes that it is practically impossible to render English acceptable into epic (dactylic) hexameter, a judgement with which we do not agree. The reader may address the question by means of the author's working carried in Chapter Two above or search out a now rare translation by H.

---

[1] *Greek Meter* (trans. from German ed;, 1927 and addenda, by H. Lloyd-Jones, Oxford: Clarendon Press, 1962), p. 59.

[2] *Ibid.,* pp 1-2.

[3] *Ibid,* pp. 3-4.

B. Cotterill done in 1911.

The rewards of metric and phonetic analysis of the Love Affair may appear slender. One can listen time after time to tapes of it recorded by a trained actor without the rhythms registering more than the serious, singsong, long-drawn tread of the epic narrative. The sophistication of the rhythm finds itself in the length of the line and the large variety of subordinate rhythms that emerge from the counterpoint of whole-word against metric division, producing a harmonic unity and disunity at the same time. No doubt it was this last that induced Aristotle and others to affirm that the basis of poetry was the syllable; but the syllabic structure, taken alone, would collapse unless coordinated with the word structure, phonetic structure, and meaning structure. These all confirm the belief that Homer's form is "advanced," technically, as Maas asserts, in consistency with the total state of his culture, regardless of the remanent social chaos of his times.

A little more is to be learned by investigating the technique of metaphor. One might expect that, if there is a second level of meaning to the passages of the Love Affair, it would crop up in the guise of metaphor. W. B. Stanford writes that Homer generally engages heavily in metaphor but that his metaphors are ordinary and uninspired; "with a very few exceptions, Homer seems always stilted and even deliberately archaistic [liturgical] in his use of metaphors."[4] In the Love Affair, we find only three "genuine" metaphors among the hundred lines: "fine as a Spider's web" refers to Hephaestus' net; Aphrodite "bridles not her passion" is an expression that may well have had the ordinary meaning of "restrain" and therefore not be metaphorical; and Poseidon speaks "winged words," a favorite hackneyed Homericism.

Hephaestus goes home "with a heavy heart," but one may regard this as literal, especially given Homeric physiological theory. And the lovers "shamed the bed" of Hephaestus, which illustrates a displaced object rather than a metaphor. Also there are epithets that refer to the gods - Poseidon, "the earth-enfolder," among others - but these we again see as literal adjectives and part of the divine names; the gods are described "as they are."

Moreover, only the single simile is to be found in the passage. Yet it would have been easy to conceal catastrophe in one of Homers' famous

---

[4] *Greek Metaphor* (1936, reprinted New York: Johnson reprint. Corp., 1972), p. 120.

similes. He might have chanted, "and as the gods laughed, it was as when great thunderclaps and bursts of light came from the blue skies, shaking the trees and setting the rocks to trembling, alarming the shepherd to gather his flock into the shelter of the cave."

Instead, the Love Affair is completely matter-of-fact. Hence one may consider the opposite hypothesis: there must be reason for the passage to be barren of metaphor and simile. The reason is not slow to suggest itself. Since the parallelism between what is said in the lines and what is happening in the sky and on earth is so close, and, furthermore, so well-kept a secret, the need for metaphor and simile is negligible. Indeed, the whole passage is a single great simile! And similes upon similes don't go.

A second clue is intriguing. Stanford was cited to have praised Homer's similes and depreciated his metaphors. "Why," one asks, "would Homer be apt to this criticism?" A statement of Stanford deserves repetition:

> The essence of effective metaphor is a clear and definite understanding of the two constituent ideas incorporated in the metaphorical term, together with an appreciation of the new concept integrated from those constituent ideas... In order to insure that a reader or hearer will thus fully appreciate his metaphors, a poet must be certain that his audience understands clearly and precisely the meanings of words as he uses them.[5]

Then comes his thesis: "Because words lacked precise definition in Homer's time, Homer could not, even if he had wished, have used daring metaphors."[6]

Since Stanford is unaware of catastrophic theory and of this book's alternative short-term theory of the Dark Ages of Greece, he pursues his arguments in the typical manner. Homer was building a primitive language and savage customs into the dawn of Greek civilization. So again, Stanford's evidence support unwittingly the 'Crazed Survivors' theory.

Stanford quotes C. M. Bowra who holds that Homer's language is clearly not primitive but "in other ways he employs a speech which has not settled to fixed forms and uses... This inexactness of function is natural in speech which is still finding itself." Stanford agrees and adds, "This is the common experience of all readers of Homer. In his dialects,

---

[5] *Ibid.*, p. 121.

[6] *Ibid.*, p. 121.

grammar, prosody, and syntax, everything points to the growth of conciliatory order out of chaos and not to deliberate variation of an existing uniformity."[7] Demetrius long ago had written, "Homer impresses his hearers greatly by the employment of words descriptive of inarticulate sounds, and by their novelty above all." Homer had to make the meaning of many words - "to combine," as Stanford puts it, "with his poetic gifts the work of a pioneer grammarian, semiologist, and rhetorician." Another facet of the greatly and eternally confused "Homeric question," it appears, is resolved by our theory. Homer is too sophisticated to be a primitive minstrel, yet he is first and foremost of the Greek poets, and nobody feels that he stood upon the shoulders of great predecessors. Many contradictions, both technical and sociological, characterize his work, his subjects, his times. These are largely resolved if Homer is regarded to be part of his times, at one with his subjects and their fathers and grandfathers, and working in a new alphabet upon a polyglot, untutored Hellenic population surviving from a set of recent natural and social disasters.

HOMER: EDITOR & PUBLISHER

Scholars have arrived at a fair concert of opinions about Homer. "The prevalent theory today" is that the *Odyssey* is not the full creation of one person.[8] Since it would be senseless for Homer to have put on a somewhat different vocabulary for each story, this evidence is weighty.

The *Odyssey's* language is more consistent than the *Iliad's*, hence it is considered to be the later work. Its concepts are more abstract, another sign of its being written later. However, both these facts would also jibe with the two-author theory.

Page makes the telling point that the *Iliad* and the *Odyssey* do not refer to each other. He repeated Monro's claim that the *Odyssey* "never repeats or refers to any incident related to the *Iliad*."[9] They neither boost nor

---

[7] *Ibid.*, p. 65.

[8] D. Page, *The Homeric Odyssey* pp. 52, 72 *et passim*. The *Iliad* and the *Odyssey* do not seem to have written by the same person either. The two epics have divergent vocabularies. *Ibid.*. pp. 149-57.

[9] *Ibid.*, p. 158.

knock each other. Yet they are consistent; there is no discrepancy between them. Some of the characters overlap, of course, and some of the statements correspond.

Further, both epics are written from the same perspective of time. Their parallelism with regards to the events described extends beyond coincidental probability, whether these events were 400 years or 30 years before Homer.

Both poems carry a style that is agreed to be oral. That is, they were intended for oral recitation, in parts and as wholes, extending over some days of recitation, if needs be. The major internal evidence of this rests in the great number of formular phrases that are employed time after time. "If the poet wishes to begin his verse with the thought 'But when they arrived...,' he has one way, and one only, of expressing this..." He has to deny himself all other ways.[10] In a sense unappreciated by modern writers, who search unendingly for an expanded, particularistic vocabulary and a way of avoiding clichés, the Greek epics were built upon collections of phrases, not words. The conclusion is that "the creation of the vast number of formulas, adaptable to almost all possible emergencies, must have been the work of many generations of poets... This is the memory technique of verse-making." But many formulas might be adapted to any long poem; ancient formulas would be the bricks that a mason could use quickly to erect a house; more closely similar is the practice of popular musical composers of folk, rock, fox trot and blues music in America who turn out great numbers of songs from a certain number of stock romantic lines and musical phrases.

A number of elements of both poems were explicitly Mycenaean. They are idiomatic, even identical, They are so tightly linked with the Mycenaean culture that they could not all have been carried orally over 500 or 400 devastated, savage years. But they could represent what was destroyed one or a couple of generations before and still obtruded in the culture of the Homeric people. Further, it is agreed that many elements of the poems were non-Mycenaean, meaning contemporary or Near Eastern or Western Mediterranean.

Here, our explanation is that the shocked society of Homer carried various cultures within itself, having no control over their incongruities. The oral technique would have been a continuation of centuries of

---

[10] Page, *The Homeric Odyssey.*, p. 139.

recitation from memory that can prosper alongside any bureaucratic society, such as the Mycenaean, in which scribes could write, but the people could not.

C. M. Bowra believes of Homer "that since he himself was alive when the wonderful art of writing returned to the Greeks in the form of the Phoenician alphabet, he dictated his poems to someone who knew it and the written texts were guarded by professional bards who recited them to later generations."[11]

Page puts the *Odyssey* not later than -700. We would guess its composition at about -650, its transcription soon thereafter. He mentions the possibility that the poet of the *Odyssey* may have been a contemporary of Archilochus, Callinus, and Alcman, two generations or more later.[12] He says there may in fact not have been any written version of the *Odyssey* before the sixth century.[13] The *Iliad* would have preceded this event by several generations. We suggest that just as the *Iliad* preceded the wanderings of Odysseus, the *Iliad* preceded the story of them. One then arrives at dates for the composition of the *Iliad* in several stages between -700 and -670.

The great literary historian, Aristarchus, places Homer some sixty years after the return of the Heraclids, whom we have assigned to the late Eighth Century. Arie Dirkwager, in an unpublished manuscript lent to this author, has reasonably calculated that Homer "lived somewhere between 715 and, let us say, 640;" he connects Homer with Archilochus, whose grandfather Odysseus is supposed to have encountered when he visited Hades, and with Lycurgus, the "Spartan lawgiver, who we think owes his fame to his work in social reconstruction following upon natural disaster."

Despite the ancient's insistence upon the single identity of Homer, Page considers finally "the relation between the two poems to be that of father and son: is it not much more probable that they are elder and younger brother, living in different places and developing in different ways? I suggest that this is so, and that it can be proved to be so."

Of course he does nothing of the kind, but the concept of a family

---

[11] "Problems Concerned with Homer and the Epics," in Thomas, op. cit.. pp. 16. 18. 42.

[12] W. B. Stanford, *Greek Metaphor* (Oxford, Eng.: Blackwell, 1936), , pp. m147-8.

[13] *Ibid.,* p. 97.

shop is congenial. It reminds one of Robert Graves' effort, possibly heuristic only, to place the authorship of the *Odyssey* in the hands of a daughter of Odysseus, named Nausicaa! The opinion of the present study is that Homer was unique. This is maintained not so as to ride free on the wagon of the traditionalists but because of what has already been said in this section and in this book.

Homer was a trained Greek bard living in the seventh century in Asia Minor. The skies were settled and society was coming out of a century of shocks. Like Shakespeare, not only could he act but he could also invent poetry. His age was not like ours, an age of personalized authorship and copyrights. His inheritance of poetry was both his and non-his; it mattered little. Homer was alert to the future. Thus he succeeded well in binding up the past. Moreover, he witnessed the new alphabetization of Greek.[14] Excitedly he seized upon its practice and went to work. Like an editor of today, he brought into the shop what he regarded as the most vendable story in Greek culture - "Achilles and The Siege of Troy." It was an epic that he himself could recite, checking now and then its lines with another bard, discovering frequent inconsistencies and correcting as many as he could, losing patience often perhaps with the scribes of the new alphabet who must have had to make hundreds of linguistic decisions in collaboration with him.

The epic in writing was an instant success. In the beginning, he who writes things down is the author, with all due regard to the gods and muses. So Homer was the author. He was more the creative editor and publisher. Probably no sooner had the original version been produced than it was copied - under his supervision for he would not have let out his treasure.

If the *Iliad* was such a success, would there be a second epic of like proportions to transcribe? There would be. Homer, Editor and Publisher, would be sought after by other bards who lacked his editorial genius and workmanship in the new literary genre. Would he help them - at a price, of course? The work would be in his name, but his patronage would be valuable. So one may conjecture that after he had created the

---

[14] A. J. B. Wace writes in the Foreword to M. Ventris and J. Chadwick's *Documents in Mycenean Greek* (Cambridge, Eng.: Cambridge Univ. Press. 1959), XXViii. that Linear B probably carried over until driven out by the more efficient Phoenician alphabet. We would agree that both alphabets were concurrently used, and, moreover, the success of the new alphabet was precipitated by the natural disasters and social destruction.

Iliad in written form, he sought out and selected a second epic coming from another part of the Greek world, singing of Odysseus, a character whom he favored beyond all others.

The signs of a common editorial hand in the two works exist; they have encouraged the belief in a unique "author" over the whole time. There is evidence of deliberate tampering with the two poems to make them consistent and related, but never duplicative. Thus Nestor's story of his early life in Pylos, found in the *Iliad*, is "remarkably Odyssean in style."[15] The *Odyssey*, coming from another bard or geographical area than the *Iliad*, would not be so familiar to Homer and a number of inconsistencies would escape his editorial scrutiny. Or perhaps he was anxious to complete its transcription and get it out on the market. The major inconsistencies of plot and dialogue are found in the meshing of the Telemachus story into Odysseus' return, although Professor Page adds analyses of other contradictions and lapses.[16]

Inconsistencies of general outlook, ethics, theology, and philosophy scarcely exist. Homer may have made his greatest contributions here. He would have been not only copy-editor, but also moralist, bent upon securing the larger Greek cultural community to its ultimate values in human relations and the human in relation to the divine. It is for reasons like these, and because the terrors of continuous disaster stretch their penumbra over the actors, that Mircea Eliade diverges from his contemplation of the remotest antiquities and calls the *Iliad* a kind of creation epic. It is a new age whose story Homer reorders and edits for publication, one that begins a century before he deals with it.

TRADUTTORE TRADITTORE

By the time the first Greek grammarians went to work, the language of Homer was quaint. The language changes. The references of words change. Associations are formed and join in the same word. Words expand their meanings and simultaneously contract them. Words are invented by new combinations of sounds, relating to the events referred

---

[15] Page, *The Homeric Odyssey.*, p. 161, fin. 8.

[16] Summarized, *Ibid.*, p. 159, 53 ff.

to, and to familiar sounds of nature, and previously exciting words of like character.

Take the word "brazen." It connotes 'bronze.' It also means 'hot.' This is easy enough.

Examine the epithet "golden-bridled Ares." It means to Murray, "Ares of the golden rein." Both are "correct." Why, as the authoritative translator (Murray) would have it, does it mean the latter, when a translation bearing in mind the hidden construction could picture Ares as a darkly ruddy planet with electric flashes and belts playing across its face, bridling it like the head of a warhorse?[17] Alexander Pope, puzzled, finds it: "He glows, he burns," (with love, of course). Fitzgerald gives simply "golden Ares."

Graves discovered that Hephaestus can be rendered as "He who Shines by Day." Phaethon, of the same root, means "shining, the shining one, radiant" and was the name of the mythical son of Helios who, paralyzed by fright, let the chariot of the Sun scorch the Earth and plunged to a fiery death, an occasion that quite probably corresponded to an earlier catastrophe, associated with the planet Venus. One should also note that Phaeacia is the Shining Land, land of Fire, the Phaeacians being "Phaecixikos." The words of "shining" and "fire" are dear to Homer. He uses them on hundreds of occasions in his epics, perhaps ninety percent of the time in symbolism of passion, heroism, and death.[18] He calls Hephaestus "the fire of the world."

The early Greek philosophers, reports Burnet, called the planet Saturn "Phaenon," the planet Jupiter "Phaethon," Mercury "Stilvon" (Brilliant), Venus "Phosphoros" (light-bearer), and Mars "Pyroeis" (Fiery one).[19] Perhaps someday a scholar will go back to the symbol and root of the ψ and find there only "fire, feuer, fuoco, feu, phaeton, etc." with

---

[17] This construction is supported as conceivable in an electric encounter in the study by Franz Xavier Kugler of the Sibylline oracles, Stecchini, op. cit., p. 143. "The Battle of the stars began with the appearance in the eastern sky of a body as bright as the sun and similar in apparent diameter to the sun and the moon. The light of the sun was replaced by long streams of flame crossing each other."

[18] Cedric H. Whitman, "Fire and Other Elements;" in Steiner and Fagles, op. cit., pp. 40 ff. Cf. also D. page, *The Homeric Odyssey*, 152-3.

[19] J. Burnet, *Early Greek Philosophers* (London, 1920), 3rd ed., p. 23; Plato's *Epinomis* (Harvard edition, Oxford: Clarendon press, 1928, lines 986a-987d) first gives the planets their Greek Present names.

perhaps an astral significance in the birth of the language and perhaps even search out the origins of other root sounds in the same vein. We should know, however, that ψ seems to have had phallic associations as a letter of the Greek alphabet.[20] And ψϋσις means creativity, talents, and the penis. At Lemnos, in probable reference to Hephaestus, there was found a medal with the inscription, "kabeireia *pythia phi*," or "the *strong one*, python, phi."[21]

Moreover, the (φ) of Hephaestus is close to the modern symbol of the planet Venus. But this is also close to the apparition of a comet, with its tail; a planet could better be a circle or a star. Many ancients designated the planet Venus by the same symbol. And Aphrodite contains in her name the same letter, and, generally, is described by a number of words conveying brilliance and light.

The symbol of a circle with a tail pointing downwards is a hieroglyph of Egypt but is also found around the globe, in ancient Mexico, for example. In Egypt it may also be rendered ♀. And as it was ascribed phallic meaning in Greece, so it was in Egypt. The statue of Horus at Coptos has a phallus in his hands which is said to have been taken from Typhon (the monster, the part of Venus-Hephaestus, that crashed into Earth).

Isis-Athena and Typhon-Hephaestus are recalled unconsciously in the symbol of the ankh, both as comets and as dismembered comets. It then recalls terror and can join with the castration fear, so that the phallic symbol and the astronomical symbol unite in a syllable that is both pornographic and anxiety-causing. But, with typical ambivalence, the ankh (crux ansata) comes down to us in a long procession led by the Christian church, where the ankh is the symbol of "life." Still, the Egyptian 'Ankh', the symbol of life, is a combination of male and female.

Moving to line 273, one finds a complicated sentence; Hephaestus fashions a device to capture the secret lovers *in flagrante delictu*. No translator feels the need to indicate that the original meaning of *akinon* is thunderbolt, not anvil (from which sparks fly). It also means a meteoritic stone. The mundane word derives from the astral; the significant aspect

---

[20] W. B. Stanford, *Greek Metaphor* (Oxford, Eng.: Blackwell, 1936), 67, 81, citing Franz Dornsieff, *Pindars Stil* (1921). Cf. *supra*, p. 175.

[21] Isaac N. Vail citing Eckhel, p. 45, of *Mythic Mountain* (Santa Barbara, Calif.: Annular publications. 1972). see also above. p. 160.

here is not the precedence, but the insistent astral atmosphere of the passages. Hephaestus, after all, might have woven a net of cord, or dug a collapsing pit; or "bummed a ride" on Helios' chariot: he is a versatile genius, not only a blacksmith. The device is of copper, again not of fibre, as fishing nets are.

A slightly different sentence emerges than the other translators, who are in rough consensus, give. Murray studiously emerges with "But straightaway one came to him with tidings, even Helius, who had marked them as they lay together in love. And when Hephaestus heard the grievous tale, he went his way to his smithy, pondering evil in the deep of his heart, and set on the anvil block the great anvil and forged bonds which might not be broken or loosed, that the lovers might bide fast where they were."

And we read:

Straightaway then went with the news, of course, Helios, who'd spotted them loving,

Shocked and dismayed was Hephaestus to hear of the painful story.

Deep down below the depths of his forge he proceeded; there, placing a thunderbolt stone on the block of the anvil, he struck and

struck off unbreakable fetters that no one could hope to dissolve, for

fixing the lovers in bondage, right where they loved, was his fierce aim.

Little can be done with the most common verb of the passage; Εϱχοαι meaning simply "to go and come," and Homer uses almost no other word of movement. "Why not 'fly'?" one asks, for, in general, Homer is fond of metaphors of birds and flight. Or even "rushed." Alexander Pope translates the word into airy and flighty language, indeed gives the whole play a fully heavenly treatment. Still, although the language openly describes events in the skies, the word "go and come" is just that and one has to be resigned to the correct perception that these heavenly bodies did not fly; they came, moved, stood, departed. The personages were huge masses, not birds or "shooting stars."

To conclude, a slight tendency exists for the translators to reduce the instances when the words and phrases of the original might have suggested hidden parallels of an astral and catastrophic character. To this they are driven not only by their own preoccupation with the evident and conventional, but by lexicons that are a product of the establishment, in effect, a guarantee that when in doubt they will follow the consensus.

It is of little use to appeal to "The Original," dismissing all translations. A thoroughly versed classicist would be similarly tempted to "read" or "explain" in classical Greek the meanings of the words in their singular romantic sense. One can imagine Homer himself, half composing, half reporting the story; even he must have contributed to its integrity as romance at the cost of greater ambiguity as history.

For basically all words describing events are a translation *ab initio* (See above, page 29). Even the most rigorous scientific language begins to wash out meanings through metaphors. Only in the subconscious minds of the earliest singers of the song and their audience would there exist openly sensible connections between the event and the signs, and between the denoting signs and the connotating signs. And soon only these latter were permitted to bubble up into awareness.

THE THROES OF ORIGINAL PLOT

Thrusting at these arguments from another point, a critic may offer the reasonable observation that the Love Affair is only an instance of the ever popular plot of the love triangle. Two people owe each other love. A third in fact captures the love of one of the pair. The third is outraged at being excluded from the prior love. And, naturally, preceding this plot came many familiar personal histories from time immemorial.

At the risk of offering a theory of literary creativity that cannot be amply defended here, I would say that we are treating of time immemorial and even of the rise of language and literary forms. Long before the Love Affair could be composed, there had to be a language; that language, to be invented, had to be preceded by and based upon a ritualized culture fascinated by repetitions and order.

The "obvious plot" had not only to be experienced, but had also to be perceived as important in two regards: to be certified by higher authority (i. e. the behavior of the gods); and to be translated from common occurrence into Symbolic form. (More will be said of this later.)

The Oedipus story, from which the important psychiatric complex derived its name, had occurred innumerable times in the dawn of humanity. But it took a particular episode of Egyptian history, involving a God-Pharaoh, which I. Velikovsky has brilliantly detected in *Oedipus and Akhnaton,* to sponsor the translation and elevate into literature, first

THE USES OF LANGUAGE

spoken and then written, the general human experience and anxiety over the sexual love between mother and son.

Among the several facets of Homer's genius is that he carried wars, sex and feasting into the humanly experienced life of the gods so that divine behavior could be at least partly understood, though full of contradictions that themselves created, including a contemporary practical wisdom and a later "rational" philosophy. Too late after the events, in the third century A. D., Quintillus wrote a sequel to the *Iliad*. It is insipid, uninspiring. It affords no sense of the presence and reality of the gods when compared with the *Wrath of Achilles* or the "Return of the Heroes" sung to Odysseus before he hears of the Love Affair. It is as if our primeval myth-maker knew the crude principle of stardom in Hollywood. "If they can't remember the story, they'll remember who starred in the movie."

Hence one speculates that the enduring plots and themes of the arts, including history, were invented with great effort and through a real-perceived event, sparking a combustible mixture of instruments and institutions - linguistic, behavioral, and technical.

HUMAN STRESS & LANGUAGE

A child likes to repeat words, phrases, and sentences. One will chant the same line indefatigably. It may be newly invented or a thousand years old. It may or may not "make sense". A relief of anxiety occurs in the repetition. The speech of the old and dying often becomes repetitive, and an old person who has spoken an acquired language will often revert to the sole use of the language he first learned. When pinned down by enemy fire, a soldier will often chant words incoherently, or if he had instruction, say, in the Catholic Church, will repeat the "Hail, Mary" prayer times without end. Sad folk ballads and neurotic "rock-and-roll" songs are obsessively simple in word and beat and prolong themselves to the agony of anyone not afflicted who must endure them. The language of sudden grief and disaster is often "No! No! No!..." or "She can't be dead! She can't be dead..."

The sacred dream recital and liturgy, plus many institutional offshoots, are a repetition of events that once occurred. That the original event was a terrible event followed by great anxiety is evidenced in many ways, as in the punitiveness with which unbelievers are regarded, for the unbeliever is saying that "the tragedy that once happened to you is insignificant." In the realm of rhetoric and linguistic pragmatics, the sacred expression is using symbols as a way of regressing to stress, re-enacting it, rememorizing the events, and ultimately releasing tensions.

Insistence upon correctness in detail prolongs the generation of memory and at the same time insures that the gods realize how faithfully these humans have remembered their lesson. The repetitiveness, another aspect of obsession, and another means of insuring memorization, progressively fixates the ritual participant upon the root of his ailment. "She can't stop scratching her mosquito bite," "He wallows in his misery;" these are trivial obsessive actions. The original recital of the Love Affair would have taken hours; Homer cut it and shaped it to a new form of art, but note well that he lets one know that it is far from the original version; he did not steal, abridge it, and present it as original.

The sacred originates in a stressful and tragic condition. In the process of sublimation, the tragic stress gives way to liturgical language, promoting the development of language itself, in both "hieratic" (priestly) and popular (" demotic") forms. Tragedy is never lost. Its final triumph is to give birth to comedy.

THE RULES OF MYTHICAL LANGUAGE

The rules of scientific language are well-known. They should actually be called "ideals," since they cover far less of science than they "should," and necessarily so, because scientific language cannot generate its highest flights unless it resort to philosophic language. To the scientist, the rule is: "one event should receive one signification." Further: "the signification should be the same for anyone to whom it is communicated." Moreover, "the signification should be testable, by repetition of the event sequence in experiment, etc." Finally, "events should be described and combined in forms of signification that do not add external meanings;" that is, no extraneous feelings or meanings should slip in by design or surreptitiously to spoil the purity of the generalization. All of this began with Aristotle's nominalism (words are distinct from, and refer to, objects) and has arrived at Whitehead's operationism (the meanings of words can only lie in the events they describe).

Aristotle had another side, also. He understood rhetoric and pragmatics. While developing a rational grammar of science, he was preparing a science of influencing. Given a particular audience, what symbols should be chosen and manipulated to produce a desired effect? Here words are signs of mental affections, not exclusively of the dualities of things. Once pursued, this line of thought has ever more fearful implications. Not until the latest stage of the modern scientific outlook has a body of scientific work been permitted to arise that would inquire into the reasons for reasoning, the meaning of meaning, the ideology behind every body of action, including the activities of science itself.

When science has come this far, it is capable of analyzing the language of myth scientifically. The first rule for the interpretation of myth is that symbols in their content will have a determined and possibly determinable meaning. The second is that "what the symbols mean" contains, besides other things, "the psychological effects produced by them." Thirdly, there is an "unconscious science of myth," as well as certain principles of the "conscious" science of myth that we have dug out and can apply with predictable effects. Just as the athlete, poet, orator, and composer may not know the scientific rules of their successful performances, so the myth-teller and myth-hearer will not usually understand what rules of linguistics and psychology he is applying.

The most important of these unconscious rules, all of them practiced and evident in the Love Affair, are perhaps the following:

1. Make a myth of any collectively experienced event that had tragic consequences in order to give symptomatic relief to the perpetual illness. (The myth of the Love Affair exemplifies this rule.)

2. Remain steadfastly true to the event. As the consensus that perceived the event then and there defined it, so relate it. (As a result of this rule, many generations later, we can behave as cryptographic detectives in relation to the historical character of the myth. We are trying to *replay* this rule as it guided the producers of the Love Affair.)

3. Conceal the truth of the event insofar as it is disturbing. (We are seeking the truth of the Love Affair in many areas, not the least of which is in the language, where we observed a number of techniques of concealing the truth while telling it.)

4. Use methods of concealment that contribute symptomatic relief. (We find in the Love Affair a thoroughly satisfactory plot that amuses, a suggestive language, reiteration, ritual, collective reassurance.)

5. The therapy should last for the duration of the pain. (Over a span of forty memorial generations and eighty reproductive generations some portion of humanity has obtained symptomatic relief from the Love Affair. However, the myth has lost impact steadily from the settling of heaven, and from more philosophical methods of coping with the symptoms. The doctrines of the eternal constancy of the heavens, the practical timelessness of earthly change, and the gradual evolution of humans - sometimes referred to altogether as the ideology of uniformitarianism - have proven a more effective repressor and a partial therapy in the long run. They have made the Love Affair mainly a salacious tale, told in a thousand forms, whose insistent threats and memories linger only vaguely.

As for adults, so for babies.

> So turkey-lurkey turned back, and walked with gander-lander, goose-loose, drake-lake, duck-luck, cock-lock, hen-len, and chicken-licken. And as they were going along, they met fox-lox. And fox-lox said "Where are you going, my pretty maids?" And they said, "Chicken-Licken went to the wood, and the sky fell upon her poor bald pate, and we are going to tell the king." And fox-lox said, "Come along with me, and I will show you the way." But fox-lox took them into the fox's hole, and he and his young ones soon ate up poor chicken-licken, hen-len, cock-lock, duck-luck, drake-lake, goose-loose, gander-lander, and turkey-lurkey, and they never saw the king to tell him that the sky had fallen![22]

The story is much longer, of course, because one after another of the little animals is added to the fearful procession following chicken-licken, and the list is repeated liturgically. The sky is beginning to fall; the people are frightened; they seek the religio-secular authority to ease their fears or perhaps to do something about it.

But they encounter the fox who, ancient myths relate, "nibbles continuously at the thong of the yoke which holds together heaven and earth" (Proclus) and "German folklore adds that when the fox succeeds, the world will come to its end." This same fox can also be a wolf, and a

---

[22] This last part of the typically repetitious (liturgical) story for tiny children called "Chicken-Licken," is quoted from James O. Halliwell-Phillips, *Popular Rhymes and Nursery Tales* (London: J. R. Smith, 1849), p. 31. The story is found in Africa, India, all over Europe. Cf. my own note in *The Burning of Troy*.

dog. It is a star. It is also called "Electra, mother of Dardanus, who left her station among the Pleiades, desperate because of Ilion's (Troy's) fall, and retired above the second star of the beam... others call this star 'fox.'" So write Santillana and von Dechend, from their sources, calling finally upon the great expert on ancient astronomy, F. X. Kugler who had said: "The star at the beam of the wagon is the fox star: Era, the powerful among the gods. In astrological usage, it represents above all the planet Mars/Nergal."[23]

The same story, whose origins disappear into the immemorial (read "memorial") past, has been altered over the last century of time. Today, people may read to their three-year olds in a new version[24] that the little animals encounter, not a fox, but a wise owl, and that the owl skeptically asks to be shown the fallen piece of sky: heaven cannot fall; it turns out that it was only an apple that had fallen. They found the apple and Chicken-Licken ate it and was happy.

Alas, they are back to the owl, which happens to have been a paramount symbol of "owl-eyed" Athena,[25] and they are eating the forbidden apple in the Garden of Eden. Once more, "success through failure."

---

[23] G. de Santillana and II. van Dechend, *Hamlet's Mill: An Essay on Myth and the Frame of Time.(* Boston: Gambit, 1969), p. 385.

[24] *Chicken Little* (Racine, Wisc.: Whitman Publ. co., 1958).

[25] The owl is a marvelous tranfiguration of a blazing-eyed twin comet that may have been one source of the duality of Athena-Hephaestus and the many twin serpent symbols of antiquity.

CHAPTER FIFTEEN

THE BIRTH & DEATH OF MEMORY

In Pieria, Memoria, ruler of the hills of Eleuther, gave birth to the Muses out of union with Zeus, son of Chronos, and thus of the forgetting of ills and a rest from sorrow.

So writes Hesiod, a contemporary of Homer in his Genealogy of the Gods. The *Theogony* was composed after 730 B. C., that is, during or after the era of troubled skies; but it was a mythical work, "reporting" on events that had occurred hundreds and thousands of year before. "The ordered pantheon of Hesiod ended in supplanting the anarchic society of the Homeric Gods."[1]

A functional psychology rests in the quoted passage. "Remembering" was no mere scratching of experience upon a *tabula rasa* of the mind. Memoria or Mnemosyne or "Recollector," is the mother of history (Clio). She has as her progeny the means of controlling herself, for Zeus is the ordering paternal force. There are nine (some said three or five)

---

[1] Mireaux, *Daily Life in the Time of Homer,* p. 429, who acutely perceives that Hesiod is a "futurist," not a" reactionary," and that his book on farming and farm life, *Works and Days,* was a treatise searching for justice and orderly existence.

muses governing the arts and sciences - dancing, music, and singing, but also history and astronomy. They will lend human memory its possibilities of selective attention, delusion, illusion, abatement, extension, a shadowing and heightening - all that is necessary to achieve that combination of remembering and forgetting which makes social life possible on a level that is higher than the level of non-remembering or total amnesia. Significantly, Memoria is the daughter of Uranus, who was the grandfather of Zeus; she is no mere sprite. Her Eleutherian Hills are the realm of freedom, so she governs freedom.

Without further ado, we may assert that the muses were created "by Zeus" to control the human memory so that humans should forget their catastrophes, and in so doing get surcease from sorrows. The word "muse" by itself has a meaning of happiness. And that the Muses will achieve this by transforming events through art and song, through myth. The memory of disasters is doctored "by Zeus" ultimately to brainwash humanity and to present the new order of heaven as proper, lawful, and beautiful. Hesiod, reciting this profound truth, goes on to describe how the muses work, reminding us of a combined team for domestic propaganda and psychological warfare.

As a result, all the arts and sciences have been manipulated by the muses. What we know of the catastrophes must come from a "natural history" - geology, biology, physics and astronomy - and a politics, philosophy, and theology that have been censored by the Muses. Additionally, we must obtain our historical material from myth, song, dances, and drama that are similarly screened. It is well to insist upon this premise, whether we come to the problem from an acquaintanceship with the natural sciences or the social sciences. The gods and especially Zeus, who seems under various names to have developed the patterns of anthropological psychology among most cultures, have required this premise of us.

The science of remembering and forgetting - what shall it be called - mnemonology? Its scope ranges from the ridiculous to the sublime; from the "psychopathology of everyday life," as Freud put it, to the "collective amnesia" that Velikovsky asserts of ancient catastrophes and that German educators observe as they try to teach the history of Nazism. It must deal with the Love Affair of Ares and Aphrodite that masks a world disaster, and with nursery songs that mask the murder of kings.

We may quote what Katherine Elwes Thomas found when she

explored *The Real Personages of Mother Goose:*

> The lines of Little Bo-Peep and Little Boy Blue, which to childish minds have only quaint charm of meaning, which suggest but the gayest of blue skies and rapturous-hearted creatures disporting in daisy-pied meadows, hold in reality grim import. Across all this nursery lore there falls at times the black shadow of the headman's block and in their seeming lightness are portrayed the tragedies of kings and queens, the corruptions of opposing political parties, and stories of fanatical religious strife that have gone to make world history.

For instance, the child sings of "four and twenty blackbirds, baked in a pie." And "when the pie was opened the birds began to sing," now, "wasn't that a tasty dish to put before the King?" The child is singing of actual history that was never heard or learned, of an incident in the grim struggle between the English Crown and the Church, during which, to appease the greed and hostility of the King, twenty-four deeds of church land were sealed into a pouch of dough and delivered to his castle. In old slang, the dough was handed over; in new slang, the "bread." The elapsed time from event to amnesiac song might have been less than a century.

The Oedipus myth, to take another instance, is capable of providing an accurate account of an episode in the history of Egypt. Its central figure was the Pharaoh Akhnaton. The story survived its original obliteration at the hands of the theocracy of Egyptian Thebes. It held intact as it was transferred across cultures, probably via Ugarit whose King Nikomedes may have founded Grecian Thebes, as Cadmus. By the time of Sophocles' tragedy, *Oedipus Rex,* seven mnemonic or fourteen reproductive generations had passed, that is, about four hundred years.[2]

Heavy trauma, it is here proposed, is at the source of many features of the higher intellectual operations and "advanced" social institutions of humankind.

> An experience which we call traumatic is one which within a very short space of time subjects the mind to such a very high increase of stimulation that assimilation or elaboration of it can no longer be effected by normal means, so that lasting disturbances must result in the

---

[2] Cf. I Velikovsky, *Oedipus and Akhnaton* (New York: Doubleday. 1960); Cyrus Gordon, "Oedipus and Akhnaton," II *Pensée,* no. 2(1972), p. 30: also notes in the same issue. We are using Velikovsky's revised chronology; John Holbrook, Jr. interprets this in III Pensee, no. 2(1973). I use term "mnemonic generation" to denote a sixty-year "memorial generation" in which the oldest members of a group can convey information to young children.

distribution of the available energy of the mind.³

TRAUMATIC ORIGIN OF MEMORY

In a prescient passage Friedrich Nietzsche (*Genealogy of Morals*, 1887) stabs into the heart of the matter. He asks, "How can one create a memory for the human animal? How can one impress something upon this partly obtuse, partly flighty mind, attuned only to the passing moment, in such a way that it will stay there?"⁴

And he continues,

> "One can well believe that the answers and methods for solving this primeval problem were not precisely gentle; perhaps indeed there was nothing more fearful and uncanny in the whole prehistory of man than his mnenotechnics. If something is to stay in the memory it must be burned in; only that which never ceases to hurt stays in the memory - this is a main clause of the oldest (unhappily also the most enduring) psychology on earth. One might even say that wherever on earth solemnity, seriousness, mystery, and gloomy coloring still distinguish the life of man and a people, something of the terror that formerly attended all promises, pledges, and vows on earth is still effective: the past, the longest, deepest and sternest past, breathes upon us and rises up in us whenever we become 'serious.' Man could never do without blood, torture and sacrifices when he felt the need to create a memory for himself; the most repulsive mutilations (castration, for example), the cruelest rites of all the religious cults (and all religions are at the deepest level systems of cruelties) - all this has its origin in the instinct that realized pain is the most powerful aid to mnemonics."⁵

Unfortunately, after this amazing passage, Nietzsche's genesis collapses. Although he immediately goes hunting for the acts that provoked such mnemotechnics, he shoots a little rabbit: the primitive forms of contract between buyers and sellers. In order to trade, men had to keep promises; in order to ensure obligations, the failure to repay had to be punished severely: thus the genealogy of morals.

One is reminded of Sigmund Freud's alternate route to fundamental

---

³ Sigmund Freud, *General Introduction to Psychoanalysis* (1916-7: Eng. trans. 1929), New York: Washington Square press, 1935), p. 286.

⁴ p. 496 of the Kaufman edition.

⁵ *Ibid.*, p. 497. Cf. Carl J. Jung, "Approaching the Unconscious," in *Man and His Symbols* (New York: Dell, 968), 1-94, for related material on fear, and on memory, pp. 34, 52-3.

error in *Totem and Taboo:* that in the oedipal conflict and the slaying of the father, man achieved a (bad) conscience and the need to justify and to punish. The Oedipus myth, as was said above, has much breadth and staying power, but a still greater and universal fear had to be imposed to support its recollection, and this was the fear of (devotion to) the god of Akhnaton. And it is difficult to conceive of anything more grand and durable than the catastrophes attendant upon encounters between Earth and other heavenly forces.

It is significant that Freud, perceiving an inadequacy of general sexual theory, moved *Beyond the Pleasure Principle,*[6] searching out a deeper fear that he termed the death instinct and observed to be present especially in veterans suffering from "shell-shock," whose nightmares and hallucinations found them continuously repeating what, after all, could hardly be called a pleasurable wish. Nor did such "symptoms vanish when their unconscious antecedents have been made conscious," as Freud remarks concerning obsessive fixations, following his earlier theory.[7] He and many others would have done well to stick with Nietzsche's brilliant premise and continue the search for historical psychological experiences of great stress befalling humankind when it had arrived at a complex state of organic potential.

The Love Affair involves both a disgraced contract and a disgraced sexuality. But these are cover-ups for a disaster too great to talk about. Indeed, by the time that the Love Affair occurred, only sexual imagery and violence were sufficiently eloquent to use as disguises, at least in literature; beyond that, one would have to resort for the patterning and recapitulation of such traumas to religious and political institutions - hierarchic, obsessed with the symbolism of violence, compulsively repetitive. The Love Affair, one must bear in mind, was only the latest in a series of catastrophes over thousands of years, from which human nature as we have known it was born and which shaped the physical world in which we live today.

Man's memory itself, the prototypical remembering, is a consequence of catastrophe more than of any other incidental or habitual interest of humanity. The Love Affair, in reflecting a catastrophe, reflects a late

---

[6] 1920, published in English, 195-, rev. ed. 1961, New York: Liveright; *Psycho-Analysis and the War Neuroses(* 1919), Stand. Ed:, XVII, 207;

[7] *General Introduction, op. cit.,* p. 291, 287.

event in a series of catastrophes that *created* memory. It was perhaps the last of the qualitatively distinct mass events on the basis of which memory was institutionalized, routinized, and socialized. Humans now remember (and forget) according to rules in which social forces play a continuous role, but this role evolved from catastrophes.

THE RULES OF MEMORY

All memory occurs under conditions that guarantee its imperfection. Given its mode of creation, remembering must function compatibly. No datum will enter the mind photographically. Rather the inputs will be screened not only by the senses, which themselves, in large part, perceive because of their prior social conditioning, but by the willingness to admit only censored data. This holds true, as many careful studies have shown, for the most noncontroversial and trivial kinds of experiences. Who says *remember* says *select*, who says *memory*, says *forgetting*. By the time of Homer, numerous natural disasters had befallen humanity; the perfect ease of the whole Phaeacian episode, including the Love Affair, attests to the approaching achievement of "perfect imperfection:" nothing of the original truth need be omitted, so well under control are the conditions creating imperfections. We are on our way to the climax of artistic sublimation.

The concept of "perfect memory" is a useful fiction. One is compelled to say that it is a theocratic fiction. For the content of what is remembered is in the broadest sense religiously and politically determined. The ideal canons of registering and remembering, set by modern science, are evidence in themselves that "you cannot trust your memory" and "independent observers have to confirm the same facts." But also the establishment of scientists as a social system lays down the rules of what is to be watched for, what is to be ignored, and what is to be distorted. The Homerids were the practitioners and teachers of "accurate memory" as defined to protect society against its anxieties.

The intensity of remembering is directly proportional to the gravity of a trauma. By intensity is meant sharpness, detail, and durability in conscious and unconscious form. By gravity is meant how deeply and adversely one is affected in the major regions of his life: his physical being, his cherished ones, his group, his wealth, his control, his beliefs about the good and the true. Machiavelli said to the rulers: it is better to be feared by the people than to be loved, if you cannot be both. Fear and anxiety drove primeval humanity to invent and to organize. Fear mixed itself early with love, and produced the continuous ambivalence towards sexuality that is exhibited in the Love Affair.

The most intense memories are likely to occur without "willing" them. This is understandable once we consider that no one will willingly subject himself to the conditions that produce intense memories. But one will try to will a pleasant memory. How many times do people think: "I shall never forget this beautiful sunset... I shall always remember this kindness... I shall never forget this orgasm," only to lose their grasp of the memory shortly thereafter. If a person remembers "a kind act" done to him long ago, it is in the context of a generally unkind and fearful environment of acts. The most that can be done to "will" the memory is to tie it consciously and unconsciously to disasters and especially institutionalize the disasters so that the group will continuously re-enact them. All great historical religions are based upon these psychological operations.

The most intense memories are most likely to be unavailable to the conscious mind, and to be buried in dreams and myths. These latter act to suppress and control anxiety. The dream and myth language is likely to approach as close as possible to the ultimate universal, traumatic experiences, without becoming unbearable. It rides on the tracks of birth throes, the fearful side of sexual copulation, death scenes, violence and conflict, including all the conventional transformations of these materials into religious and social activities, routines and institutions. This "step-down" principle works on the descent into the depths of the unconscious; it works, that is, on the depth of burial, and it brings about the selection of the next less traumatic kind of material as the screen for the more traumatizing type.

The speed of remembering is proportionate to the intensity of the trauma. "The experience burned itself indelibly upon my mind," one says. A single experience is enough to cause remembering, if it is grave enough. If it is too grave, physical collapse occurs and no further memorization is possible. At the other extreme, in the absence of fear, interest or even recognition - as in most classrooms, an abundance of knowledge moves, as they say, "from the notes of the teacher to the notes of the student without passing through the minds of either." If our physical analysis is correct, the astral Love Affair occupied a few hours among many years of experiencing all sorts of things.

The phenotypes of the myth are functions of the archetypes of the cultural personality, which is merely to say that the kind of story told, together with its details, are characteristic of the culture. Some more ancient pre-Greek and proto-Greek cultures practicing group marriage would have had to find a different plot and details to screen the reiteration of the Moon and Mars encounter. It is characteristic of "Western man's" partially Greek-born culture, and a proof of his cultural ancestry, that the adulterous love triangle, descended from the Greeks, is still a favorite artistic theme.

FORGETTING

Forgetting is subject to the same rules as remembering. We remember to forget. That is, amnesia is activated in the same way as memory. Glancing at the list of rules of remembering, one can substitute *forgetting* for *remembering* and get the following rules of forgetting.

Like remembering, forgetting is guaranteed to occur under all conditions, and to be imperfect, never complete. Nor is forgetting accurate: it is ragged, affected by many particular causes. If the popular metaphor speaks of the stream of memory, one can speak as well of the stream of forgetting. Forgetting occurs proportionate to the gravity of a trauma, and forgetting occurs without willing to forget.

The most intense forgetfulness is most likely to be available to the conscious mind; one must admit "we cannot recall what it is that we have forgotten," when the thing forgotten is a matter of grave threat to the mind.

Forgetting, too, speeds up with the intensity of the trauma. For this reason one can believe that events that occurred perhaps only a generation before Homer, or even in his lifetime, might achieve a complete aesthetic screen at his hands. Of course, a multitude of local scenarios are possible; but let us imagine what may have happened in a typical disaster of the "Age of Mars" that is, in the eighth and seventh centuries.[8]

An ordinary person is alerted and examines the sky with a foreboding of evil. A brilliant speck grows larger from day to day. He is told that it has done so before, with terrible consequences. The memory is already excited. Calendars are studied and worked over. Oracles are consulted. All group efforts are mobilized to control the menace: rituals of subservience and devotion; the stricter punishment of any suspected deviants in all areas of law and conduct; the destruction of enemies if they can be promptly engaged; the sacrifice of more and more valuable properties and persons.

Relentlessly the menace approaches. The sky is full of lights, shapes and turbulence. The Earth begins to respond - to live, to move, to smoke, to blow up strong winds, to shriek, to take fire. Thunderbolts strike on all sides. Our hero watches, bemused. He is exceedingly frightened, as are his family and neighbors. There may be a pandemonium in which he faints or is struck dumb; he may scramble into a temple or house or cave; he will cover his head. The young will observe more than the old. "The disaster occurs in successive kinds of turbulence, in all the various destructive forms of earth, air, fire, and water, the primordial elements. Animals, both tame and wild, crowd in upon people, terrified, unaggressive, unhungry. Eardrums are blown in or sucked out by abrupt pressure changes. Some are struck blind, others gassed. Strange objects and lifeforms drop from the sky. The sky reels. The waters gyrate madly and rush to and fro."

The vista is one of unmitigated disaster. There is nowhere to go. The survivors regroup after each incident. They are partially paralyzed with fear and despair, partly striving for survival and control.

"What god is angry?" they wonder, if they don't already know. What other gods can they appeal to and how? What trait of a god should they address themselves to? The most important religious and political decisions of their lifetimes are made; the most sacred instruments and skills of the immemorial past are called upon in the crisis. Nothing, nobody, will ever persuade him to behave differently, or his children or, if they can help it, their descendants into the eternal future.

When the disasters subside, the survivors are crazed. They must regroup, recollect their thoughts, and do something about the memory. This is not a task for an astronomer sitting in the air-conditioned hall of a giant telescope in Arizona. Nor for a sober historian. It is a task for any surviving priest rulers: "We have been visited by the gods. The figures they strike in the sky are their various apparitions when destructive and punitive... Good gods and spirits fight evil ones. Our conduct displeases them: we must strengthen our observance of rituals: purify ourselves; expiate our sins; sacrifice ever more precious possessions; kill more enemies; control the libertarian; guard the names by which we call a god; and remind ourselves forevermore of the events of these days while we watch for their eventual recurrence."

---

[8] Frank W. Lane's book, *The Elements Rage* (Philadelphia: Chilton Books, 1965), can be used as a kind of reference manual for all that happens when the forces of nature intensify into their disastrous forms.

Again history is quickly subverted: indeed, it has never existed. Instead memorial activities are planned by the community that will register whatever intensity on the memorial-screen is sufficient to suppress the pain of the memory of the original experience plus all the preceding related and similar traumatic experiences.

It is well to be quite explicit: No sooner is a disaster experienced than it is remembered: no sooner remembered than it is forgotten. All the rules of remembering are rules of forgetting.

What? Is memory a forgetting while to forget is to remember? One seems to be approaching this paradox; if it is not indeed an absurdity. Yet, if we resolve this paradox we shall better understand the great mystery of myth, which bids us remember ferociously in order the more firmly and securely to forget.

The paradox disappears with one fact, well appreciated. The fact is that a memory can enter the mind, but can rarely leave it. Except by organic lesion, there is little forgetting. The biological system can scarcely throw off a memory; it can readily manipulate it.

What is called "forgetting" is the eternal bookkeeping system of memory. From conception to dissolution and death, the system will always show a net profit. But, like many a bookkeeping system in commerce, memorial bookkeeping has numerous ways of casting the balance so as to conceal the surplus. It is with the forgotten material that the mind works to create myth, art, and hypothesis. The concept of forgetting is needed to describe the handling of the transactions of memory that permit consciousness, instrumentally rational conduct, and normal behavior.

Where is the balance cast that *makes these two opposites indeed opposite?* In the functional machinery of the mind, where opposites are coined according to the needs of the moment. Whatever stabilizes the organism's "normalcy" is chosen; and the organism remembers or forgets conveniently.

AMNESIAC PHILOSOPHERS

Whatever the finesse with which memory and forgetfulness may be explained, there must remain some incredulity in the modern mind. Scientists believe proudly that they can read any evidence unflinchingly.

If the human mind that experienced catastrophe should not remember consciously, and discourse liberally and frankly upon it, what then of those tough intellectuals of ancient times who conducted inquiries afterwards? Why have they not handed down frank evidence of catastrophes? The disbelief of the theory of the Love Affair that was based upon archaeological, geological and astronomical grounds may have changed to acceptance. But what of the silences of ancient history?

Though certain biases of languages and philosophy that formed after the catastrophes have already been noted - several additional suggestions may be offered as to why Hesiod, Homer, Thales, Pythagoras, Plato and other illustrious ancient Greeks do not frankly tell their curious descendants of the true deeds of Mars and the Moon.

In the first place, natural disasters and sudden change *did* occupy the minds of ancient thinkers (sticking still to the Greek-speaking area). Homer's *Iliad* is replete with accounts of god-enacted and god-caused disaster. In Aristophanes' comedy, "The Clouds," the gods reprove the Moon for having brought disasters to the calendar and their cult. Plato begs us to take him seriously when he relates the story of the destruction of Atlantis. (One may infer that there were a great many spoofers of old myth in Athens.) In *The Laws,* he asserts that mankind has been reduced to marginal survivors on numerous occasions owing to natural disasters. Conversely, he is angry at the "immorality" of Homer, which he takes at face value, and in the same dialogue he proclaims the god-given harmony and regularity of the heavenly spheres and would punish severely offenders who claim disasters have come or will come from the skies. Plato's self-contradictions in respect to catastrophism are serious. They reveal great doubts in his mind, and what in an ordinary person would be called "typical neurotic aggressiveness to resolve the tensions provoked by his doubts."

In the *Epinomis,* Plato is again exhibiting his anxieties, in a form that has not been generally appreciated. As mentioned in an earlier place, he gave the present Greek names of the planets for the first time. He offers the lame excuse that the fiery terms used for the heavenly bodies were so similar because the Greeks did not know the planets and did not want unfairly to give names to some but not to others.

Perhaps the whole matter of naming was controversial, involving as it did ancient psychological associations, theological theories, and intercultural contacts with Egyptians, Syrians, and others.

In any event, attention should be called to Plato's statement that the heavenly bodies are gods without souls. He distinguishes these from the Olympian gods, whom he dislikes, precisely because of their reputation for immorality and uncontrollability. He is, in effect, trying to rid the mundane scene of these gods, by exiling them in the eternal immutable astral regions. He would then fix the calendar of festivals to their periods. This would seem to be a major unconscious philosophical step towards controlling the gods and paving the way for a lawful universe. Thus it happened that Plato usurped the Olympian gods.

Aristotle, over three hundred years after the Love Affair, was still conscientious, if serene, in his study of the skies: heaven and the planets are self-moved movers executing perfectly regular motions; they are substances immune to change and far more perfect than man. He is nevertheless impelled to write of planets:

> Our forefathers in the most remote ages have handed down to us, their posterity, a tradition, in the form of a myth, that these substances are Gods and that the divine encloses the whole of nature. The rest of the tradition has been added later in mythical form with a view to the persuasion of the multitude and to its legal and utilitarian expedience; they say these Gods are in the form of men or like some of the other animals, and they say other things consequent on and similar to these which we have mentioned. But if we were to separate the first point from these additions and take it alone - that they thought the first substances to be Gods, we must regard this as an inspired utterance, and reflect that, while probably each art and science has often been developed as far as possible and has again perished, these opinions have been preserved until the present, like relics of the ancient treasure. Only thus, then, is the opinion of our ancestors and our earliest predecessors clear to us [9].

Moreover, the ancients were habituated to a level of natural disaster that would astonish moderns. Earthquakes, erupting volcanoes, and "rushing stars" (meteorites and comets) were much more common in the era following the settling of heaven. Earthquakes were ordinary in Rome, for instance, even five centuries later. The Greeks did not develop a tradition of geological and astronomical reporting until the scientific period began, over a century after Homer sang (seventh century). Herodotus carries remarks about disaster in his *Histories* (fifth century); Thucydides, who could describe plagues in acceptable modern medical style, flourished 250 years after the Love Affair. He reported no astral phenomena of consequence during the Peloponnesian Wars.

---

[9] *Metaphysics* (W. D. Ross trans.) Vol. II, L. 1074b.

Third, the number of survivors was small. Many storage and retrieval systems of memory were blasted or drowned out. If the many dutiful clerks of Pylos, Mycenae, Knossos, Troy, and other centers had continued their bureaucracies, the records might be ample.

Furthermore, astral encounters and an earthly turbulence would provoke dense or brilliant atmospheric conditions that would render stable observations rare. Encounters would often be obscured and only partly visible in the areas where there would be potentially competent observers. One would always expect disputation as to what occurred when the celestial armies clashed.

The printing press was unknown and only the bark of the papyrus, clay tablets, stone, and several types of leaf were the media for the inscription and transmission of messages non-orally. Although more durable than modern books and film, they lacked the widespread dissemination that can be achieved with the printed word. Records were always few and a great burden was placed upon accurate memorization and repetition to the young, to an extent quite unappreciated today.

Oral accounts, like writing to be sure, have intrinsic mnemonic techniques, which, to the discredit of our scientific age, have not been adequately analyzed, and which lend, therefore, a greater semblance of error that actually exists in the accounts told. Personification of events, for example, is a technique of illiterate memorization, as well as a psychological process that is pervasive of mental operations in nearly all cultures.

There has been an almost total destruction of records, both from the time of the catastrophes and later. Only several thousands of the clay tablets from several locations carrying the language "Linear B" have been rescued from the ruins of Mycenaean culture. These tablets, by their paucity and scorched condition offer mute testimony that a well-administered civilization became a shambles of fire, destruction and death perhaps in a few hours, and a few events.

The classical period produced thousands of volumes by scientists on most subjects. Almost all of these have been lost owing to carelessness, barbarian depredations, and political and religious fanaticism.[10] Of 150 known Greek authors of tragic drama, we have full plays by only three

---

[10] Cf. H. Bellamy, *Moon, Myths and Man* (London: Faber and Faber, 1936), pp. 44-7, for details of the destruction of ancient records.

of them and only thirty-three of the 297 creations of these three men remain. From this ancient treasure would have come a number of plays such as Seneca's *Thyestes,* which could only be a pale later replay of Sophocles' lost *Atreus,* both concerned with the devastating commotions of the globe in the period of the Love Affair.

Owing to the rules of memory and forgetting, one should not expect an elaborate literature of catastrophe to have existed in scientific form, but the writings of Pythagoras, Eudoxos, Alcmaion, Eratosthenes and many another author would have established ample foundations for a set of modern sciences that would admit of catastrophism in their theories.

When the great modern astronomer, Schiaparelli, reconstructed the planetary theory of Eudoxos (408-355), the colleague of Plato (427?-347) and Aristotle, he had this to say:

> For Jupiter and Saturn, and to some extent for Mercury also, the system was capable of giving on the whole a satisfactory explanation of their motion in longitude, their stationary points, and their retrograde motions; for Venus it was unsatisfactory, and it failed altogether in the case of Mars. The limits of motion in latitude represented by the various *hippopedes* were in tolerable agreement with observed facts, although the periods of the deviations and their places in the cycle were quite wrong." [11]

We would surmise that Eudoxos' problem arose from an absence of data concerning the classical and present celestial order. For the other planets, he may have had access to several centuries of observations from Egypt or Mesopotamia. For Venus, and even more for Mars, there may have been fewer ancient sources and less lengthy series of observations available to him. These planets, too, in their present motions, are more difficult to plot than the others. Perhaps the problem of theory was even more important than the problem of data; he might have had to disencumber himself of a theory of motions and cycles that was more adequate for an earlier sky than for a classical sky.

If this speculation about Eudoxos is tenable, one may dissever in him the factors of amnesiac relief through abstraction, a lack of fundamental data from the past and puzzlement owing to incorrect theory. Eudoxos was striving to order the cleared skies; he would in any event have found ancient evidence of erratic skies a nuisance and impediment.

---

[11] Quoted in Ross, op. cit., II, P. 390. Cf. Walter Burkert, *Lore and Science in Ancient Pythagoreanism,* trans. by E. L. Miner (Cambridge Harvard U. Press, 1972), part IV, regarding, *inter alia,* Eudoxus' influence on Plato.

These several reasons why direct scientific observations of ancient catastrophes have rarely reached us complement the primary and most striking reason that has already been discussed: massive instantaneous amnesia in direct proportion to the pain and horror of disaster, followed by heavy ritualistic, aggressive, and expressive displacement of the fear and avoidance involved. Nichomachus of Gerasa and Lucian agreed; the divine Orpheus was the founder of astronomy and the inventor of the harp. "The harp, that had seven chords, discoursed the harmony of the errant spheres."[12]

The "errant spheres;" the disasters; the memory and the forgetting; the muses; the harp for the sublimation of memory; and the "holy dreamtime songs" like the Love Affair.

---

[12] Lucian (second century, A. D.), "Astrology," in Works, Vol. V, A. M. Harmon, trans. (Cambridge, Mass.: Harvard Univ, Press, 1936), p. 355. Nichomachus (first century A. D.) was famous for his mathematical accuracy.

CHAPTER SIXTEEN

THE TRANSFIGURATION OF TRAUMA

One thunderstorm does not make a great god, nor does one volcano. Further, ordinary nature does not make a great god, neither its abundances nor its famines. The struggles of old bulls with young bulls over cows do not make a great god. A great god dwells in heaven, but can be everywhere. A people will recognize another people's great god as kindred but, too, the god is often hostile. Every great god emerges out of an apparently universal disaster in which the skies are involved, not excepting the great Mother - Earth Goddess, oldest of all, who cast off from her heaving body the oppressive Heaven, Uranus.

The gods of the Love Affair are great gods. And to the skeptic who deplores the deceit, adultery, and generally libertine and human deportment of these "stars," one might remark: "You cannot imagine how really badly these gods behaved; it was inutterably worse... Anyhow, no one is saying that these are *your* gods, and we had better not get onto *that* subject."

The gods of Demodocus opera theater behave as they do to cover up their real behavior which is infinitely more destructive, indiscriminate, and punitive. The next problem of this stage is to show how their more intolerable behavior works itself out as a bedroom farce. How was the traumatic disaster transformed?

DREAMWORK

The best available model for the interpretation of a myth is the dream. As was shown in an early chapter, the staging of the telling of myth creates a collective Holy Dreamtime. The audience is prepared to dream, to engage in dreamwork themselves, and to emerge with a sense of heightened reality. For reality is the unreality that enable people to compose their anxieties. In *The Interpretation of Dreams,* his admitted masterwork,[1] Sigmund Freud told how dream functions to keep one asleep, and one can only stay asleep so long as the unconscious problems that bother him most are censored and reworked into a form, which, while often disgusting and disturbing upon recollection, is nevertheless better than the unconscious reality.

To discover the latent wish whose fulfillment keeps one asleep is not always easy, as many a psychiatrist will attest. Homer tried his hand at it, in an astonishing scientific leap over two millennia:

It is dark. Odysseus has returned to his palace. He presents himself to Penelope, his wife, in the disguise of an old beggar who has some knowledge of her husband, the long-wandering king of Ithaca. He wins her confidence. Penelope speaks to him (in disguise as an old beggar):

Let me ask you to interpret a dream of mine which I shall now describe. I keep a flock of twenty geese in the place. They come in from the pond to pick up their grain and I delight in watching them. In my dream I saw a great eagle swoop down from the hills and break their neck with his crooked beak, killing them all. There they lay in a heap on the floor while he vanished in the open sky. I wept and cried aloud, though it was only a dream, and the Achaean ladies, gathering around me, found me sobbing my heart out because the eagle had slaughtered my geese. But the bird came back. He perched on a jutting timber of the roof, and breaking into human speech he checked my tears. "Take heart," he said, 'daughter of the noble Icarius. This is not a dream but a happy reality which you shall see fulfilled. The geese were your lovers, and I that played the eagle's part am now your husband, home again and ready to deal out grim punishment to every man among them.' At this point I awoke. I looked around me and there I saw the geese in the yard pecking

---

[1] (1900). Vols. IV and V of the *Standard Edition* (London: Hogarth press, 1953; New York: Basic Books; Avon Books, 1972.

their grain at the trough in their accustomed place.

"Lady," replied the subtle Odysseus, "nobody could force any other meaning on this dream; You have learnt from Odysseus himself how he will translate it into fact. Clearly the suitors are all of them doomed: There is not one who will get away alive."[2]

The cunning and cautious Odysseus agrees quickly, in an uncharacteristic way. (Or can one believe that Homer was so extremely subtle as to make him here super-cunning?)

A psychiatrist does well to avoid counsel where his own private involvement is deep. Penelope's wish may not have been that her husband return and the suitors be slain, but quite the contrary, that her legendary patriarchal husband not return so that her beautiful geese could continue to play about her and eat from her board. This latent and ambivalent wish has been bothering her and making her sleep badly, we hear. Perhaps the best that the dream could contrive for her was to act out what she feared, followed by a hysterical awakening; and then came the half-asleep explanation, with which Odysseus emphatically agreed.[3]

It is perhaps one of the signal achievements of humanity to have discovered and applied the principles of collective dreamwork. The sacred conscious dreamers of ancient Phaecia *do* stay asleep and it is an amusing dream. They are awakened gently by the boys leaping into the air after a ball. Odysseus, one might think, should have been upset by the Love Affair dream. It would not stretch the imagination to put himself in Hephaestus' place, long absent, with his wife rumored to be consorting with various suitors, enjoying his bed as they were his board. Instead he was "glad at heart, following the Song of Demodocus." There was fundamentally more at stake in the dream than his Penelope and possessions.

The reduction of the gods to human terms in the Love Affair myth under examination is basically a way of coping with them. It is universal in religion, as annoying as it may be to rational philosophers. All religion is a dream; the actions here analyzed are a mere flicker played upon a

---

[2] Lines 531-590, Murray, op. cit.

[3] An alternative reconstruction, more Jungian than Freudian, is that Penelope was suffering a crisis of Character, in which the eagle (her stronger, more dictatorial, dogmatic aspect) was moving bloodily to dispose of the geese (her inner weakness), and, in the course of the resolution, identifying with her absent husband. George English, who pointed out this interpretation to me, thought as well that the transition was a bloody bridge that often is crossed at the presumed age of Penelope, between 35 and 45.

universal human screen.

Within itself, however, the present myth has an external logic that most dreams do not possess. Freud speaks of the occasional reorganization that occurs in dreams so as to reassemble the transmuted pieces into an acceptable form that fools one with its facade of "really the way things happen." The myth has been worked upon consciously. It is not Kafka-esque or Ionescu-esque; it does not double back upon itself like the theater of the absurd. Homer had gone far, but not *that* far. His myth is classical, "rational," "normal."

His handling of the material gives a clue as to how the Greek and Western mind will work from then on in transmuting its unconscious material into its fictional components: "realism," romanticism (in the vulgar sense), explicit motivation, clarity of plot. At least, this has been the leading thrust of western literature, especially of popular literature, until now.

Freud mentions also the reversal of cause and effect in dreams. One is uncertain, for example, exactly "how the gods flew." The astrophysical uncertainty leaves one uncertain whether such a reversal may have affected the myth. Since destruction was mutual among the parties, the myth-work could have enjoyed some leeway in deciding "who did what to whom" and thereby ease its task.

Other features of dreamwork that Freud analyzed have already been treated. He says that the dreamer is always present in his dream, although somewhat apart as a kind of third person, and our myth contains its dreamers as well, from Athena and Odysseus, down to the ordinary household retainer crowding at the periphery of the audience, the ordinary man beset by the disastrous conduct of the gods.

Freud says, too, that the dreamer commands symbolic language which he has never been aware of learning. And George English has neatly stated that "a dream is a tool for rubbing information against information." So, although the ordinary Phaeacian was not a master of the ceremonies, he was, as a community member, entitled to identify himself with the action; the symbolism of the myth may have meant as much to him or her as it did to Odysseus, or more.

Freud discovered that when the wakened dreamer recites the dream, he is prone to deny most vociferously those elements that are exercising the dreamwork censorship. Everything may be made clear except that which is most obvious - the purpose of the dream. What might have

The Transfiguration Of Trauma

been going on in the unconscious mental operations of the Phaeacian dreamers was described in the pages on "The Love Affair as the Mask of Tragedy." But if Odysseus or any Phaeacian were to be questioned about the myth, his most assured remark would be that it was comedy, not a tragedy; that disaster was not his concern, that the gods had everything under control and didn't mean what they were doing anyhow - in short, a total contradiction of the covert meaning of the myth.

Elsewhere in these pages, other Freudian injunctions as to the components of dreamwork were considered: the transmutation of catastrophic symbolism into the symbols of the smithy and the bedroom; the matching of plot with reality, and reality with wish; the uncovering of the levels of meaning.

Freud can help on at least one more perplexing point, because it bedeviled him too. One cannot help but wonder at the sanguine piling up of levels of different meaning upon single words, phrases and symbolic deeds; this author must seem like a table waiter setting upon his arm an alarmingly tall stack of plates. Freud talks in *The Interpretation of Dreams* of the genius of dreamwork.

> It is, indeed, not easy to form any conception of the abundance of the unconscious trains of thought, all striving to find expression, which are active in our minds. Nor is it easy to credit the skill shown by the dream-work in always hitting upon forms of expression that can bear several meanings; My readers will always be inclined to accuse me of introducing an unnecessary amount of ingenuity into my interpretations; but actual experience would teach them better.[4]

Even when the mind is carefully trained to perceive and understand by one sign only a single referent, it does so under duress. For such perception and cognition is not only inhuman; it is false to "reality." And when freed from the bonds of an everyday meaning, the mind exhibits an astonishing genius for combinations and patterns of "unreal reality." Hephaestus' lameness means all that we have said it means, and perhaps even more. The movements of the plot of the Love Affair are of the number and variety of the movements of great bodies in the sky, a double-tracked reality that scarcely strains the myth-making mind.

Given that Nineveh and Sparta were designed by their rulers to imitate various celestial archetypes, can one still be amazed that the same archetypes will have been working within the unconscious mind to

---

[4] Page 562, 332 fn., 560, 60, 534 ff.

produce many other manifestations, concealed as well as overt?

Where Freud cannot help one, or rather, where one would not want his help, given his theories, is in the interpretation of the larger framework of sexualism and catastrophe. For here, as mentioned before, Freud, like every other authority except the rare predecessors of, and those of the circle of, Velikovsky has not known or been willing to acknowledge the priority of catastrophes over other drives and behaviors in the creation of human nature and institutions as found today. Freud may have postulated an instinct for "ego-survival," but he did not conceive how catastrophically the ego had been threatened.

SEXUALITY & DISASTER

The Love Affair is especially appropriate for the analysis of the causal forces in human history because it seems on its face to show that sex is so important that even disasters are translated into sexual terms. This is true only in a quantitative sense; sexuality is a step down from catastrophe in the mental turmoil associated with it, and, as such, is a logical deflator of catastrophic anxiety. The Love Affair, paradoxically, reveals sexuality to be secondary in the definition of human nature.

At the beginning one must of course grant the obvious: the Love Affair is saturated with sexuality. It would be difficult to conceive, furthermore, of any area of behavior that would provide such a complete analogy to the latent action and at the same time one that would communicate so readily with the audience of ancient Greeks. We have already remarked on the Grecian fascination with the struggle between the sexes.

Sexuality is primeval, familiar, a continuous source of conflict. It is both marvelous and understandable, surrounded with mishap, steady, dangerous and humorous. It lends itself to moods, to sharing and exclusiveness, to love and hate. It is endlessly diverting and suggestive with respect to ordinary nature. In its reproductive aspects, it is profoundly meaningful to short-lived and disease-prone people. But, one should not forget, sexuality points "downward," to the animal kingdom, further to the plants. What has sex to do with the astral gods? No. The philosophers are right in their way, Sex is tossed by man onto the laps of gods. It is an expiative and control mechanism. "You shall have all we have, and, (cunningly) you will be controlled by it, too."

One must not go too far afield. This ground should be left for a later ploughing. One is faced in the Love Affair with a sexuality thousands of years beyond its first ramifications into human nature. Here it is necessary only to throw up a barrier against interpreting the Love Affair as a love affair because sexuality is deemed to be the fountainhead of myth.

Sexuality can also be a cloak of disaster. It stands here with all of its traditional and well-developed imagery in place of the true story. There is reason for its use. Catastrophe can be buried well beneath sexual imagery; there are enough intimations of fright, noise, violence, love, hate, strangeness, explosiveness, conflict and damage in the "primal scene," the "birth trauma," the lust to mate, and the competition for mates to inspire the most profound analogies. Still, they are partial analogies, not "the whole real thing."

And when the direction of causation is reversed, there is additional reason to believe that the catastrophes of the gods are the teachers of sexual conduct, as they are the teachers of religion, of politics, of war, of the arts and crafts. Catastrophe reinforces sexuality, provides taboos, devises perversions, excites sexual orgies, and poisons relations between the sexes even while it exalts them. That the often repeated song of Demodocus must have taught the audience something about sex, marriage and justice is quite likely. The "calloused attitude" toward such affairs may have been Dorian Greek but where did the Dorians get it from?

The sexual psychoses, which Sigmund Freud and every doctor from the shaman to the Park Avenue psychiatrist have treated, are aggravated by the uncontrolled amnesia of disaster and by many of the transfigured forms of behavior that man invented to ameliorate the symptoms of disaster. Not having yet uncovered the source of the infernal *Angst* that crouches ready to produce psychotic behavior, therapists, whether specialized in sexually oriented crises, or religiously inspired, or war-peace directed, or of any other inclination - alienation, materialism, etc. - can go on in endless circles, curing when easing of symptoms will occur in any event, curing through authority, or passing along through symptomatic relief a psychosis from one object-fixation to another.[5]

---

[5] Cf. Sebastian de Grazia, *Errors of Psychotherapy* (New York: Doubleday. 1952).

Withal one should not deny that a skillful cutting of the brain and drugging of the glands may someday excise the primeval *Angst;* it may be that the stone-age men of many areas were up to treating a catastrophically-induced psychosis with their frequent resort to trephination of the skull.

IN ILLO TEMPORE

It is common for persons who have suffered a personal disaster to have a recurrent dream respecting it. The same dream or one like it may repeat itself for years, disappear for years, and recur. Similarly, every known human group has developed in its prehistoric period various myths that have to be retold and rituals that have to be repeated. All of them go back to the great times of destruction and creation, *illud tempus,* a phrase that Mircea Eliade finds useful as a pivotal point in his far ranging studies of comparative religion.

Writing of the activities of archaic man, which would include Homeric man, he declares that "their meaning, their value, are not connected with their crude physical datum but with their property of reproducing a primordial act, of repeating a mythical example. Nutrition is not a simple physiological operation; it renews a communion. Marriage and the collective orgy echo mythical prototypes; they are repeated because they were consecrated in the beginning (in those days *in illo tempore, ab origine*) by gods, ancestors, or heroes."[6]

"We must do as the gods did in the beginning."[7] Time must be regenerated periodically, in endless cycles; in accord with the temporal period, many things are renewed: fires are put out and rekindled, the dead return to visit, the original combats between gods and devils are re-enacted, and orgies commemorating the destruction of all values are held to precede the new year. The year *in illo tempore* ended in a catastrophe of earth, air, fire, and/or water. "In fact, among many primitive people, an essential element of any cure is the recitation of the cosmogonic myth." Also, it is recited on the occasions of birth, marriage, and death, indeed

---

[6] *Myth of the Eternal Return,* p. 4.

[7] *Ibid.,* p. 21.

The Transfiguration Of Trauma 229

for practically every occasion when a person needs to build up morale.[8]

Yet this same "archaic man" dreads history. He wishes only to recapitulate his beginnings, the sacred events, not the profane events that have happened since. He is not simply a conservative, a traditionalist; he is super-conservative, obsessed with what happened *in illo tempore*. For there was a dreadful thing then, beyond all historical measure and until it is controlled, nothing else is controllable.

With all his acumen and learning, Eliade himself does not penetrate the iron curtain *illius temporis*. Something Big Happened! He writes one work entitled *Myth and Reality,* but the "reality" is not what happened; it is the interposed reality of a revisionist philosopher, not the reality of which the myths speak in deafening language and blinding imagery. And he entitles another of his works *The Myth of the Eternal Return,* but here, too, he confines himself to providing valuable illumination from all quarters of the globe on the obsessive need to make the great leap backwards to the traumatics events, not to the *actual* conditions that mankind returns to.

The terror *in illo tempore,* the fact that "for archaic men, reality is a function of the imitation of a celestial archetype," the association of the return with cures that practically scream out, "If we survived chaos and creation, we can survive anything!" the fixation upon cycles of disaster and revival and the incompetency of humanity over millennia to get onto a longitudinal temporal plane - all of these facts and many more constitute evidence that unspeakable disaster governs the so-called "archaic mind" and carries through to modernity.

Indeed, one must credit the doctrine of uniformitarianism, and all of its ramifications in the sciences and philosophy, as being the first successful counterattack of the human mind against the fetters that catastrophes imposed upon it. It was largely this modern doctrine in astronomy, geology, biology, and finally religion and politics that smoothed out the external cycles, made the proven details of history important, claimed millions of year for human development, and set up the idea of progress - all of these being achievements that would have been difficult without denying the importance of what happened *in illo tempore*.

The myth of the Love Affair is not a basic document to establish the

---

[8] *Ibid.,* pp. 66, 68, 73, 82-3.

general theory of the first days because it is not a myth of creation. That it is in direct line with cosmogony may, however, be asserted. It is a tale told in a newly settled land under semi-cosmogonic conditions of dream, dance, rhythm, and verse. The gods struggle; the Moon is renewed.

It is a second-level myth in the last series of catastrophes. Its relationship with the events *in illo tempore* is apparent, but it is of the last days of that time. In the next century and a half, the first group of uniformitarians will have appeared, with the colossal nerve to say, with Plato, that "the ruler of the universe has ordered all things with a view to the excellence and preservation of the whole."[9]

THE KERNELS OF HISTORY

Millions of words of myth have been born of the human mind through the ages. Myth is still being created, not only among the so-called primitive peoples whose numbers are so rapidly diminishing everywhere, but also in the sophisticated editorial rooms of giant newspaper and television monopolies and in the halls of law and bureaucracy. The myth that "the President works with great energy and command of information" is comparable to the myth that "Hercules cleared the Augean Stables." (Amusingly, Hercules was accused of a conflict of interest for taking pay from two sources for his work.)

This is so if we take, as the superficial rendering of the word, that myth is a factual narrative whose aim is to some important degree to stabilize the ever-flowing stream of anxiety of the organism within itself and in regard to the outer environment. It is like a dam that commands the flow of water from the rains and streams above in the interest of the consumers of the water below. By using common symbols, the system operates on behalf of a community. As a result, a myth will perform little or no functions for a person who belongs to another community, to a different hydraulic control system. One should not be put off, therefore, when a scoffer exclaims: "All these myths do nothing for me."

The greatest sources of trouble and fear are the greatest and most enduring sources of myth. The doings of the gods (nature),

---

[9] Plato, *The Laws,* book X, p. 290, loc. cit.

supplemented by the dynamics of sexuality and the competition for the other scarce values of power, respect, wealth, knowledge and health provide both the anxieties and the linguistic references used to compose myths. The combinations and permutations of expression that give rise to particular myths are infinite, especially when one adds the universal factors of *wish fulfillment,* already mentioned, and *functional design,* by which different types of myths are to be used as supplications, expiation, lessons to children, augury, dramatic entertainment, and so on. Myth is adapted, also to create the type of person a society's ideology needs.

That millions of words have been composed for such personal-social reasons over 10,000 years, say, is not at all surprising. and that most myth is untranslatable without knowledge of its culture, its language, the context in which one myth is employed, and its typical audience is also understandable. Which is to say that the problem of the historic message contained in a myth is to be solved only when these features of its expression are known.

Afterwards, the historic content of the myth can be approached directly. In this sense all myth contains history about a group; it could only come about as a result of experiences, whether one or many; and its detail contains empirical and linguistic references. Ares does not "bridle" in a horseless culture, nor does one smite a rock to get water in swampland. That Achilles is known by 36 epithets and Odin by fifty names, gives some idea of the variety of traits of a hero or god in a given culture.

But now to the most difficult problem; the portrayal of an actual event in a myth, as in the Love Affair. If one has arrived at the historic message contained in the Love Affair, what is to prevent him from putting all of Greek myth or any other body of myth through a historiographical sausage-grinder, emerging with thousands of little links of Greek history? It is conceivable. But much is trivia and repetitive. Or the history involved has such vague parameters of time, space and references *when treated as history* as to be useless.

Also, a great, if unknown proportion of myth consists of references to cultures, sub-cultures, priesthoods, temples, occupations, and schools that are lost to history. Their local contexts are missing. Furthermore, many myths are hopelessly successful in their function of telling about something while at the same time concealing it (the opposite of scientific communication which aims at telling something and only that something in a special language designed to communicate it clearly and exactly).

Still, the impression of impenetrable jungle and inescapable labyrinth that the first sight of the body of myth makes upon one retreats remarkably upon application of the tools of the sciences and the virtues of patience and imagination to particular segments.

Then the questions occur: "Who cares?" and "What resources are we willing to devote the task?" For most people, and experts, too, the use of myth is largely that of symbolic poetry: the mind reacts to it, is startled, pleased, achieves a phantasmagoria or pandemonium akin to the effects of various drugs. Enough.

On the other hand, where there exists little of other types of knowledge of important historical problems, natural or social, resort to myth analysis is necessary and its techniques will be continuously improved. To the degree that such systematic work is accompanied by an equally alert and extensive archaeology, considerable advances in a number of sciences might ensure. As the expert on Babylonian and ancient science, Otto Neugebauer, once commented to the author in a few moments of smoking of the peace-pipe between exchanges on the work of Velikovsky, we could dig up the whole ancient world with a fraction of the funds of the space program, and thus find out what it has to say to us. The art treasures to be excavated would, of course, be also of value.

CHAPTER SEVENTEEN

SETTLED SKY & UNSETTLED MIND

Great myths are the stories of human tragedy on a grand scale. If mankind no longer exists in an age of myth, it is not because of a new intelligence or style but because of the lack of terrible stimulus. Even so, the ages of myth-making have left a legacy of serious problems. *One does* relive the ancient terrors; they have left deep tracks in minds and glands, regularly revived by a horde of customs and rememorized. Furthermore, man is a myth-maker and he will always find sufficient personal and social crises to inspire individual and collective repressions of memory, though not on the original grand scale.

WHAT HOMER REMEMBERED

Earlier, we decided to place Homer's "publication" of the *Odyssey* around 630 B. C., two generations after the end of the Martian catastrophes. We mentioned in another place that amnesia can set in abruptly following a grave event and the sublimation of the troublesome subconscious memory could be accomplished quickly as well. We alluded to nursery rhymes based upon atrocious political acts for an example.

Still, the question gnaws at us: "Did Homer really not known of the disasters of the century before him?"

The catastrophist reaches, all too easily at times, for the "proof by non-existent proof," which comes close to begging the question. Thus, physical and biological destruction, if complete, makes memory non-existent, therefore impossible. Psychic destruction (total amnesia) also makes proof impossible in the sense that the remembering mind cannot remember any of the events one is called upon to remember. Total Psychic Destruction and/or Total Physical Destruction equals Zero Proof, hence zero recall of the catastrophic events. We have advanced in these pages and elsewhere many conditions approaching the Zero Proof formula, but never has history been totally obstructed. Therefore Homer must have had some means of knowing the catastrophic events of two generations earlier, even in his childhood.

We now can suppose that he did remember terrific destruction and social turmoil, directly or through his elders. Why would these memories not enter into his work directly? Why would he not attach the Greek gods (except Helios, the Sun), to their sky-bodies?

In the first place, he would not dare to or wish to tie the gods explicitly to their bodies. The gods were much more than the bodies, much older than the events in which they acted, and hostile to presumptions (hubris) of humans about them. Homer and other dramatists might also have agreed to a convention not to portray the gods in this manner.

On the subconscious level, Homer may have written of the gods in such a way as to display their natural histories, even knowing of their history in some part and consciously, without realizing that he was writing the history of the gods. He could describe Ares as Ares, actually appreciating that he was doing so, protesting (as writers accused of libel or of autobiography sometimes do), "I am only writing fiction," and furthermore they will believe it and so will their hearers.

This is no more than happens with children, who, in their play, will often re-enact disagreeable experiences with cruel attendants or playmates in a comic or brutal scenario with toys, and, when questioned, will sincerely deny that they were re-enacting the real experiences. I need only mention similar and well known behavior among persons who are mentally ill. Nor need I discuss again the technology of dreams, whereby the dreamer translates the experience into a detailed representation, which he may promptly forget, or he is unable to retranslate into real terms, or which he may refuse in either event to accept as connected with his experience.

We conclude that, behaving typically, Homer could know both subconsciously and to a degree consciously of a horrendous history, could rewrite the history as poetry, could refuse to make explicit connections that would be obviously revealing, and could deny that his story was historical. "How can you doubt me," we hear Demodocus and Homer crying, "am I not blind?" There is no end to the self-deception and deceptiveness of the schizoid human.

THE PROGRESS OF SCIENCE

Scientific theories are *metaphors* that, when pursued, place their users into a position of control and prediction. Scientific theories are also *consensuses* in as much as they cannot be communicated or believed, much less worked out and routinized, unless a number of competent persons accept them as a basis for conducting operations.

Modern science has made great efforts to put aside, first, the primitive metaphoric systems such as are found in the myth we are studying, second, the mystic metaphorism, though much more agreeable, of Pythagoreanism and Platonism, and, third, though with great reluctance, the empirical nominalism of Aristotle and of the Newtonian Laws.

Now it moves uncertainly on a stripped-down linguistic and mathematical basis, purely operational and denotative, so far as particular small areas are concerned. Ironically, the bigger the library and the greater the equipment of a university or research center, the more likely the scientists in it will be utterly specialized and isolated from each other's group. Their metaphors will communicate with the smallest number of persons.

Then it happens that many chasms are created which no one dare approach and the bridges over these chasms become and will remain forever the operational constructions of metaphor.

Pythagoras and his associates, who flourished early in the sixth century B. C., give us a crucial lesson in the transformation of "true myth" into "false science". We say that until the 7th century (687 B. C.), the planets moved erratically from time to time. This fact was known to "pre-scientific" Greeks. *Planos,* the root word, means leading astray, cheating, deceiving; a wandering, roaming, straying; (metaphorically a wandering of mind), a madness, in uncertain fits (of disease). (These all from Liddell-Scott *Greek-English Lexicon.)* Wanderer meant as Odysseus wandered - without knowing what would happen next. (And, of course, Odysseus, complemented by his mentor, Athena, is the greatest deceiver, the trickiest of men, "the born trouble-maker.")

The eminent historian of science, George Sarton, says that Pythagoras aimed to prove that the planets were not "planets". He points out that "as their Greek names implied; *planaò* means to cause to wander, to mislead; *planètès* is a wandering, erratic, misleading body."[1] To Pythagoras, " the planets cannot be 'errant' bodies; they must have circular and uniform movements of their own.. If one could not but analyze those complicated motions they would be reduced to uniform circular ones. The whole of Greek astronomy grew out of that arbitrary conviction." [2]

We begin to perceive what happened. Even though Sarton sees the origins of Pythagorean astronomy in an *idée fixe* - that heavenly bodies must move regularly and circularly, he believes that his arbitrary idea had a true result - namely to "discover" that the planets *do* have such motions.

Hence, astronomers and public now agree that, as the contemporary popularizer Asimov puts it, "the Greek astronomers realized that there must be more than one canopy. For while the 'fixed' stars moved around the Earth in a body apparently without changing their relative positions; this was not true of the Sun, Moon, and five bright starlike objects (Mercury, Venus, Mars, Jupiter and Saturn)- in fact, each moved in a separate path. These seven bodies were called planets (from a Greek word meaning 'wanderer'...")._[3]

So the word "planet" means "wanderer" but wanderer *on a path,* a

---

[1] *History of Science,* V. I, op. cit., p. 13.

[2] *Ibid.*

[3] *An Intelligent Man's Guide to Science,* p. 17.

contradiction in terms. Pythagoras asserted their paths to be regular. We know that they have been so, since then.

Two events have occurred. The first is that the planets, which were originally named correctly, have stopped acting so as to deserve their name. Pythagoras denounced the meaning of the name and postulated their orderly movement. Modern astronomers accepted *his* meaning and introduced *their* order on top of *his* order.

Pythagoras indeed was far more anxious than they to reduce the planets to order. He was obsessively concerned with the development of all abstractions in accord with fixed formulas. Not content with abstraction, he founded a secret society to contain his truths and avert public examination. Propelled by "the Great Fear," he led the search for absolutes of order, a search that led Plato less than a century later to propose imprisonment in a "House of Better Judgement," and even death for those who would deny the immutability and harmony of the heavens.

Laplace is regarded as the founder of the science of probability. Writing two centuries ago, he disposed of the providential hand that Newton had postulated to set the solar system in orderly motion and maintain it. Order there was, declared Laplace, but it may be explained as originating in natural causes and as preserving itself by regular motions whose disruption was quite unlikely.

However, he declared, in passages rarely quoted, the probability of a comet striking the earth in the course of centuries is great and its result could be devastating if the comet were very large.[4] Besides, he warned that his own calculations, reinforcing Newton's conception of regularity in the movements of the orbs, did not take into account "various causes that can be ascertained by careful analysis, but which are impossible to frame within a calculation;" such would be comets, meteors, and even electric and magnetic forces. "The sky itself, despite the orderliness of its movements, is not unalterable." So spoke Laplace.

However, because the heavens have "settled down" in recent millennia, major displacements and encounters are increasingly unlikely. The celestial encounters of 2700 years ago may have been the last for some time to come.

---

[4] Stecchini, in *The Velikovsky Affair,* p. 107.

In 1974, Robert W. Bass went beyond this self-critique of Laplace into a critique of Laplace's famous calculations of stability for the solar system.[5] Instead of confirming the practical immutability of the planetary motions, Bass emerged in agreement with W. M. Smart's thesis that the theoretical term of assured reliability of the planetary orbits is in the hundreds or few thousands of years. The fabric of mathematical "proof" of the orderly skies has been torn to shreds.

A CLAIM OF SUCCESS

When the lines of the Love Affair were read, of a summer day on the island of Naxos in July of 1968, the hypothesis of this book sprang to life. Nowhere, whether in writing or in conversation, had I come upon a parallel between the song and external events. Nor, for that matter, had there ever been, to my knowledge, a predecessor to the story itself in ancient times. Overtime, the means of providing theory occurred in three forms, each depending upon a number of theories, techniques and facts.

One method would be to draw up all parallelisms (and lacks thereof) between the Love Affair and the celestial disasters that contemporary quantavolutionists, particularly Velikovsky, had described as occurring around the time of Homer. This has been done and a close parallelism discovered.

A second method would be to translate the myth by psychological and linguistic theories into a set of events that would most closely adhere to the characters, setting, dynamics (plot), and language of the myth. This has been done and the set of events that was most satisfying to the myth was the aforesaid catastrophic period of encounters among Mars, Earth, Venus and Moon.

The third method would be to search for the effects of the events, both upon human behavior and the cosmic bodies involved. The human avenue led into a stream of effects that has been accumulating from previous disasters; indications of collective behavior expected under the circumstances of the Greek disaster were also found. In the geologic and

---

[5] "Did Worlds Collide," and "Proofs of the Stability of the Solar System," IV *Pensée* (1974), 8-20, and 21-6.

astrophysical areas, recent explorations of all three extra-terrestrial bodies, together with revised theories of cataclysmic changes on earth, tended to confirm the historicity of the Love Affair. As Isaac Newton would say, "To the same natural effects we must as far as possible assign the same causes."[6] The probability of the theory as a whole being correct is enhanced by the concordance of the three results of the three methods. One should remain critical, however because in each area of method, theories are being developed and employed that are controversial, and also because in each methodological area, much less than an "ideal" amount of factual material is available.

Also this study attempted to do what Laplace avoided doing, to introduce many factors whose quantification for the purposes of a calculus of probabilities was impossible. Considering the confusion of theories and the onrush of incompatible facts in every related area of knowledge, it may appear to have done rather well.

From time to time, in the course of research, a question would return to haunt the author: suppose that an older version of the Love Affair were to be discovered.

If there were a predecessor to the Love Song of Demodocus, it would be Homer's work, a work well known to Homer, and/or a fable known to other contemporary cultures or preceding ones. Thus far, none has appeared. However, the effects of such a hypothetical discovery would be considerable. It would undercut my logical insistence that this particular plot is a screen for historical events of the early seventh century.

Almost certainly "love triangles" were observed and caused trouble for millennia before Homer. For that matter, walruses and apes snorted and grunted their way through similar affairs. Adultery found itself condemned under laws that were promulgated before Homeric times; Deuteronomy bans it, and also Genesis. Depending upon the culture, the emotions evoked by such triangles might be no less than the outrage of Hephaestus. The fearfulness of earlier catastrophes may have helped to build up the emotions. So the preconditions of the particular plot - the triangle and the emotional charge - were known and diffused.

In order to nullify the theory, however, the structure of the pre-existing plot would need to be closely parallel, and analogous gods would

---

[6] *Principia,* Bk. III, Chap. V.

need to participate in it. An Egyptian creation myth, much older than "the Love Affair," has a marriage between the Sun (Re) and the Heaven god (Nut, Roman Uranus) that is disturbed by copulation between Heaven and Earth (Geb). The Sun forbids Heaven giving birth to children during the year (360 days), but clever Thoth (Mercury) gambles with the Moon for Time, wins 1/72 part of the day, and hands over to Heaven five extra days (365) in which to give birth, whereupon Heaven bore Osiris (Saturn), Horus (Jupiter), Set, Isis, and Nephthys (the last three Venus-connected) on 5 successive days. Many events are incorporated here, but the major characters are from an earlier age and the plot is not analogous or homologous with the plot of "The Love Affair".

Respecting divine participation in Genesis, God does intervene against Abimelech to prevent his consummation of a relationship with Abraham's wife, Sarah, whom he has taken in good faith and with the consent of Abraham. It is plausible that other plots of adultery of a historical and fictional character, involving deities, should have existed.

There is no reason to believe that Homer had written (as Patroni insists) or knew of an original Opera Ballet of the Love Affair, parallel to the plot found in the *Odyssey,* and including the same gods as characters. The details of the story of the song are stuck off so firmly that a complete version resounds from behind the lines. Assuming that Homer or another had presented the Opera Ballet before, would this fact preclude a late dating of the underlying historical catastrophe? I think not, if it is in the same generation, and especially if it were the work of a younger Homer. Hence, the haunting question can be answered by a denial: this certain plot probably did not exist before the celestial events that it represents in disguise took place.

FROM SAVAGERY TO SUBLIMITY

If it is true that mankind suffers infinitely from the gods, it has become human because of them. They are in a sense, then, entitled to do with man what they will. As the old-fashioned property-owner used to say: "It's my property. I can dispose of it as I please." Many will assert that man would have been better off without the gods. No. This is a materialistic, mechanical view of human origins and human nature, more in keeping with tight suppression of memory and uniformitarian ideology, than with the lessons of catastrophe. Man was created by catastrophes and made to some degree what he is by them. This is a point on which pragmatists, phenomenologists, and idealists may agree.

But - it is more doubtful that the species would have become human if it had not humanized the gods. It is almost impossible to conceive that humans would have become humanly intelligent if they had been physiologically capable of experiencing the disasters mechanically, "in cold blood". They could have forgotten the disasters more easily over the generations. They would not have developed the arts and sciences. That is, there are few, if any, grounds for believing that they could have become scientific before they had passed through a stage of being monstrously human.

If people are able now to become "rational" and view ancient catastrophes and natural history as truly natural, it is only because they did not have the capacity for viewing events as natural in the first place.

The first humanoid who pointed at an active natural force with a capacity to impress a whole people and said: "There is our god. He made us and is now sending us a message" - that humanoid became the first person.

After the dreamtime dance and song of the Love Affair ends, and the dance of the spheres completes the ceremony, a peaceful and generous mood pervades the audience. King Alcinous announces that all the nobles must give fine personal gifts to Ulysses. This they do: cloaks and tunics and bars of gold. Euryalus, who has slandered Ulysses, gave the best gift of all, a gleaming copper sword with a silver belt in an ivory sheath. All these are heaped before the visitor. A hot bath is prepared for him and preparations for dinner are made.

I allude to these lines to stress once more the effects of the dance. The sublimation of unconscious effect has been well-nigh perfect. The ancients who heard these passages would imagine the full and blissful original scene, the way in which a sacred song and dance should ideally be conducted, the effects upon the participants and audience that should ideally occur.

This no one may deny. All that may be said by way of criticism is that such is the intent and result of great literature, of music, of dance, of plastic art, of liturgies, indeed of all constructive crowd behavior whose aim is social internalization. In the group, an anxiety is present whose specifications are hidden for fear of their depressive and disruptive effects. A spell must be cast; the symptoms will be displaced, discussed and alleviated; and everyone will feel better afterwards.

Objectively one can appraise the effect; it is good therapy; people are kinder to each other; possible alternative means of handling the anxieties are rendered unnecessary. Amidst the frequent crowd panic and madness of the *Iliad* and the *Odyssey,* of the *Bible,* of aggressive, ritualized, stupefied, and senseless self-sacrifice and others' sacrifice, the Song of Demodocus in its context, for all that the gods misbehave, is superior therapy.

It is well that those ancient censors who called the story false and sacrilegious and would have ripped it out of the *Odyssey* did not have their way. This is said, not alone on behalf of many bored and salacious schoolboys, not even for the sake of Truth, but for the realization it can bring of how ancient cultures, no less than primitive and modern ones, strove for alternatives to the labyrinthine rites, collective murder and bloody offerings by which societies sought to extirpate the hidden anxieties of catastrophe.

The present age is fraught with anxiety; still it has not reached the levels of our ancestral disasters. Up to this moment, the settled skies have allowed scientists and poets in free countries to move ever more boldly in exploration of the world within and the world without. The most radical investigations of nature and human nature have been permitted. The most radical experiments in the expressive arts have been tolerated. It is no longer true that the human mind cannot face, at least intermittently and "for the record," the evidence of ancient catastrophes. On this account one may predict that, within a few years, much more proof than is presently available will be collected and advanced in favor of the general theory of quantavolution and catastrophes and that the theoretical reconstruction will proceed apace.

When Odysseus is about to complete the slaughter of the suitor's relatives, Athena gives him pause: enough of bloodshed.[7] And when Eurycleia caught sight of the slain suitors in the palace hall, "she was about to cry out in exultation, beholding so great a deed. But Odysseus restrained her... 'Rejoice in your heart, old woman, and restrain yourself

---

[7] Even if someone later than Homer wrote these last lines of the *Odyssey* (D. Page, op. cit.) and they lack poetic merit, their moral function is apparent.

Settled Sky & Unsettled Mind

and do not cry aloud. It is an unholy thing to glory over slain men. These men the destiny of the gods and their own merciless deeds have overcome.'"[8]

The Hero resigns. The Moon is in place. The Goddess Athena is in her heavenly sphere. And Mars in his. Mercy begins once more.

And 2500 years later, the philosopher, Immanuel Kant, writes: "Two things fill the mind with ever-increasing wonder and awe, the more often and the more intensely one's thoughts are drawn to them: the starry heavens above me and the moral law within me."[9]

---

[8] Rieu trans., ls. 411-17.

[9] Quoted by Stecchini, in *The Velikovsky Affair*, p. 44.

APPENDIX

CHARACTERS OF THE BOOK

GODS

Athena (also Athene, Pallas Athene): Greek Goddess of wisdom, war, and the arts and sciences, "officially" declared to be the same as the Roman goddess, Minerva; identifiable in her planetary aspect with the planet Venus. In other cultures, she carries many names, including Ishtar (Babylonia), Quetzalcohuatl (Mexico), Lucifer (Rome), Helel (Judea), Aten (? Egypt), Subari (India). Protector of Odysseus.

Hephaestus (Hephaistos): Husband of Aphrodite. Greek god of fire and of the crafts and sciences, comparable to many smith-gods, also a solar deity; called Vulcan by the Romans and probably is Tuchulcha of the Etruscans. Identifiable with Athena and planet Venus.

Ares: Lover of Aphrodite. Greek god of war, called Mars by the Romans, Nergal by the Babylonians. Identifiable with the planet Mars.

Aphrodite: Lover of Ares. Greek goddess of the Moon and of love. Also, Greeks called the Moon "Selene" and partially transferred Aphrodite from the Moon to planet Venus and called the planet Aphrodite; meanwhile, the later Romans transported the name of the Italian goddess, Venus, to the Goddess Aphrodite and named the planet Venus. The Roman "Selene" was "Luna".

Hermes: Messenger god and god of luck. Identified with the Planet Mercury.

Apollo: God of Far-Distances and music. Personifies detached Wisdom. May represent a destroyed planet, now the meteoroid belt. Was later identified with the Sun.

Zeus: Son of Kronos and called the Father of the Olympian Gods in Homer. Identifiable with the Planet Jupiter.

Poseidon: God of the Sea, of Earthquakes, and ultimately of the Earth. Brother of Zeus. Enemy of Odysseus.

Helios (Helius): God of the Sun.

HUMANS

Demodocus (Demodokos): Great singer and harpist of Phaeacia, who recites the story of The Love Affair, and may be a self-portrait of Homer.

Odysseus: Hero of Homer's *Odyssey*. Epic poem of wanderings after the Trojan War. Known in Western Europe also as Ulysses. Guest of King Alcinous. His name, in American vernacular, would be "the born trouble-maker."

Penelope: Wife of Odysseus.

Alcinous (Alkinous): King of Phaeacia.

Nausicaa: Daughter of Alcinous.

Halius: Son of Alcinous. Dancer.

Laodamas: Son of Alcinous. Dancer.

PLACE & TIME

The ancient Mediterranean and the ancient skies above, possibly 687 B. C.

Phaeacia:

Realm of King Alcinous, probably based on real places in the Western Mediterranean, but fictionalized by Homer.

Scheria:

The larger land of which Phaeacia formed part.

Troy:

Fabled site of the Trojan War, identified by most archaeologists and classicists on the site of the town of Hisarlik in Turkey, near the Dardanelles Straits.

Lemnos:

Island in the upper Aegean Sea where the Sintians lived, favorites of Hephaestus.

www.ingramcontent.com/pod-product-compliance
Lightning Source LLC
Chambersburg PA
CBHW022355040426
42450CB00005B/195